best of
Hometown Cooking

For more delicious recipes
visit betterrecipes.com

Meredith₀ **Books**
Des Moines, Iowa

Meredith Books
1716 Locust Street
Des Moines, Iowa 50309–3023
meredithbooks.com

Printed in China.

Library of Congress Control Number: 2007921711
ISBN: 978-0-696-23630-3

Pictured on the back cover (top to bottom):
Coconut Shrimp (page 179), Apple Crumb Pie (page 352),
and Festive Fall Chili (page 267)

Table of Contents

Introduction

✦ ✦

You know the recipe. It's the one you carefully copied on a paper napkin at the family potluck 10 years ago—the recipe you tasted once and fell in love with forever. The recipe you just had to have and were lucky enough to get because your aunt, sister, mother, or friend happened to remember it on the spot. It's the dish you've been making ever since, putting it together once a week for dinner, bringing it to every party and picnic you're invited to—it's the cherished recipe you have now memorized.

And now, here's a cookbook filled with more than 350 recipes just like the ones you hold so near and dear to your heart! Compiled from the best of the best dishes submitted to the online recipe-sharing community at betterrecipes.com, these are the snacks, meals, and desserts that define great cooking. These dishes come from hometown cooks across the country—people just like you who have created their own unique meals or tweaked and perfected classics given to them by friends and family. These are their go-to recipes—the soups, sandwiches, and suppers their families beg for, as well as the appetizers, snacks, and desserts they're proud to bring to gatherings and get-togethers. The recipes on these pages were so well loved by the people in your community, they couldn't wait to put them online (and now in a cookbook!) to share with you.

As you flip through the pages, you'll find many special features. In several chapters, prizewinning recipes from the category are featured on the opening pages—singled out because they're so delicious, as well as practical and reliable. (Check out betterrecipes.com for more information on recipe contests.) Additionally, many recipes come with special notes from the cook, containing instructions and personal information about that dish. If you're looking for fast and easy weeknight dinners and other foods, keep your eye out for the "quick" icon at the top of certain recipes—when you see this you know it can be made in 30 minutes or less! And located throughout the book you can find useful hints and tips that will make your cooking adventures fun, easy, and safe. The best part? More recipes are just a click away. Whenever you need a great dish for any occasion, visit betterrecipes.com for all your cooking needs! There's no end to the great recipes available to you. Enjoy!

Chapter 1
Appetizers & Snacks

6

This rich smoothie recreates the silky texture of flan using cream cheese, caramel ice cream topping, and butter pecan ice cream.

Butter Pecan Flan Smoothies ❖quick❖

Kathy—Cambria, CA

Ingredients

2   **3-ounce packages cream cheese, softened**

2   **cups butter pecan ice cream**

1   **cup milk**

¼   **cup caramel ice cream topping**

6   **large ice cubes**

2   **tablespoons chopped pecans, toasted**

   Freshly grated nutmeg

Start to finish: 10 minutes

Method

1. In blender combine cream cheese, butter pecan ice cream, milk, caramel topping, and ice cubes. Blend until smoothie consistency is reached. Pour into chilled glasses. Top with toasted pecans and nutmeg.

Makes 4 servings

Cook's Notes
I absolutely LOVE flan, so I decided to create a wonderful smoothie that would reflect that creamy flavor. And it really does!

Rolled in a creamy blue cheese mixture, then coated in chopped nuts, these grapes are a bite-size nibble perfect for any get-together.

Blue Cheese–Pistachio Grapes

Jeanne—Des Moines, IA

Prep: 25 minutes   **Chill:** 30 minutes

Method

1. In a small bowl combine cream cheese, blue cheese, and, if desired, wine. Roll grapes in cheese mixture to lightly coat each (if necessary, remove excess with a knife). Roll grapes in chopped nuts. Cover and chill grapes for 30 to 60 minutes or until serving time.

Makes 10 to 15 servings (about 4 grapes per serving)

Cook's Notes
These are so quick and yummy.

Ingredients

1   **3-ounce package cream cheese, softened**

2   **ounces blue cheese, crumbled**

2   **teaspoons port wine (optional)**

1   **large bunch seedless red or green grapes (40 to 60 grapes)**

⅓   **cup finely chopped pistachio nuts, pecans, or almonds**

7

These pitted dates are packed with a mixture of sweetened cream cheese, orange peel, and dried cranberries, then sprinkled with chopped pecans.

Cranberry-Stuffed Dates ❖quick❖

Carole—Cleveland, OH

Ingredients

4   ounces cream cheese, softened

1   tablespoon sugar

1   teaspoon finely shredded orange peel

1   tablespoon orange juice

1   teaspoon vanilla

2   tablespoons dried cranberries, finely chopped

16 to 18 large dates, pitted and split

2   tablespoons finely chopped pecans

    Orange peel strips (optional)

Start to finish: 20 minutes

Method

1. In a medium bowl combine cream cheese, sugar, finely shredded orange peel, orange juice, and vanilla. Beat with an electric mixer on low to medium speed until smooth. Stir in cranberries.

2. Stuff dates with cream cheese mixture; sprinkle with pecans. Transfer to a serving plate. If desired, garnish with strips of orange peel.

Makes 16 to 18 dates

Cook's Notes
These are very easy and very tasty.

Ranch salad dressing mix is the secret ingredient in these luscious appetizers. No party is complete without a grab-and-gab treat like deviled eggs!

quick Ranch Deviled Eggs

Sheryl—Apopka, FL

Start to finish: 20 minutes

Method

1. Halve eggs lengthwise; remove yolks. In a small bowl use a fork to crumble yolks. Mix in dry dressing mix, mustard, and Worcestershire sauce; add enough mayonnaise to make creamy.

2. Use a teaspoon to refill egg halves with yolk mixture; sprinkle with paprika.

Makes 10 servings

Ingredients

5	hard-cooked eggs
½	of a packet ranch salad dressing mix
¼	teaspoon yellow mustard
¼	teaspoon Worcestershire sauce
2	teaspoons mayonnaise (or as needed)
	Paprika

9

Stuffed mushrooms are a favorite of many, but when you pack them full of sausage and cheeses, they're irresistible. Another time, try a lower-fat sausage.

Fabulous Stuffed Mushrooms

Tiffany—San Antonio, TX

Ingredients

1½	pounds large white button mushrooms
4	scallions, finely chopped
3	cloves garlic, minced
2	tablespoons olive oil
8	ounces pork sausage
1	to 2 teaspoons crushed red pepper
	Kosher salt
	Freshly ground black pepper
4	ounces reduced-fat cream cheese (Neufchâtel), softened
½	to 1 cup soft bread crumbs
½	cup freshly grated Parmesan cheese

Prep: 40 minutes   Bake: 30 minutes

Method

1. Preheat oven to 400°F. Clean mushrooms and remove stems. Place mushroom caps in single layer in a baking dish. Finely chop mushroom stems and set aside. In large skillet lightly saute scallion and garlic in hot olive oil.

2. Add pork sausage to garlic and onion mixture. Add red pepper. When sausage is slightly brown, add chopped mushroom stems. Add kosher salt and black pepper to taste. Continue to cook and stir until most of the liquid evaporates.

3. Remove skillet from heat; add cream cheese and ½ cup of the bread crumbs. If mixture still has a lot of liquid, add enough of remaining bread crumbs, ¼ cup at a time, to absorb all of the liquid. Stir until well mixed.

4. Place 1 heaping teaspoon of the sausage mixture into each mushroom cap. Top mushrooms with Parmesan cheese. Bake for 30 minutes.

Makes 10 to 12 servings

Cook's Notes
Our friends have no idea that I've used low-fat cream cheese! Also, you can substitute different mushrooms such as portobellos—if the mushroom has a cap, you can use it.

Tip

Cleaning Mushrooms The best way to clean mushrooms is to rub them gently with a damp paper towel or soft brush. If you soak them or put them under running water, they can easily become waterlogged and mushy. When buying fresh mushrooms look for firm white caps with tightly closed, fresh-looking gills (the fanlike underside of the cap).

These ground turkey meatballs in a peanutty lime sauce work well to make ahead and reheat just before your party.

Thai Turkey Meatballs

Christine—Windsor, CA

Prep: 25 minutes **Bake:** 30 minutes

Method

1. Preheat oven to 350°F. In a large bowl combine ground turkey, green onion, egg, bread crumbs, garlic, lime zest, and cilantro. Form turkey mixture into meatballs. Place meatballs in a single layer in a baking pan. Bake for 30 minutes.

2. Meanwhile, in a small saucepan combine peanut sauce, lime juice, and mayonnaise. Heat mixture over low heat, adding more lime juice if necessary to achieve desired consistency.

3. Place meatballs and sauce mixture in a slow cooker; keep warm on low until ready to serve (it takes about 30 minutes for flavors to blend).

Makes 8 servings

Cook's Notes
If you love cilantro, feel free to add more than 1 tablespoon to the meatballs.

Ingredients

1 **pound ground turkey**

1 **bunch green onions, chopped**

1 **egg**

¼ **to ⅓ cup panko bread crumbs**

3 **cloves garlic, minced**

  Zest of 1 lime

1 **tablespoon chopped fresh cilantro**

1 **8-ounce bottle Thai peanut sauce**

  Juice of 1 lime

2 **tablespoons mayonnaise**

Tip

What's Panko? Japanese panko bread crumbs are a favorite of cooks everywhere because of the light texture that the coarse and airy crumbs give to ground meat dishes and the crisp, crunchy coating they give to breaded and fried or baked foods. If you can't find them at your supermarket, look at Asian markets.

With three easy steps, you can have your own Buffalo wings for any occasion. Be sure to serve them with plenty of blue cheese dressing! See photo on page 209.

Knock-Your-Socks-Off Buffalo Wings

Staci—Brooksville, KY

Ingredients

Cooking oil for deep-fat frying

2½ pounds chicken wing portions

⅓ cup butter

½ teaspoon garlic powder

¼ teaspoon ground cumin

¼ teaspoon chili powder

1 cup bottled hot pepper sauce

Bottled blue cheese salad dressing

Prep: 15 minutes Cook: 10 minutes per batch

Method

1. In a deep-fat fryer heat 2 inches of cooking oil to 375°F. Fry chicken wing pieces, in batches, about 10 minutes or until wings are crisp and juices run clear.

2. Meanwhile, in a microwave-safe medium bowl combine butter, garlic powder, cumin, and chili powder. Microwave on 100% power (high) until butter is melted. Stir in hot sauce.

3. Transfer cooked chicken to a large skillet. Pour hot sauce mixture over chicken; turn to coat chicken. Cook over medium heat until sauce thickens. Serve with blue cheese dressing.

Makes 6 to 8 servings

Cook's Notes
When I take these to parties, I always come home with an empty platter!

Loaded with cheese and plenty of herbs, this toasted bruschetta will be gone before it hits the table.

quick Italian Herb Cheese Bruschetta

Joann—Bradenton, FL

Prep: 15 minutes **Bake:** 12 minutes

Method

1. Preheat oven to 375°F. Cut bread on the diagonal into ¼-inch slices.

2. Place bread on two baking sheets; drizzle with olive oil. Sprinkle with salt and pepper. Bake for 12 to 15 minutes or until crisp and golden. Remove from oven and set aside.

3. Meanwhile, in a medium bowl combine cheese spread, salami, basil pesto, and parsley. Stir well to combine. Spread the herb and cheese mixture on the toasted bread slices.

Makes 6 servings

Ingredients

1   long narrow loaf Italian semolina bread

½   cup olive oil

1   teaspoon salt

1   teaspoon ground black pepper

1   8-ounce container herb cheese spread

8   slices Italian salami, finely chopped

¼   cup purchased basil pesto

1   tablespoon chopped fresh parsley

For a super-simple, utterly elegant appetizer, spinach, prosciutto, and Swiss cheese are piled on pumpernickel cocktail bread and broiled.

Spinach Prosciutto Canapés

Janet—Bricktown, NJ

Ingredients

1   10-ounce package frozen spinach

4   ounces prosciutto

½   cup mayonnaise

¼   cup grated Parmesan cheese

½   of a 2.8-ounce can french-fried onion rings

1   8-ounce loaf pumpernickel cocktail bread

4   ounces Swiss cheese, shredded

Start to finish: 15 minutes

Method

1. Preheat broiler. Thaw spinach; drain and pat dry with paper towels. Cut prosciutto into small pieces.

2. In a medium bowl combine spinach, prosciutto, mayonnaise, Parmesan cheese, and onion rings.

3. Broil pumpernickel until slightly toasted. Spread spinach mixture on bread; top with Swiss cheese. Broil until cheese melts.

Makes 16 servings

The zesty taste of green chile peppers combined with delicious smoked salmon makes a tasty, crowd-pleasing appetizer.

Santa Fe Pinwheels

Marla—Moriarty, NM

. . . .

Prep: 20 minutes **Chill:** 1 hour

Method

1. In a bowl combine cream cheese and herb cream cheese.

2. Lay a tortilla flat and spread with one-fourth of the cream cheese mixture, leaving a 1-inch space all around the edges. Place one-fourth of the smoked salmon on top of the cream cheese; top with one-fourth of the chile peppers. Roll up. Cover with plastic wrap and refrigerate for at least 1 hour or up to 2 days.

3. Immediately before serving, unwrap; cut into ½-inch slices. Arrange on a plate or platter and serve.

Makes 12 servings

Cook's Notes
I served these at the open house for my husband's new business and there wasn't a crumb left! Since I have a wheat allergy, I made them using spelt tortillas available at my local natural foods store, and everybody thought they were fabulous. All ingredients should be at room temperature for easy handling.

Ingredients

- 4 **ounces reduced-fat cream cheese (Neufchâtel), softened**
- 3 **ounces light herb cream cheese (at room temperature)**
- 4 **10-inch flour or spelt tortillas**
- 6 **ounces smoked salmon, thinly sliced**
- 2 **4-ounce cans diced green chile peppers, drained**

Impressive as puff pastry is on its own, it's even better when topped with chopped olives and cheese in these quick-to-make bread twists.

Cheese and Olive Twists

Donna—Gray, ME

Ingredients

1   **17.3-ounce package frozen puff pastry, thawed**

1   **egg yolk mixed with 1 teaspoon water**

⅓   **cup grated Romano cheese**

⅓   **cup pitted oil-cured olives, chopped**

Prep: 20 minutes   Bake: 10 minutes

Method

1. Preheat oven to 400°F. Unfold pastry sheets on lightly floured surface. Brush pastry with egg mixture and sprinkle with Romano cheese. Evenly distribute olives on top of cheese; press down gently. Cut each pastry sheet into 12 strips. Lift each strip by both ends and twist.

2. Place strips on ungreased cookie sheet. Bake about 10 minutes or until light brown and puffed.

Makes 24 servings

Cook's Notes
For extremely sharp cheese flavor, choose Caprino Romano; for a quieter but sharp and tangy cheese flavor, choose pecorino Romano. Serve with dips and salsas, salads, and stews, or let these nibbles stand alone as appetizers at cocktail parties.

In Italy, a common dip for bread is flavored olive oil—a healthful alternative to butter. In this version, the olive oil is mixed with garlic and a variety of herbs.

quick Tuscan Bread Dip

Laura—Pinckney, MI

Start to finish: 15 minutes

Method

1. Mix oregano, basil, rosemary, crushed red pepper, garlic powder, black pepper, salt, and thyme; grind together. Place 2 teaspoons of the herb mixture into each of eight or nine shallow dipping bowls and set aside.

2. Put olive oil in small saucepan and heat. Add minced garlic and stir for 15 to 20 seconds just to flavor the oil but not to brown the garlic. Remove from heat and promptly ladle 2 to 3 tablespoons of the olive oil mixture into each of the shallow dipping bowls of herbs; mix together.

Makes 8 to 9 servings

Cook's Notes
Serve with slices of crusty French or Italian bread for dipping.

Ingredients

1   tablespoon dried oregano

1   tablespoon dried basil

1   tablespoon dried rosemary

1   tablespoon crushed
    red pepper

1   tablespoon garlic powder

1   tablespoon freshly ground
    black pepper

1   teaspoon salt

½   teaspoon dried thyme

1   cup plus 2 tablespoons
    olive oil

3   cloves garlic, minced

Need a great appetizer for your next tailgate party? This simple taco dip will satisfy even the heartiest appetites.

Touchdown Taco Dip *quick*

Pamela—Parkersburg, WV

Ingredients

2   pounds ground beef

1   14.5-ounce can refried beans

¼   cup water

1   package taco seasoning mix

2   cups shredded cheddar cheese

1   16-ounce carton sour cream

1   16-ounce jar salsa

2   cups shredded lettuce

1   large tomato, diced

4   green onions, chopped

2   cups shredded co-jack cheese

   Tortilla or corn chips

Start to finish: 25 minutes

Method

1. In a large skillet brown ground beef. Drain off fat. Add refried beans, water, and taco seasoning to beef.

2. Stir well and heat on low. Spread the mixture into a 13×9×2-inch baking dish. Sprinkle cheddar cheese on top. Spread sour cream and salsa over to cover. Top with shredded lettuce, tomato, and green onion. Sprinkle with co-jack cheese. Serve with tortilla chips.

Makes 12 servings

Cook's Notes
I have been making this since about 1975. My children are grown, but they prepared this recipe all the time while they were in college and still make it for their parties now.

Since this tasty dip needs time to chill, you can make it up to a day before a party. Then just pull it out of the refrigerator to serve!

Cowboy Caviar
Michelle—Citrus Heights, CA

Prep: 20 minutes   **Chill:** 2 hours

Method

1. In a large bowl, combine all ingredients. Let chill at least 2 hours or overnight. Serve with tortilla chips.

Makes 10 to 15 servings

Cook's Notes
If you like a little more spice, add a finely chopped jalapeño.

Ingredients

1   16-ounce can corn, drained

1   15-ounce can black beans, rinsed and drained

3   avocados, halved, pitted, peeled, and cubed

6   plum tomatoes, diced

1   bunch fresh cilantro, coarsely chopped

    Juice of 1 lime

2   to 3 teaspoons bottled hot pepper sauce

1   teaspoon minced garlic

    Salt

    Ground black pepper

    Tortilla or corn chips

Avocado Hints An avocado is rarely ripe enough to eat straight from the supermarket. When you buy an avocado, it should feel firm to the touch. Take it home and let it sit on the counter for a few days. When it's ready, it should yield to gentle pressure. To cut an avocado open, run a knife around the fruit horizontally to the pit, then twist to separate.

The name of this recipe says it all—it's the best! Serve with lime-flavored tortilla chips for an over-the-top taste sensation.

The Best Crab Dip EVER

Kathy—Athens, GA

+ +

Ingredients

1   **pound crabmeat**

½   **cup mayonnaise**

2   **ounces sharp cheddar cheese, shredded**

1   **ounce chili sauce**

1   **tablespoon Worcestershire sauce**

½   **teaspoon prepared horseradish**

½   **teaspoon lemon juice**

½   **teaspoon bottled hot pepper sauce**

     Crackers, pita chips, or tortilla chips

Prep: 15 minutes   **Chill:** 1 hour

Method

1. Combine the first eight ingredients and mix well. Cover and refrigerate for at least 1 hour so the flavors can blend.

2. Serve with crackers.

Makes 8 servings

On their own, shrimp and cheesecake are the favorites of many. Bring the two together and top with a tangy glaze for a taste sensation like no other!

Shrimp Cheesecake with Tomato Glaze

Cheryl—Elizabeth City, NC

Prep: 20 minutes Bake: 1 hour

Method

1. Preheat oven to 350°F. Lightly coat sides and bottom of an 8-inch springform pan with nonstick cooking spray; set aside. In a large bowl beat softened cream cheese and eggs with an electric mixer on low to medium speed until mixed. Add Gouda cheese, whipping cream, flour, seafood seasoning, and parsley. Beat for 2 minutes; fold in shrimp. Pour mixture into prepared pan; bake for 1 hour.

2. Meanwhile, to make the glaze, in a medium saucepan combine drained tomatoes, balsamic vinegar, and brown sugar. Bring to a simmer; cook about 20 minutes or until thickened, stirring occasionally. Cool glaze to room temperature.

3. Remove cheesecake from oven and allow to come to room temperature. Run a knife around the inside of the pan to loosen the cheesecake; carefully remove from pan. Cut cake into 10 to 12 wedges; spread glaze over the top. Serve with toasted baguette slices.

Makes 10 to 12 servings

Ingredients

Nonstick cooking spray

1 8-ounce package cream cheese, softened

2 eggs

1 pound smoked Gouda cheese, shredded

½ cup whipping cream

1 tablespoon all-purpose flour

1 tablespoon seafood seasoning

1 tablespoon chopped fresh parsley

8 ounces frozen, cooked baby shrimp, thawed

1 14.5-ounce can fire-roasted diced tomatoes, drained

1 cup balsamic vinegar

¼ cup packed brown sugar

Toasted baguette slices

Cookie Dough Cheese Ball

Bev—Brunswick, MO

Ingredients

1   17.5-ounce package chocolate chip cookie mix

1   8-ounce package cream cheese, softened

2   cups chopped pecans

½   cup butter, softened

    Vanilla wafers or graham crackers

Prep: 15 minutes   Chill: 3 hours

Method

1. In a large bowl combine dry cookie mix, cream cheese, 1 cup of the pecans, and the butter. Beat with an electric mixer on low speed for 1 minute; beat on medium speed until well mixed.

2. Shape into a ball; roll in remaining 1 cup pecans. Wrap in plastic wrap; chill for at least 3 hours. Serve with vanilla wafers.

Makes 12 servings

Cook's Notes
This dessert cheese ball tastes great scooped on wafers, graham crackers, or other thin cookies.

On a hot day, indulge in this smoothie that is reminiscent of a banana split.

quick Banana Split Smoothies

Tanya–Paragould, AR

Start to finish: 10 minutes

Method

1. In a blender combine first five ingredients; cover and process until smooth. Gradually add ice cubes, blending until slushy. Pour into chilled glasses.

2. Garnish with whipped topping, chocolate syrup, and maraschino cherries.

Makes 3 servings

Ingredients

2   **medium ripe bananas**

1   **8-ounce can crushed pineapple, drained**

1½   **cups milk**

½   **cup fresh or frozen unsweetened sliced strawberries**

2   **tablespoons honey**

5   **ice cubes**

   Whipped topping, chocolate syrup, and maraschino cherries

23

This frosty drink can be served any time of day. It blends cooled coffee, two kinds of ice cream, and milk.

Wake-up Frosties 〈quick〉

Sarah—Waco, TX

Ingredients

1	**cup strong brewed coffee, cooled**
1	**scoop chocolate ice cream**
1	**scoop vanilla ice cream**
1	**cup whole milk**
½	**teaspoon vanilla**

Start to finish: 10 minutes

Method

1. In a blender combine all of the ingredients and process until smooth. Pour into glasses and serve.

Makes 2 servings

Cook's Notes
Garnish with whipped cream and grated chocolate, if desired.

This cool beverage combines brewed coffee, milk, vanilla, and almond extract, poured over ice and topped with cinnamon-dusted whipped cream.

quick Almond Iced Coffee

Lillian—Gainesville, FL

Start to finish: 5 minutes

Method

1. Combine coffee, milk, sugar, vanilla, and almond extract. Taste for sweetness and, if desired, add more sugar. Pour into 4 ice-filled 10-ounce glasses. Top with a spoonful of whipped cream and a sprinkle of ground cinnamon.

Makes 4 servings

Cook's Notes
For coffee-holics this simple summer drink will fit the bill.

Ingredients

2   cups strong brewed coffee
    (at room temperature)

2   cups milk

2   teaspoons sugar or to taste

1   teaspoon vanilla

½   teaspoon almond extract

    Ice cubes

    Whipped cream

    Ground cinnamon

Savor this hot apple cider with a little butter, a little rum, and a cinnamon swizzle stick to stir it all together.

Spiced Rum Cider quick

Donna—Gray, ME

Ingredients

1 **cup apple juice or apple cider**

2 **teaspoons packed light-brown sugar**

1 **tablespoon butter**

4 **teaspoons light rum**

2 **cinnamon sticks (each about 4 inches long)**

Start to finish: 15 minutes

Method

1. In a small saucepan combine apple juice, brown sugar, and butter. Heat but do not boil.

2. Pour 2 teaspoons rum into each of two teacups. Fill with hot juice mixture. Stir with a stick of cinnamon (one stick for each cup).

Makes 2 servings

Cook's Notes
When the kids are home from trick-or-treating, the party's over, the costumes are in the laundry, and the makeup is removed, this one's for you! Happy Halloween!

Chapter 2
Sandwiches & Wraps

This behemoth sandwich is heaped with layers of Caesar dressing, smoked turkey, ham, two cheeses, and more. Wow! See photo on page 210.

Caesar Chef Salad Sandwiches quick

Mary—Ada, OK

Ingredients

1   1-pound loaf French bread

¾   cup bottled Caesar salad dressing

2   cups baby spinach leaves

8   ounces thinly sliced deli-style smoked turkey breast

4   thin slices red onion, separated into rings

4   slices provolone cheese

8   ounces thinly sliced deli-style ham

1   medium tomato, sliced

4   slices co-jack cheese

6   sandwich picks with whole black and green olives

6   sandwich picks with small cherry tomatoes

Start to finish: 20 minutes

Method

1. Cut bread horizontally into three slices. Spread cut sides with dressing. Layer 1 cup of the spinach leaves, the turkey breast, onion, and provolone cheese on bottom slice. Cover with center bread slice. Layer ham, tomato slices, co-jack cheese, and the remaining 1 cup spinach on top. Place top slice of bread on sandwich. Press down lightly.

2. To serve, cut into six pieces, securing each with an olive pick and a tomato pick for garnish.

Makes 6 servings

Cook's Notes
This delicious family-style sandwich can be prepared 1 to 2 hours in advance and chilled. Other cheeses and meats may be substituted according to taste preferences.

For this easy twist on the typical Caesar salad, the lettuce, chicken, and Parmesan cheese are tossed with Caesar dressing, then sandwiched between toasted bread.

quick Caesar Sandwiches

Surita—Seagull Row, CA

Start to finish: 15 minutes

Method

1. Preheat broiler. In a bowl toss together desired amounts of chicken strips, romaine, and Parmesan cheese with enough dressing to coat.

2. Broil bread slices 3 to 4 inches from heat for 2 to 3 minutes or until toasted, turning once. Spoon chicken mixture on and serve.

Makes as many servings as desired

Cook's Notes
You can make as many of these sandwiches as you want. The toasted bread acts as a crouton—the favorite part of a Caesar salad. Adding red onion slices is a great option.

Ingredients

Grilled chicken strips (purchased or homemade)

Romaine lettuce

Shredded Parmesan cheese

Bottled Caesar salad dressing

Sandwich bread slices

A chicken salad mixture with hard-cooked eggs, onion, celery, Dijon mustard, and seasoned salt is spread on sourdough bread and topped with Muenster cheese.

Lemon Chicken Salad Sandwiches

Betsy—Fayetteville, AR

Ingredients

8	cups water
4	skinless chicken breast halves
1	medium onion, chopped
2	stalks celery, chopped
1	large lemon
2	hard-cooked eggs, coarsely chopped
2½	tablespoons mayonnaise
1	tablespoon Dijon-style mustard
1	teaspoon seasoned salt
1	teaspoon paprika
8	slices sourdough bread
4	to 8 slices Muenster cheese

Prep: 30 minutes Cook: 25 minutes

Method

1. In a Dutch oven combine water, chicken, half of the onion, and half of the celery. Bring to boiling; reduce heat. Cover and simmer about 25 minutes or until chicken is tender. Transfer chicken to a plate; let stand until cool enough to handle. Remove chicken from bones; chop chicken.

2. Grate zest from the lemon; juice the lemon. In a large bowl combine chicken, lemon zest, lemon juice, and hard-cooked eggs. Add mayonnaise, mustard, seasoned salt, and paprika; mix just until combined.

3. Spread chicken mixture on half of the bread slices; top with cheese. Top with remaining bread.

Makes 4 servings

Cook's Notes
For an even tastier sandwich, place on a grill pan heated to medium and press with a skillet. Flip after 2 to 3 minutes and press again, cooking until bread is golden brown and cheese is melted. Serve warm.

Pita sandwiches with chicken get refreshingly cool and crunchy from the cucumber and mint in the dressing.

Cucumber Chicken Pita Sandwiches

Shelly—Sherwood, OH

Start to Finish: 20 minutes

Method

1. For dressing, in a small bowl stir together yogurt, cucumber, dillweed, and mint. Set aside.

2. For each sandwich, place a pita bread round on a plate. Top with lettuce, chicken, tomato, and feta cheese. Spoon dressing on top. Roll up pita bread. Secure with wooden pick. Serve immediately.

Makes 4 servings

Cook's Notes
If you like, you can prepare the dressing, then cover and chill it up to 6 hours.

Ingredients

½ cup plain yogurt

¼ cup finely chopped cucumber

½ teaspoon dried dillweed

¼ teaspoon dried mint, crushed

4 large pita breads

4 lettuce leaves

6 ounces thinly sliced cooked chicken breast

1 small tomato, thinly sliced

⅓ cup crumbled feta cheese

This hot, Tuscan-inspired sandwich is packed with flavorful grilled chicken, savory veggies, and provolone cheese.

Grilled Tuscan Chicken Sandwiches

Pamela—Parkersburg, WV

Ingredients

4 skinless boneless chicken breast halves

½ cup bottled zesty Italian salad dressing, plus additional for drizzling

1 teaspoon salt

1 teaspoon black pepper

2 tablespoons olive oil

1 red sweet pepper, cut into thin bite-size strips

1 green sweet pepper, cut into thin bite-size strips

1½ cups sliced fresh mushrooms

1 red onion, cut in thin slices

1 teaspoon minced garlic

8 submarine buns, split, or 2 loaves specialty bread, split

8 slices provolone cheese

Mayonnaise (optional)

Lettuce (optional)

Prep: 25 minutes Marinate: 4 hours Grill: 14 minutes Stand: 5 minutes

Method

1. Place chicken in a large resealable plastic bag; pour the ½ cup Italian salad dressing over chicken. Seal bag; turn to coat chicken. Marinate in the refrigerator for 4 hours, turning bag occasionally.

2. Drain chicken, discarding marinade. Sprinkle chicken with salt and black pepper. Place chicken on rack of an uncovered grill directly over medium coals. Grill for 12 to 15 minutes or until chicken is tender and juices run clear (170°F).

3. Meanwhile, in a large skillet heat olive oil over medium heat. Add sweet pepper, mushrooms, and red onion; cook for 4 minutes. Add garlic; cook for 2 to 3 minutes more or until vegetables are tender.

4. When chicken is done, transfer to a plate; let stand for 5 minutes. Cut chicken into bite-size strips; arrange chicken strips on bun bottoms. Top with vegetable mixture. Drizzle with additional Italian dressing; top with cheese. If desired, spread bun tops with mayonnaise. Place bun tops on sandwiches. Wrap sandwich in foil; grill about 2 minutes more or until bread is warm and cheese is melted. If desired, add lettuce to sandwiches after grilling.

Makes 6 to 8 servings

Cook's Notes
These are so good with the specialty breads. I like to try a different one each time I make this. I especially like Asiago cheese bread.

Chicken breasts are sprinkled with taco seasoning mix, baked, topped with cheese, and served in a bun with sour cream, onion, and avocado.

quick Mexican Chicken Sandwiches

Connie—Shelby, OH

Prep: 15 minutes Broil: 13 minutes

Method

1. Preheat broiler. Coat unheated rack of broiler pan with nonstick cooking spray. Sprinkle taco seasoning mix on chicken. Place chicken on prepared broiler pan.

2. Broil 4 to 5 inches from the heat for 12 to 15 minutes or until chicken is tender and no longer pink (170°F).

3. Top chicken with cheese; broil about 1 minute more or just until cheese is melted.

4. Place chicken on bun bottoms; top with avocado, onion, sour cream, and bun tops.

Makes 4 to 5 servings

Cook's Notes
You may also chop the ingredients and put them in a tortilla for a wrap.

Ingredients

Nonstick cooking spray

1   **1.25-ounce package taco seasoning mix**

4   **or 5 skinless boneless chicken breast halves**

4   **ounces cheddar cheese, shredded or thinly sliced**

4   **or 5 hamburger buns, split**

1   **avocado, halved, pitted, peeled, and sliced**

1   **onion, sliced**

¼   **cup sour cream**

Cubed cooked turkey is combined with dried cranberries and celery, tossed with a mixture of mayonnaise and yogurt, and spooned onto split croissants.

Turkey-Cranberry Salad Sandwiches

Mireya—North Richland Hills, TX

Ingredients

2 cups cubed cooked turkey

½ cup dried cranberries

½ cup finely chopped celery

3 green onions, thinly sliced

½ cup mayonnaise

¼ cup plain yogurt

2 tablespoons lemon juice

  Salt

  Ground black pepper

4 croissants, halved

  Lettuce leaves

Prep: 20 minutes Chill: 30 minutes

Method

1. In a medium bowl combine turkey, dried cranberries, celery, and green onion; mix well. In a small bowl stir together mayonnaise, yogurt, and lemon juice. Season to taste with salt and pepper.

2. Pour mayonnaise mixture over turkey mixture; stir together. Chill for 30 to 60 minutes.

3. Spread turkey mixture on bottom halves of croissants. Top with lettuce and croissant tops.

Makes 4 servings

Rum, lime juice, cilantro, papaya, and black beans dress up this unusual—yet supertasty—steak sandwich.

Brazilian Steak Sandwiches

Roxanne—Albany, CA

Prep: 20 minutes   **Marinate:** several hours to overnight   **Grill:** 14 minutes

Method

1. Place steak in a large resealable plastic bag. For marinade, in a small bowl combine rum, lime juice, olive oil, garlic, salt, and cayenne pepper; pour over steak in bag. Seal bag; turn to coat steak. Marinate in the refrigerator several hours to overnight, turning bag occasionally.

2. Drain steak, discarding marinade. Place on rack of an uncovered grill directly over medium coals. Grill for 14 to 22 minutes or until done as desired, turning once halfway through grilling.

3. Meanwhile, in a medium bowl combine mashed black beans, sour cream, cilantro, almonds, coriander, and cumin.

4. Thinly slice steak across the grain. Spread bread slices with the bean mixture. Arrange steak slices on half of the bread; top with spinach, papaya, and remaining bread slices, bean mixture side down.

Makes 6 servings

Cook's Notes
This hearty, healthful sandwich would pair well with a bowl of soup.

Ingredients

- 1 **pound boneless beef sirloin steak, cut 1 inch thick**
- 2 **tablespoons rum**
- 2 **tablespoons lime juice**
- 2 **tablespoons olive oil**
- 1 **large clove garlic, crushed**
- ½ **teaspoon salt**
- ¼ **teaspoon cayenne pepper**
- 1 **15-ounce can black beans, rinsed, drained, and mashed**
- ¼ **cup sour cream**
- 1 **tablespoon chopped fresh cilantro**
- 1 **tablespoon chopped smoked salted almonds**
- ¼ **teaspoon ground coriander**
- ¼ **teaspoon ground cumin**
- 12 **slices hearty country-style bread, toasted**
- 1 **cup shredded fresh spinach**
- 1 **large ripe papaya, peeled and sliced**

Tender filet mignon steaks are marinated, then grilled, sliced, and spooned into buns with fresh veggies and cheese.

Montreal Grilled Filet Mignon Subs

Pamela—Parkersburg, WV

Ingredients

2 beef tenderloin steaks, cut 1-inch thick

1 0.71-ounce package Montreal steak marinade mix

¼ cup water

¼ cup cooking oil

2 tablespoons red wine vinegar

2 tablespoons olive oil

2 cups sliced fresh mushrooms

1 medium red onion, cut into thin slices

½ of a green sweet pepper, cut into thin bite-size strips

½ of a red sweet pepper, cut into thin bite-size strips

   Salt

   Black pepper

4 submarine buns or two 6-inch loaves specialty bread, split

¼ cup mayonnaise

6 to 8 slices provolone cheese

Prep: 35 minutes **Marinate:** 30 minutes **Grill:** 15 minutes **Stand:** 5 minutes

Method

1. Place steaks in a large resealable plastic bag. In a small bowl whisk together dry marinade mix, water, cooking oil, and red wine vinegar; pour over steaks in bag. Seal bag; turn to coat steaks. Marinate in the refrigerator for 30 minutes to 2 hours, turning bag occasionally.

2. In a medium skillet heat the olive oil over medium heat. Add mushrooms, red onion, and sweet pepper; cook for 8 to 10 minutes or until vegetables are tender. Set aside.

3. Drain steaks, reserving marinade. Sprinkle steaks with salt and pepper. Place steaks on rack of an uncovered grill directly over medium coals. Grill for 10 to 15 minutes or until done as desired, brushing with reserved marinade during the first 5 minutes of grilling. Discard any remaining marinade. Transfer steaks to a plate; let stand for 5 minutes. Thinly slice steaks across the grain.

4. Spread buns with mayonnaise. Fill buns with sliced steak, vegetables, and cheese. Wrap in foil. Grill about 5 minutes or until buns are warm and cheese is melted. If using bread, cut into wedges to serve.

Makes 4 servings

Cook's Notes
These are delicious, especially when using Asiago cheese loaves or a focaccia bread with pesto and herb.

Who doesn't love meatball subs? In this version the meatballs are stuffed with cubes of mozzarella cheese before baking for a yummy surprise! See photo on page 210.

Meatball Subs

Staci—Brooksville, KY

+ +

Prep: 25 minutes   **Bake:** 25 minutes

Method

1. Preheat oven to 375°F. In a large bowl combine ground beef, bread crumbs, Parmesan cheese, Italian seasoning, and salt. Shape beef mixture into 2-inch balls. Using your fingers, make a hole in the center of each meatball; place a cube of mozzarella cheese in center of each. Shape meat around cheese to cover.

2. Coat a 2-quart square baking dish with nonstick cooking spray. Arrange meatballs in baking dish. Bake for 20 to 25 minutes or until cooked through.

3. While meatballs are baking, place butter in a small microwave-safe bowl; microwave on 100% power (high) until butter is melted. Stir garlic powder into melted butter. Brush cut surface of rolls with butter mixture; place roll tops and bottoms, cut sides up, on baking sheet.

4. Remove meatballs from oven. Place rolls in oven; bake for 5 to 10 minutes or until brown.

5. Meanwhile, in a large saucepan combine spaghetti sauce and meatballs. Heat until warm. Place meatballs on rolls; top with sliced sweet pepper.

Makes 4 servings

Ingredients

1   **pound ground beef**

⅓   **cup fine dry bread crumbs**

¼   **cup grated Parmesan cheese**

1   **tablespoon dried Italian seasoning, crushed**

½   **teaspoon salt**

   Cubed mozzarella cheese

   Nonstick cooking spray

2   **tablespoons butter**

1   **teaspoon garlic powder**

4   **hoagie rolls, split**

1   **14-ounce jar spaghetti sauce**

1   **green sweet pepper, sliced**

Cook's Notes
It doesn't take long to make these sandwiches. They are a warm tummy pleaser. Everyone will be surprised to bite in and find the cheese inside.

Ground beef is cooked with onion and flavored with salsa, then spooned into halved pita bread and topped with cheese.

Mexican Party Pita Pockets ◆quick◆

Juanita—Moultrie, GA

Ingredients

1 **pound lean ground beef**

½ **of an onion, chopped**

1 **cup bottled hot salsa**

Dash salt

3 **or 4 whole wheat pita breads, halved**

½ **cup shredded Mexican blend or cheddar cheese**

Start to finish: 20 minutes

Method

1. In a large skillet combine ground beef and onion; cook until meat is brown. Drain off fat. Stir salsa and salt into beef mixture.

2. Spoon beef mixture into pita halves. Sprinkle with cheese.

Makes 3 to 4 servings

Cook's Notes
This is a quick and easy meal that's good for busy families.

Draining Ground Meat There are several ways to drain fat from cooked ground meat. One of the most effective: Use a slotted spoon or skimmer to transfer the cooked meat to a large plate lined with several paper towels. Lay several more paper towels on top of the cooked meat and press gently to absorb as much fat as possible.

Chicken gumbo soup adds flavor to these incredibly easy sloppy joes. Try them the next time you need to make quick sandwiches for dinner or lunch.

quick Jeannie's Sloppy Joes

Jeannie—Durham, NC

Start to finish: 20 minutes

Method

1. In a large skillet cook ground beef over medium heat until brown, breaking up meat with a wooden spoon. Add chicken gumbo soup and ketchup. Cook for 5 to 10 minutes or until mixture reaches desired consistency. Spoon onto buns.

Makes 4 servings

Cook's Notes
This is so easy and it tastes so good!

Ingredients

1   pound ground beef

1   10.75-ounce can condensed chicken gumbo soup

2   tablespoons ketchup

4   hamburger buns, split

Make these calzones filled with sausage and three kinds of cheese for a fast, easy, and superdelicious dinner.

Cheesy Sausage and Artichoke Calzones

Julie—Marietta, GA

Ingredients

1 **pound bulk Italian sausage (or use links with casing removed), cooked and drained of fat**

1 **14-ounce can quartered artichoke hearts, drained**

2 **cups diced plum tomatoes**

1½ **teaspoons beef bouillon granules dissolved in 1 tablespoon water**

1 **teaspoon dried Italian seasoning, crushed**

½ **teaspoon onion powder**

½ **teaspoon sugar**

½ **teaspoon dried minced onion**

2 **10- to 13.8-ounce cans refrigerated pizza dough**

1 **cup shredded mozzarella cheese**

1 **cup shredded Asiago or fontina cheese**

1 **cup ricotta cheese**

1 **cup marinara or spaghetti sauce (optional)**

Prep: 20 minutes   Bake: 25 minutes

Method

1. Preheat the oven to 400°F. In a large bowl combine cooked sausage, drained artichoke hearts, tomato, beef bouillon mixture, Italian seasoning, onion powder, sugar, and minced onion.

2. Divide pizza dough into 4 pieces and press into ¼- to ½-inch-thick rounds. Place two rounds on each of two greased baking sheets. Divide the sausage mixture among the dough rounds, spreading on half of each round to within ¾ inch of the edge. Top each round with some of the mozzarella cheese, Asiago cheese, and ricotta cheese. Fold the uncovered portion of dough over the filling; using your fingers, roll and crimp edges.

3. Bake for 25 to 30 minutes or until crusts are golden brown. If desired, serve calzones with warm spaghetti sauce.

Makes 4 servings

Cook's Notes
I created this recipe as an easy dinner version of my favorite soup. These terrific calzones go over well with both kids and adults.

Try this version of the legendary Greek pita pockets for sandwiches that are full of flavor—without all of the calories!

quick Reduced-Calorie Gyros

Marjorie—Skaneateles, NY

41

Prep: 20 minutes Broil: 10 minutes

Method

1. Preheat broiler. In a small bowl combine yogurt, cucumber, the finely chopped onion, the 2 cloves garlic, the sugar substitute, and dried mint; refrigerate until needed.

2. In a large bowl combine lamb, turkey, oregano, the 1 clove garlic, the onion powder, salt, and pepper. Shape meat mixture into six ½-inch-thick patties. If desired, place in freezer to firm.

3. Place patties on unheated rack of a broiler pan. Broil 3 to 4 inches from the heat for 10 to 12 minutes or until done (165°F). Halve patties crosswise.

4. Place lettuce, tomato, and sliced onion in pita halves. Place half of a meat patty in each pita half. Top with yogurt mixture.

Makes 6 servings

Ingredients

8 ounces fat-free plain yogurt

⅓ cup finely chopped seeded cucumber

2 tablespoons finely chopped sweet onion (such as Vidalia)

2 garlic cloves, minced

½ packet sugar substitute

½ teaspoon dried mint, crushed

8 ounces lean ground lamb

8 ounces uncooked ground turkey breast

1½ teaspoons dried oregano, crushed

1 clove garlic, minced

1 teaspoon onion powder

1 teaspoon salt

¾ teaspoon ground black pepper

Shredded lettuce

Sliced tomatoes

Sliced sweet onions (such as Vidalia)

6 pita breads, halved

Packed with oodles of delicious ingredients, this grilled sandwich is a real crowd-pleaser.

Portobello, Spinach, and Crab Panini (quick)

Anne—Des Moines, IA

42

Ingredients

¼ cup mayonnaise

2 tablespoons bottled roasted red sweet peppers, drained and chopped

2 6-inch portobellos or several smaller ones

1 tablespoon olive oil, plus additional for brushing

2 cloves garlic, crushed

6 ounces fresh spinach

12 very thin slices provolone or Swiss cheese

6 large slices French bread or sourdough bread

8 ounces cooked crabmeat

¼ cup thinly sliced red onion (optional)

Start to finish: 30 minutes

Method

1. In a small bowl combine mayonnaise and roasted peppers; refrigerate until ready to use.

2. Slice portobellos at an angle. In a large skillet heat the 1 tablespoon olive oil over medium heat. Add portobellos and garlic; cook for 3 to 4 minutes or until mushrooms are tender, stirring frequently. Remove portobello mixture from skillet. Add spinach to skillet; cook just until it wilts. Remove from heat; cool. Squeeze spinach dry; chop spinach.

3. Divide half of the cheese slices among half of the bread slices. Spread mayonnaise mixture over cheese. Layer with crabmeat, red onion (if desired), spinach, and portobello mixture. Top with remaining cheese and remaining bread. Brush bread with additional olive oil.

4. Grill on a covered indoor grill until cheese is melted. (Or cook on a griddle or in a large skillet until brown on bottom, using a heavy pan to weigh down the panini. Turn panini. Cook until cheese is melted.)

Makes 3 large or 6 small servings

A waffle sandwich? It's true—and it's delicious! Layered with crisp bacon, scrambled eggs, and American cheese, this is great for breakfast, lunch, or dinner.

quick Waffle Breakfast Panini

Robyn—Easton, PA

Start to Finish: 20 minutes

Method

1. Place one of the cheese slices on one of the waffles; add bacon, scrambled eggs, and remaining slice cheese. Top with remaining waffle.

2. Place panini in a panini press or on a covered indoor grill. Press and cook about 2 minutes or until waffle turns golden and cheese is melted. (Or cook on a griddle or in a large skillet until brown on bottom, using a heavy pan to weigh down panini. Turn panini. Cook until cheese is melted.)

3. Place on serving plate; top with butter and serve with maple syrup.

Makes 1 serving

Cook's Notes
This is great as a grab-and-go sandwich.

Ingredients

2 slices American cheese

2 frozen waffles, thawed

2 slices bacon, cooked crisp

2 eggs, scrambled

1 tablespoon butter

¼ cup maple syrup, warmed

Ground turkey is mixed with onion, garlic powder, parsley, barbecue sauce, American cheese, tomato, and lettuce and served on a bun.

Ground Turkey Onion Burgers

Sonya—Douglasville, GA

44

Ingredients

2   **tablespoons olive oil**

1   **sweet onion (such as Vidalia), chopped**

2   **teaspoons dried parsley flakes, crushed**

1½   **teaspoons garlic powder**

1   **to 1¼ teaspoons salt**

1   **teaspoon sugar**

1¼   **pounds uncooked ground turkey**

  Nonstick cooking spray

  Bottled barbecue sauce

4   **or 5 hamburger buns, split**

  Tomato slices

4   **or 5 slices American cheese**

  Lettuce leaves

  Pickle slices (optional)

Prep: 15 minutes   Cook: 12 minutes   Cool: 5 minutes

Method

1. In a medium skillet heat olive oil over medium heat. Add onion; cook until tender and just starting to brown. Remove from heat; stir in parsley flakes, garlic powder, salt, and sugar. Let cool for 5 minutes.

2. In a large bowl combine ground turkey and onion mixture. Shape turkey mixture into four or five ¾-inch-thick patties.

3. Coat skillet with nonstick cooking spray. Preheat skillet over medium heat. Add patties; cook for 12 to 14 minutes or until juices run clear (165°F).

4. Spoon barbecue sauce onto cut sides of buns. Top bun bottoms with a turkey patty. Top with tomato, cheese, and lettuce. If desired, top with pickles. Add bun tops.

Makes 4 to 5 servings

Cook's Notes
These are great with french fries, potato chips, or any other simple side dish.

Tip

Ground Turkey Types Ground turkey comes two ways. One kind is made from white meat, dark meat, fat, and skin; the other is made from all-white breast meat. The first kind is higher in fat and darker in color. The all-breast ground meat is pink in color and more healthful. Choose the mixed variety for more flavor and the all-white kind for less fat.

Take ground turkey to the next level with these spunky burgers! The refreshing topping is a mixture of diced mango, mint, lime juice, and lime zest.

Thai Turkey Burgers
Roxanne—Albany, CA

Prep: 20 minutes **Grill:** 15 minutes

Method

1. In a large bowl combine turkey, yogurt, green onion, ginger, soy sauce, garlic, and curry paste. Shape turkey mixture into six ¾-inch-thick patties. Place patties on rack of an uncovered grill directly over medium coals. Grill for 15 to 19 minutes or until juices run clear (165°F).

2. Meanwhile, in a small bowl combine mango, mint, lime zest, lime juice, and toasted sesame oil. Set aside.

3. For the last minute of grilling, place roll halves, cut sides down, on grill. Grill about 1 minute or until toasted.

4. To serve, place lettuce on roll bottoms. Top with burgers. Spoon mango mixture over. Add roll tops.

Makes 6 servings

Cook's Notes
This Asian-style burger goes well with a salad of pickled raw vegetables and green tea.

Ingredients

1 ½ **pounds uncooked ground turkey**

¼ **cup plain yogurt**

2 **tablespoons minced green onion**

1 **teaspoon minced fresh ginger**

1 **teaspoon soy sauce**

1 **clove garlic, crushed**

1 **teaspoon curry paste**

1 **cup diced peeled mango**

2 **tablespoons chopped fresh mint**

½ **teaspoon grated lime zest**

1 **teaspoon lime juice**

1 **teaspoon toasted sesame oil**

6 **sesame seed rolls, split**

6 **lettuce leaves**

Curry Paste Thai curry paste comes in three colors—red, yellow, and green—and varying degrees of hotness. Small jars of it can be found in the Asian or gourmet section of your supermarket and at Asian food markets. Read the label for how much heat it packs and experiment if you're adventuresome.

Lamb is seasoned with garlic, curry, rosemary, and pepper and marinated in soy sauce for a sensational flavor combination.

Garlic Lamb Burgers

John—Monroeville, PA

Ingredients

1 **pound ground lamb**

6 **cloves garlic, minced**

¼ **teaspoon curry powder**

¼ **teaspoon dried rosemary, crushed**

¼ **teaspoon ground black pepper**

¼ **cup soy sauce**

   Nonstick cooking spray

4 **slices Swiss, cheddar, or American cheese**

4 **kaiser rolls, split and toasted**

4 **slices onion**

   Dijon-style mustard

Prep: 15 minutes Marinate: 10 minutes Cook: 9 minutes

Method

1. In a large bowl combine lamb, garlic, curry powder, rosemary, and pepper; mix well. Divide into four equal portions; shape into ½-inch-thick patties. Place patties in shallow glass dish. Pour soy sauce over; marinate at room temperature for 10 minutes.

2. Coat an unheated large skillet with nonstick cooking spray. Preheat over medium-high heat. Add patties to hot skillet. Reduce heat to medium. Cook for 9 to 12 minutes or until juices run clear (160°F).

3. Turn off heat. Place cheese on burgers; cover and let stand for 1 minute. Place roll bottom on plate; top with burger and onion. Spread tops of rolls with mustard; place on onion-topped burgers mustard side down.

Makes 4 servings

These small hamburgers are dressed up with french fries, sliced cheese, olives, and ketchup for monstrous fun. Just be sure to remove the toothpicks before eating!

Mini Monster Burger Plates

Pamela–Parkersburg, WV

Prep: 30 minutes **Cook:** 12 minutes

Method

1. Divide ground beef into 12 equal portions; shape each portion into a ¾-inch-thick patty. Sprinkle patties with salt. In a very large skillet cook patties over medium heat for 12 to 15 minutes or until done (160°F).

2. Meanwhile, arrange potatoes in a single layer on a large baking sheet; bake according to package directions.

3. Place burgers on bun bottoms; place each on a small white paper plate. Cut each cheese slice into six strips. Arrange six strips on each burger to resemble the legs of a spider. Top with bun tops.

4. Cut each french fried potato-spiral in half. Run toothpick through half of the halved spirals; arrange on bun tops to look like antennae or ears. Arrange two or three olive slices on each bun to look like eyes.

5. Place remaining halved potato-spirals under sides of buns to look like arms. Garnish plate with ketchup to look like blood.

Makes 12 servings

Cook's Notes
These are so adorable, and my grandchildren love them. They also make a nice little lunch with just the right size burger for children.

Ingredients

1 ¼	pounds lean ground beef
1	teaspoon salt
24	frozen french fried spiral-cut potatoes
12	rich butter rolls (such as King's Hawaiian brand), split
12	slices American cheese
4	to 6 small pimiento-stuffed green olives, sliced
	Ketchup

All the delicious flavor of a BLT sandwich—in a grilled wrap! Flour tortillas are loaded up with ranch dressing, cooked bacon, tomatoes, lettuce, and Gruyère cheese.

BLT Grilled Wraps quick

Elaine—Dallas, TX

48

Ingredients

16   slices bacon

4   large flour tortillas

½   cup bottled ranch salad dressing

2   large tomatoes, thinly sliced

4   ounces Gruyère cheese, thinly sliced

2   cups shredded Boston lettuce

2   tablespoons finely chopped red onion

½   teaspoon sea salt

½   teaspoon freshly ground black pepper

Start to finish: 25 minutes

Method

1. In large skillet cook bacon over medium heat until golden and crisp. Remove crisped bacon from skillet; place on paper towels and lightly blot to absorb excess grease.

2. Place tortillas on work surface and spread ranch dressing in center of each tortilla. Place four bacon slices along one edge of each tortilla. Top with tomato, cheese, lettuce, and red onion; sprinkle with sea salt and pepper. Fold to form a wrap.

3. On a griddle or in a large skillet place wraps, seam sides down. Cook over medium-high heat for 4 to 5 minutes or until golden, turning once. Serve immediately.

Makes 4 servings

Cook's Notes
For extra flavor, I like to use applewood smoked bacon.

Sautéed onions, peppers, and black beans are encased in whole wheat tortillas and served with plenty of chunky picante sauce.

quick Quick Black Bean Wraps

Kim—Kingwood, TX

Start to finish: 25 minutes

Method

1. In a nonstick saucepan heat olive oil over medium heat. Stir in onion; cover and cook for 5 minutes. Stir in sweet pepper; cover and cook for 5 minutes more. Stir in black beans, chile peppers, and ½ cup of the picante sauce; cook, uncovered, for 5 minutes more.

2. In a toaster oven lightly toast the tortillas. Scoop about ½ cup of the bean mixture onto each tortilla; roll up and serve warm. Top wraps with the remaining picante sauce.

Makes 4 servings

Cook's Notes
This isn't fancy, but it's very quick to make and quite delicious!

Ingredients

1   teaspoon olive oil

1   onion, thinly sliced

1   red sweet pepper, sliced

1   15-ounce can black beans, rinsed and drained

1   4.5-ounce can chopped green chile peppers

1   cup thick and chunky picante sauce

4   whole wheat tortillas

Serve these yummy chicken sandwiches with deli coleslaw or potato salad for an easy lunchtime treat.

Honey Mustard Chicken Wraps

Patti—Islip, NY

50

Ingredients

1   pound skinless boneless chicken breast halves, cut into bite-size strips

½   cup bottled honey-Dijon salad dressing, plus additional for drizzling

4   slices Swiss cheese

4   large flour tortillas

10 slices turkey bacon, crisp-cooked, drained, and crumbled

2   tomatoes, sliced

1   cup shredded lettuce

½   cup chopped red onion

Prep: 20 minutes Marinate: 30 minutes Cook: 3 minutes

Method

1. Place chicken in a large resealable plastic bag; pour the ½ cup honey-Dijon dressing over. Seal bag; turn to coat chicken. Marinate chicken at room temperature for 30 minutes.

2. Drain chicken, discarding marinade. In a large skillet cook and stir chicken for 3 to 4 minutes or until it is tender and juices run clear (170°F).

3. To assemble wraps, place one slice of the cheese on each tortilla. Divide cooked chicken among the tortillas. Divide bacon, tomato, lettuce, and red onion among wraps. Drizzle with additional honey-Dijon dressing. Roll tortillas up tightly; cut in half crosswise.

Makes 4 servings

Shredded chicken in hot sauce is combined with celery, carrot, and blue cheese dressing, then wrapped in flour tortillas with onion and lettuce.

Buffalo Chicken Wraps

Desmond—New Carrollton, MD

Prep: 25 minutes **Cook:** 8 minutes

Method

1. In a medium bowl combine celery and carrot; stir in blue cheese dressing and set aside.

2. Sprinkle chicken breasts with garlic powder, thyme, salt, and pepper. In a large skillet heat oil over medium-high heat. Add chicken; cook for 8 to 12 minutes or until chicken is tender and juices run clear (170°F), turning once. Transfer chicken to a plate; let stand until cool enough to handle.

3. Meanwhile, in a small microwave-safe bowl combine hot pepper sauce and butter; microwave about 1 minute or until butter is melted. Whisk hot sauce mixture until combined.

4. Using two forks, shred chicken breasts; fold into hot sauce mixture.

5. Cover tortillas two at a time, with a wet paper towel; microwave on 100% power (high) for 10 to 15 seconds to warm.

6. Place lettuce and a few strips of onion at one edge of each tortilla; top each with approximately 1½ tablespoons of the chicken mixture. Top with celery mixture. Fold in sides; roll up to form wraps.

Makes 4 servings

Cook's Notes
Serve the wraps with chips and salsa or with a pasta salad.

Ingredients

2   stalks celery, thinly sliced

1   carrot, grated

½   cup bottled blue cheese salad dressing

2   skinless boneless chicken breast halves

⅛   teaspoon garlic powder

⅛   teaspoon dried thyme, crushed

    Salt

    Ground black pepper

1   tablespoon cooking oil

¼   cup bottled hot pepper sauce

¼   cup unsalted butter

8   9- to 10-inch flour tortillas

    Torn leaf lettuce

1   red onion, halved and thinly sliced

There's plenty of flavor in these luscious tortilla wraps! Cream cheese, Jarlsberg cheese, turkey, lettuce, egg slices, and broccoli spears all make an appearance.

Turkey Broccoli Roll-Ups quick

Deborah—Lilburn, GA

Ingredients

- 6 ounces chive and onion cream cheese spread
- 4 8-inch sun-dried tomato flour tortillas
- 4 ounces Jarlsberg cheese, sliced
- 12 ounces very thinly sliced deli turkey
- 4 lettuce leaves
- 2 hard-cooked eggs, sliced
- 1 10-ounce package frozen broccoli spears, cooked according to package directions and well drained

Start to finish: 15 minutes

Method

1. Spread cream cheese on the top half of each tortilla; top with sliced cheese, turkey, lettuce, egg slices, and broccoli (trimming to fit if needed).

2. Fold the bottom half of each tortilla over the top half to within 1½ inches of the top edge. Fold in sides; roll up. Secure with decorative toothpicks.

Makes 4 servings

Chapter 3
Salads

This eye-catching salad combines the colors and flavors of mixed greens, strawberries, orange sweet pepper, red onion, and diced pears.

Over-the-Rainbow Salad

Mary—Ada, OK

54

Ingredients

¼ cup white balsamic vinegar

¼ cup olive oil

1 tablespoon lime juice

1 teaspoon lemon-pepper seasoning

¼ teaspoon garlic powder

¼ teaspoon salt

8 cups torn mixed salad greens

1 pint fresh strawberries, hulled and quartered

½ cup slivered almonds, lightly toasted

¼ cup chopped orange sweet pepper

3 tablespoons chopped red onion

2 firm yellow pears

Prep: 20 minutes   Chill: 1 hour

Method

1. For dressing, in a screw-top jar combine balsamic vinegar, olive oil, lime juice, lemon-pepper seasoning, garlic powder, and salt. Cover and shake well. Set aside.

2. In a large bowl gently toss together salad greens, strawberries, almonds, sweet pepper, and red onion. Chill for 1 hour.

3. Dice pears; add to salad greens mixture. Shake dressing well; pour over salad. Gently toss to coat.

Makes 4 to 6 servings

Cook's Notes
This colorful salad goes hand in hand with grilled chicken or seafood for a healthy meal. It is easy to make as well as delicious.

This light salad with a sugar-free syrup relies on a variety of fruits and a little bit of white wine for its sweetness.

Fruity Sangria Salad

Corvilia–Renton, WA

Prep: 25 minutes **Chill:** 1 hour

Method

1. For syrup, in a medium saucepan combine water, wine, sugar substitute, quartered lime, and ginger. Cook and stir over medium heat for 3 to 4 minutes or until sugar substitute is dissolved. Discard lime and ginger. Cool to room temperature.

2. In a large bowl combine apples, grapes, melon cubes, nectarines, and lemon juice. Pour cooled syrup mixture over fruit and stir lightly to combine. Chill for 1 to 2 hours. Divide among serving bowls and top with whipped topping and lime zest.

Makes 6 to 8 servings

Ingredients

1 ¼	cups water
½	cup dry white wine or sparkling white wine
⅓	cup sugar substitute blend (such as Splenda brand)
1	lime, quartered
1	1-inch piece fresh ginger, peeled
3	medium Granny Smith apples, cored and chopped
2 ½	cups seedless green grapes
2	cups cubed honeydew melon
2	cups cubed cantaloupe
2	nectarines, peeled (if desired), pitted, and sliced
1	tablespoon lemon juice
1	cup frozen light whipped dessert topping, thawed
1	teaspoon grated lime zest

Prepare this salad when you're expecting a crowd for supper. It's full of your favorite taco ingredients, such as ground beef, tomatoes, and cheese. See photo on page 211.

Taco Salad *quick*

Lisa—Austin, TX

Ingredients

1 ½   pounds ground beef

1   8-ounce jar mild taco sauce

1   1.25-ounce envelope taco seasoning mix

1   head lettuce, shredded

1   cup chopped onion

1   cup chopped celery

4   medium tomatoes, chopped

¾   cup chopped green sweet pepper

3   cups shredded cheddar or taco blend cheese

1   8-ounce package taco-flavor tortilla chips, coarsely crushed

1   8-ounce bottle Russian salad dressing

Start to finish: 25 minutes

Method

1. In a large skillet brown ground beef; stir in taco sauce and taco seasoning mix. Let cool.

2. In a large salad bowl combine lettuce, onion, celery, tomato, and sweet pepper. Add ground beef mixture, cheese, and chips. Pour salad dressing over; toss to coat.

Makes 10 servings

Cook's Notes
Russian salad dressing is actually American in origin. It includes mayonnaise, pimiento, chili sauce, chives, and other herbs. Its name may have come from the fact that it used to contain caviar—a famous Russian delicacy.

You can make the blue cheese salad dressing a few days in advance. Keep it covered in the refrigerator.

quick Chicken Salad with Blue Cheese Dressing

Beth—Silver Spring, MD

Start to finish: 25 minutes

Method

1. For dressing, in a blender combine buttermilk, the 1 cup blue cheese, the sour cream, mayonnaise, mustard, lemon juice, and garlic. Cover and blend until smooth. Season to taste with pepper. Set dressing aside.

2. In a large skillet cook bacon over medium heat until crisp. Drain bacon on paper towels, reserving 2 tablespoons drippings in skillet. Crumble bacon. Add pecans to drippings in skillet; cook pecans until brown.

3. In a large bowl toss romaine with pecans, crumbled bacon, and apple; divide among dinner plates. Arrange chicken slices on top of salad. Top with red onion and, if desired, additional blue cheese. Serve with the dressing.

Makes 4 servings

Cook's Notes
All the ingredient amounts in both the salad and the dressing can be adjusted according to taste. This is great served with corn bread!

Ingredients

2 **cups buttermilk**

1 **cup crumbled blue cheese, plus additional for garnish (optional)**

1 **cup sour cream**

¼ **cup mayonnaise**

¼ **cup Dijon-style mustard**

1 **tablespoon lemon juice**

2 **to 3 cloves garlic, minced**

Ground black pepper

8 **slices bacon**

1 **cup chopped pecans**

3 **to 4 cups torn fresh romaine, arugula, and/or spinach**

1 **cup finely chopped apple**

2 **large skinless boneless chicken breast halves, cooked and sliced**

½ **of a small red onion, thinly sliced**

Grilled chicken tenderloins are tossed with artichoke hearts, romaine, and an oil-and-vinegar dressing for a satisfying yet light main course. See photo on page 211.

Grilled Chicken-Artichoke Salad

Toniann—Centennial, CO

58

Ingredients

1   pound chicken breast tenderloins

    Salt

    Black pepper

6   tablespoons olive oil

1   9-ounce package frozen artichoke hearts, thawed

1   head romaine lettuce, chopped

2   tomatoes, halved and sliced

1   sweet pepper (any color), sliced

1   cucumber, sliced

⅓   cup balsamic vinegar

Prep: 20 minutes Grill: 8 minutes

Method

1. Sprinkle chicken with salt and black pepper. Place chicken on oiled rack of an uncovered grill directly over medium coals. Grill for 8 to 10 minutes or until chicken is tender and no longer pink (170°F). Cut chicken into bite-size pieces.

2. Meanwhile, in a medium skillet cook artichoke hearts in 1 tablespoon hot olive oil about 5 minutes or until tender; sprinkle with salt and black pepper. In a large bowl combine romaine lettuce, tomato, sweet pepper, and cucumber. Add chicken and artichoke hearts; gently toss to combine.

3. For dressing, in a small bowl whisk together the remaining 5 tablespoons olive oil, the balsamic vinegar, ⅛ teaspoon salt, and ⅛ teaspoon black pepper. Pour dressing over chicken mixture; gently toss to combine.

Makes 2 to 4 servings

First marinated in a mixture of taco seasoning mix, lemon juice, and oil, these chicken breasts are then broiled, sliced, and served on lettuce with all the extras.

Southwest Chicken Salad

Gail—Covina, CA

Prep: 15 minutes **Marinate:** 20 minutes **Broil:** 12 minutes

Method

1. In a small bowl stir together oil, lemon juice, water, and taco seasoning mix. Place chicken in a large resealable plastic bag. Pour oil mixture over chicken. Marinate at room temperature for 20 minutes.

2. Preheat broiler. Drain chicken, discarding marinade. Place chicken on unheated rack of a broiler pan. Broil 4 to 5 inches from the heat for 12 to 15 minutes or until chicken is tender and no longer pink (170°F). Cool slightly; thinly slice chicken.

3. Divide lettuce among dinner plates. Top lettuce with chicken, salsa, cheese, sour cream, and olives.

Makes 6 servings

Cook's Notes
This meal lends itself well to a buffet because of all the topping options. Allow guests to select from the choices provided in the recipe—and your own favorites, such as crushed tortilla chips.

Ingredients

¼   cup cooking oil

¼   cup lemon juice

¼   cup water

1   1-ounce package taco seasoning mix

1½   pounds skinless boneless chicken breast halves

8   cups torn lettuce

1   cup purchased salsa

1   cup shredded cheddar cheese

½   cup sour cream

¼   cup ripe olives

This flavorful turkey salad with sweet peppers, peas, Swiss cheese, and creamy horseradish dressing is perfect for lunch. It's a great way to use up turkey leftovers.

Turkey Salad with Horseradish Dressing

Betty—Atlanta, GA

60

Ingredients

- 12 ounces roasted turkey breast, cut into thin bite-size strips
- 4 ounces Swiss cheese, cut into thin bite-size strips
- 1¼ cups cooked fresh or frozen peas
- ⅓ cup chopped red sweet pepper
- 2 tablespoons chopped fresh chives or 2 small green onions, sliced
- ⅓ cup mayonnaise
- ⅓ cup sour cream or plain yogurt
- 1½ to 2 tablespoons prepared horseradish

  Freshly ground black pepper

  Butterhead lettuce or romaine lettuce leaves

Start to Finish: 20 minutes

Method

1. In large bowl toss together turkey, Swiss cheese, peas, sweet pepper, and chives. For dressing, in a small bowl combine mayonnaise, sour cream, and horseradish.

2. Add dressing to turkey mixture; gently toss to coat. Season to taste with black pepper.

3. Arrange lettuce leaves on four dinner plates. Spoon turkey mixture over lettuce.

Makes 4 servings

Looking for a healthful dinner? Try this turkey and feta salad. It has lots of nutritious veggies and is low in fat.

◆quick◆ Turkey-Feta Cheese Salad

Rose—Campbell, CA

+ +

Prep: 15 minutes   **Cook:** 15 minutes

Method

1. Coat an unheated large skillet with nonstick cooking spray. Preheat over medium heat. Add ground turkey, seasoned salt, onion powder, garlic powder, black pepper, and crushed red pepper; cook about 15 minutes or until turkey is brown.

2. In a large serving bowl combine salad greens, cherry tomatoes, red onion, and feta cheese. Spoon turkey mixture over. Sprinkle with crushed tortilla chips.

Makes 3 to 4 servings

Ingredients

Nonstick cooking spray

1   pound uncooked ground turkey breast

1   teaspoon seasoned salt

½   teaspoon onion powder

½   teaspoon garlic powder

½   teaspoon ground black pepper

¼   teaspoon crushed red pepper

1   16-ounce package torn mixed salad greens

12   cherry tomatoes

½   of a red onion, chopped

½   cup crumbled feta cheese

1   cup crushed baked tortilla chips

This salad, which is served over torn fresh spinach, is dressed with a mixture of olive oil, balsamic vinegar, garlic, lemon juice, oregano, and parsley.

Mediterranean Lamb and Barley Salad

Patricia—Baden, PA

Ingredients

2   cups water

1   cup quick-cooking barley

¼   cup olive oil

1   teaspoon grated lemon zest

2   tablespoons lemon juice

1   tablespoon white balsamic vinegar

1   tablespoon chopped fresh flat-leaf parsley

1   teaspoon chopped fresh oregano or ½ teaspoon dried oregano, crushed

1   clove garlic, minced

½   teaspoon salt

⅛   teaspoon freshly ground black pepper

2   cups chopped cooked lamb

½   cup peeled, seeded, and chopped cucumber

½   cup seeded and chopped plum tomato

2   ounces crumbled feta cheese with basil and tomato

6   cups torn fresh spinach

Prep: 25 minutes Cook: 10 minutes Chill: 1 hour

Method

1. In a medium saucepan bring water to boiling; add barley. Reduce heat; cover and simmer for 10 minutes. Remove from heat; let stand for 5 minutes. Chill about 1 hour or until cool.

2. Meanwhile, for dressing, in a small bowl whisk together olive oil, lemon zest, lemon juice, balsamic vinegar, parsley, oregano, garlic, salt, and pepper. Set aside.

3. Add lamb, cucumber, tomato, and feta cheese to barley. Pour dressing over lamb mixture; toss to coat.

4. To serve, divide spinach among dinner plates. Spoon lamb and barley mixture into center of spinach.

Makes 4 servings

Cook's Notes
Remember this salad when you have leftover lamb. In fact, this recipe may help you finish off several odds and ends in your pantry and/or refrigerator.

 Tip

Seeding a Cuke The best way to seed a cucumber is, of course, to first peel it. Cut off the ends, then cut it horizontally down through the center. With the tip of a teaspoon or other small spoon, scrape the seeds out, top to bottom. You'll wind up with a hollowed-out cucumber half that resembles a canoe.

Salad greens, sweet pepper, and Italian salad dressing turn an ordinary meat and cheese tray into an extraordinary salad your guests will love.

quick Easy Antipasto Salad

Pamela—Parkersburg, WV

Start to finish: 15 minutes

Method

1. Arrange salad greens and sweet pepper on a serving platter or in a large bowl. Arrange ham, salami, provolone cheese, Colby cheese, and pepperoni over greens and pepper. Drizzle salad dressing over salad.

Makes about 6 servings

Ingredients

1 16-ounce package torn mixed salad greens

1 green sweet pepper, chopped

8 ounces cooked ham, cut into bite-size pieces

8 ounces salami, cut into bite-size pieces

8 ounces provolone cheese, cut into bite-size pieces

8 ounces Colby cheese, cut into bite-size pieces

12 pepperoni slices

Bottled Italian salad dressing

This main dish salad combines cubes of flavorful broiled pork tenderloin with shredded cabbage and avocado and a drizzle of a zesty dressing.

Pork and Cabbage Salad

Laura–Fort Wayne, IN

Ingredients

1 **pound pork tenderloin**

¼ **cup soy sauce (reduced-sodium, if desired)**

2 **cloves garlic, minced**

1 **teaspoon minced fresh ginger**

1 **16-ounce package shredded cabbage with carrot (coleslaw mix)**

1 **avocado, peeled, pitted, and cubed**

¼ **cup olive oil**

Juice of 1 lime

2 **green onions, sliced**

Honey-roasted peanuts

Prep: 25 minutes Broil: 16 minutes

Method

1. Preheat broiler. Split the pork tenderloin lengthwise to butterfly (do not slice all the way through). Place tenderloin on unheated rack of a broiler pan.

2. In a small bowl combine 1 tablespoon of the soy sauce, half of the minced garlic, and half of the minced ginger. Spread soy sauce mixture over tenderloin; rub in with your fingers. Broil tenderloin for 16 to 20 minutes or until done (160°F). Cool and cube pork.

3. In a salad bowl layer coleslaw mix, pork, and avocado. In a screw-top jar combine olive oil, lime juice, the remaining 3 tablespoons soy sauce, the remaining garlic, and the remaining ginger. Cover and shake well. Pour dressing over salad; gently toss to coat. Sprinkle with green onion and peanuts.

Makes 4 servings

Cook's Notes
To make this salad easier and quicker to throw together, broil the pork the day before and refrigerate.

This make-ahead layered salad combines lettuce, peas, green onion, and water chestnuts. Just before serving, add tomato, crumbled bacon, and eggs.

Supereasy Salad Stack

Mary—Ada, OK

Prep: 20 minutes **Chill:** 8 hours

Method

1. In a deep 2-quart clear glass bowl or serving dish layer salad greens, peas, celery, green onion, and water chestnuts. Spread mayonnaise evenly on top. Sprinkle with Parmesan cheese, sugar, seasoned salt, and garlic powder. Cover and chill for 8 to 24 hours.

2. Just before serving, top with tomato, bacon, and egg. Toss to serve.

Makes 8 to 10 servings

Cook's Notes
I have been preparing this "make-ahead" salad for years. It is a family favorite that is perfect to take to reunions and other get-togethers.

Ingredients

1   **16-ounce package torn mixed salad greens**

1   **10-ounce package frozen peas, thawed**

½   **cup finely chopped celery**

4   **green onions, thinly sliced**

1   **8-ounce can sliced water chestnuts, drained**

2   **cups mayonnaise**

¼   **cup grated Parmesan cheese**

2   **teaspoons sugar**

1   **teaspoon seasoned salt**

¼   **teaspoon garlic powder**

2   **tomatoes, diced**

8   **slices bacon, crisp-cooked and crumbled**

3   **hard-cooked eggs, quartered**

This Asian-inspired spinach salad showcases shiitake mushrooms, water chestnuts, rice wine vinegar, soy sauce, and toasted sesame oil.

Allison's Asian Spinach Salad quick

Allison—Plano, TX

Ingredients

1 **10-ounce package fresh baby spinach**

4 **ounces fresh shiitake mushrooms (or other variety), sliced**

1 **8-ounce can water chestnuts, drained and chopped**

2 **grapefruit, sectioned and cut up**

¼ **cup toasted sesame oil**

2 **tablespoons rice wine vinegar**

2 **tablespoons grapefruit juice**

1 **tablespoon soy sauce**

1 **teaspoon sugar**

1 **teaspoon bottled hot pepper sauce (or to taste)**

¼ **teaspoon salt**

¼ **teaspoon dry mustard**

Start to finish: 20 minutes

Method

1. Gently rinse the spinach; drain well and put into large salad bowl. Add mushrooms, water chestnuts, and grapefruit.

2. In a small bowl whisk together toasted sesame oil, vinegar, grapefruit juice, soy sauce, sugar, hot pepper sauce, salt, and dry mustard. Toss with spinach mixture just before serving.

Makes 6 to 8 servings

Cook's Notes
This is awesome served with chicken or fish.

Tip

Prepping Shiitakes You don't want to eat the stem of a shiitake mushroom—it's hard and woody. Always cut the stems of shiitake mushrooms completely off before you slice them.

Goat cheese, dried cranberries, red pear, and toasted walnuts make this tossed green salad extra-special.

quick Romaine and Spinach Salad

Jodie—San Antonio, TX

Start to finish: 20 minutes

Method

1. In a salad bowl combine romaine, baby spinach, pear, goat cheese, walnuts, and dried cranberries; set aside.

2. For vinaigrette, whisk together balsamic vinegar, olive oil, poppy seeds, garlic, salt, brown sugar, and pepper; pour over salad. Gently toss to combine.

Makes 6 servings

Ingredients

3 cups torn romaine lettuce

3 cups torn baby spinach

1 red pear, chopped

4 ounces goat cheese, crumbled

4 ounces walnuts, toasted and coarsely chopped

½ cup dried cranberries

½ cup balsamic vinegar

½ cup olive oil

1 tablespoon poppy seeds

1 tablespoon minced garlic

1 teaspoon salt

1 teaspoon packed brown sugar

½ teaspoon ground black pepper

Tote this cabbage salad to your potluck or picnic! The delightful crunch comes from three sources—ramen noodles, almonds, and sesame seeds.

Mama's Best Chinese Cabbage Salad

Jennifer—River Vale, NJ

Ingredients

½ **cup butter**

½ **to 1 cup slivered almonds**

3 **tablespoons sesame seeds**

1 **large head Chinese cabbage (napa), sliced and then chopped**

2 **bunches green onions, chopped**

2 **3-ounce packages uncooked ramen noodles (any flavor), broken (discard seasoning packet)**

1 **cup sugar**

1 **cup cooking oil**

½ **cup cider vinegar**

1 **tablespoon soy sauce**

Prep: 20 minutes Chill: 1 hour

Method

1. In skillet melt butter over medium heat. Add almonds and sesame seeds; cook until toasted. Let cool.

2. In a large bowl combine cabbage and green onion. Add almond mixture and broken ramen noodles; gently toss to combine.

3. For dressing, in a medium bowl whisk together sugar, oil, cider vinegar, and soy sauce. Pour over cabbage mixture; gently toss to coat. Cover and chill for 1 to 2 hours before serving.

Makes 8 servings

Cook's Notes
This is a real crowd pleaser! Do not expect leftovers as this delights even the most jaded of palates.

Tip

What is napa cabbage? Napa cabbage is a Chinese cabbage that resembles romaine lettuce. The leaves are upright and tightly compact with curly edges. They're pale green and crinkly with a wide white center stalk.

Tossed with a sweet-and-sour dressing, this broccoli salad highlights crumbled bacon, raisins, and water chestnuts.

quick Broccoli Slaw

Marjorie—Skaneateles, NY

Start to finish: 20 minutes

Method

1. Break broccoli into small florets. Peel broccoli stalks and slice crosswise. In large skillet cook bacon until crisp; drain well and crumble.

2. In a large bowl combine broccoli, bacon, water chestnuts, cheese, onion, and raisins. In a small bowl stir together mayonnaise, sugar, and vinegar. Pour mayonnaise mixture over broccoli mixture; gently toss to coat.

Makes 6 to 8 servings

Ingredients

1   large bunch broccoli

8   ounces bacon

1   8-ounce can sliced water chestnuts, drained

1   cup finely shredded Colby cheese

½   cup chopped sweet onion (such as Vidalia)

½   cup raisins

1   cup mayonnaise

½   cup sugar

2   tablespoons vinegar

Creamy and delightful, this red potato salad gets its kick from Italian salad dressing, capers, horseradish, and ripe olives.

Italian Red Potato Salad

Karyn—Henderson, NV

70

Ingredients

- 5 large red potatoes, peeled and cut into large chunks
- ½ cup bottled Italian salad dressing
- ½ cup sour cream
- ¼ cup mayonnaise
- 2 tablespoons creamy horseradish
- 2 7.5-ounce cans pitted ripe olives, drained and chopped
- 1 cup finely chopped celery
- ¼ cup finely chopped onion
- ¼ cup capers, drained
-   Salt
-   Ground black pepper

Prep: 35 minutes **Stand:** 45 minutes **Chill:** 1 hour

Method

1. In a covered large saucepan cook potato in a generous amount of boiling salted water about 15 minutes or just until tender. Drain. In a large bowl gently toss together potato and Italian dressing. Let stand about 45 minutes or until cooled to room temperature.

2. Add sour cream, mayonnaise, and horseradish; gently toss to combine.

3. Add drained olives, celery, onion, and capers; gently toss to combine. Season to taste with salt and pepper. Cover and chill for 1 hour before serving.

Makes 10 servings

Cook's Notes
You may have to add more or less sour cream depending on the size of your potatoes.

Shrimp, strawberries, raisins, almonds, bacon, and hearts of palm are tossed with raspberry vinaigrette and served on Boston lettuce leaves.

◆quick◆ Summer Shrimp Salad

Alicia—Olathe, KS

Start to finish: 20 minutes

Method

1. In a large bowl combine shrimp, chopped hearts of palm, sliced strawberries, golden raisins, green onion, bacon pieces, and sliced almonds. Pour raspberry vinaigrette over the mixture; gently toss to coat.

2. Place a single Boston lettuce leaf on dinner plates. Spoon one-fourth of the shrimp mixture into the center of each lettuce leaf.

Makes 4 servings

Cook's Notes
Heart of palm is the edible portion of the stem of the cabbage palm tree, which is the state tree of Florida. It is white and tastes similar to artichoke hearts.

Ingredients

20   medium cooked shrimp, peeled and deveined

½   cup canned hearts of palm, drained and chopped

10   fresh strawberries, sliced

¼   cup golden raisins

1   green onion, sliced

2   tablespoons cooked bacon pieces

1½   tablespoons sliced almonds

½   cup bottled raspberry vinaigrette salad dressing

4   Boston lettuce leaves

Crab salad gets a power boost from spaghetti, cauliflower, and broccoli. Cheese, mayonnaise, and two types of salad dressing ensure every bite is divine.

Crab Salad quick

Tim—Bondurant, IA

Ingredients

12	ounces dried spaghetti
8	to 12 ounces flaked cooked crabmeat
1	cup shredded co-jack cheese
½	cup chopped onion
½	cup chopped cauliflower
½	cup chopped broccoli
½	cup frozen peas
½	cup mayonnaise or salad dressing
¼	cup bottled Italian salad dressing
¼	cup bottled ranch salad dressing
	Salt
	Ground black pepper

Start to finish: 25 minutes

Method

1. Cook spaghetti according to package directions. Drain in colander and rinse with cold water.

2. In a large bowl combine cooked spaghetti, crabmeat, cheese, onion, cauliflower, broccoli, and peas. In a small bowl stir together mayonnaise, Italian salad dressing, ranch salad dressing, and salt and pepper to taste. Pour mayonnaise mixture over spaghetti mixture; gently toss to coat.

Makes 4 to 6 servings

Looking for a cool salad for a hot summer day? Try this sensational flank steak and soba noodle mixture. An Asian-style vinaigrette finishes it off perfectly.

Flank Steak Pasta Salad

Melissa—Studio City, CA

Prep: 20 minutes **Broil:** 15 minutes

Method

1. Preheat broiler. Cook soba noodles according to package directions; drain and set aside.

2. Meanwhile, brush both sides of the steak with olive oil; sprinkle with salt and black pepper. Place on unheated rack of a broiler pan. Broil for 15 to 18 minutes or until it reaches medium doneness (160°F). Let stand for 15 minutes. Thinly slice steak across the grain, cutting longer strips in half.

3. In a large bowl combine cooked noodles, steak, sweet pepper, green onion, and carrot. For salad dressing, in a small bowl whisk together sesame oil, rice wine vinegar, ginger, soy sauce, hot pepper sauce, and garlic. Pour dressing over noodle mixture; gently toss to coat. Serve immediately or chill before serving.

Makes 6 servings

Cook's Notes
Soba noodles are Japanese noodles made from wheat flour and buckwheat flour, which gives them a golden color. You can find them in the Asian section of your supermarket or at Asian food stores.

Ingredients

1   10.5-ounce package soba noodles

1½ pounds beef flank steak

1   tablespoon olive oil

1   teaspoon salt

½   teaspoon black pepper

1   red sweet pepper, cut into thin bite-size strips

6   green onions, chopped

½   cup shredded carrot

½   cup toasted sesame oil

¼   cup rice wine vinegar

2   tablespoons minced fresh ginger

2   tablespoons soy sauce

2   teaspoons bottled hot pepper sauce

2   teaspoons minced garlic

This Greek pasta salad is filled with vibrant vegetables and enlivened with Italian dressing. Make it as a stunning side dish for your next picnic.

Greek Orzo Salad

Cindie—Andover, MA

Ingredients

½   cup dried orzo or rosamarina pasta

1   15-ounce can garbanzo beans (chickpeas), rinsed and drained

1½   cups chopped cherry or grape tomatoes

1   cup chopped green sweet pepper

1   cup chopped cucumber

⅓   cup sliced black olives

½   cup bottled Italian salad dressing

Crumbled feta cheese (optional)

Prep: 30 minutes   Chill: 1 hour

Method

1. Cook pasta according to package directions; drain, rinse, and cool.

2. In a large bowl combine cooked pasta, drained garbanzo beans, tomato, sweet pepper, cucumber, and olives. Pour Italian dressing over; gently toss to coat. Cover and chill for 1 to 2 hours.

3. If desired, sprinkle with feta cheese before serving.

Makes 6 servings

Red tomatoes, orange and yellow sweet peppers, green herbs, and white feta cheese make up the five colors in this refreshingly simple salad.

Five-Color Orzo Salad

Kelly—Houston, TX

Prep: 25 minutes **Stand:** 20 minutes

Method

1. Cook pasta according to package directions; drain well and rinse with cold water.

2. In a large bowl toss together cooked pasta, tomatoes, feta cheese, sweet pepper, red onion, basil, and parsley.

3. In a medium bowl whisk together lemon juice, olive oil, salt, black pepper, and garlic; pour over salad and toss. Let stand at room temperature for 20 minutes. Toss again before serving.

Makes 6 to 8 servings

Cook's Notes
Add boiled peeled shrimp to make this a main dish.

Ingredients

1 ½   cups dried orzo or rosamarina pasta

1   cup cherry tomatoes, halved

1   cup crumbled feta cheese

½   cup finely chopped orange sweet pepper

½   cup finely chopped yellow sweet pepper

¼   cup finely chopped red onion

2   tablespoons chopped fresh basil

2   tablespoons chopped fresh parsley

¼   cup lemon juice

3   tablespoons olive oil

½   teaspoon salt

¼   teaspoon ground black pepper

1   clove garlic, minced

Here's a delicious way to use ramen noodles! This salad combines celery, green onion, water chestnuts, radishes, and peanuts with a zesty dressing.

Peanut-Powered Pacific Rim Salad ◆quick◆

Margee—Trout Lake, WA

Ingredients

4	3-ounce packages uncooked ramen noodles (any flavor)
¼	cup creamy peanut butter
3	tablespoons seasoned rice vinegar
2	tablespoons reduced-sodium soy sauce
2	tablespoons lime juice
1	tablespoon toasted sesame oil
2	teaspoons grated fresh ginger
1	teaspoon chili powder
1	teaspoon minced garlic
½	cup chopped celery
⅓	cup chopped green onions
⅓	cup chopped radishes
¼	cup canned sliced water chestnuts, drained
½	cup honey-roasted peanuts

Start to finish: 25 minutes

Method

1. Stir two of the seasoning packets from the ramen noodles into a large saucepan of boiling water. Discard remaining seasoning packets. Add all of the ramen noodles to the boiling water; cook for 2 minutes. Drain and cool.

2. Meanwhile, for dressing, in a food processor or blender combine peanut butter, seasoned rice vinegar, soy sauce, lime juice, toasted sesame oil, ginger, chili powder, and garlic. Cover and process or blend until smooth.

3. In a large bowl gently toss together cooled noodles, celery, green onion, radishes, and water chestnuts. Drizzle dressing over; gently toss to coat. Sprinkle with peanuts.

Makes 6 servings

Cook's Notes
Although you can serve this delightful salad immediately, if there's time allow the salad to stand at room temperature for 30 minutes so that the flavors can blend and develop.

Refreshing, delicious, and nutritious! This tasty blend of blueberries, cranberries, and raspberries is accompanied by a creamy yogurt-cardamom dressing.

Berry Wild Waldorf

Carolyn–Lacey, WA

Prep: 15 minutes **Chill:** 1 hour

Method

1. In a medium glass bowl combine blueberries, the 1 cup cranberries, the raspberries, celery, raisins, and pecans.

2. In a small bowl stir together yogurt, sugar, and cardamom. Stir into berry mixture, mixing well to coat. Cover and chill for 1 to 2 hours.

3. Just before serving, stir again. If desired, garnish with mint and Frosted Cranberries.

*Frosted Cranberries: To prepare, pat cranberries dry with paper towels. In a small plastic bag shake berries with powdered sugar.

Makes 6 servings

Cook's Notes
This is a very colorful and quick salad that is good on warm days. My children really enjoy it!

Ingredients

2   **cups fresh blueberries**

1   **cup chopped fresh cranberries**

1   **cup fresh raspberries**

½   **cup chopped celery**

½   **cup golden raisins**

¼   **cup chopped pecans**

2   **8-ounce cartons low-fat vanilla yogurt**

2   **tablespoons sugar**

¼   **teaspoon ground cardamom**

    Fresh mint leaves (optional)

    Frosted Cranberries* (optional)

Pineapple, maraschino cherries, coconut, and pecans shine when combined with a luscious cream cheese dressing.

Decadent Tropical Fruit Salad

Mary—Ada, OK

Ingredients

2   6-ounce cartons lemon yogurt

1   8-ounce package cream cheese, softened

¾   cup sugar

3   bananas, diced

1   20-ounce can crushed pineapple (juice pack), drained

1   10-ounce jar maraschino cherries, drained and chopped (if desired, reserve one whole cherry for garnish)

1   cup chopped pecans

½   cup flaked coconut

Fresh mint leaves (optional)

Prep: 15 minutes   Chill: 1 hour

Method

1. In a large bowl beat together yogurt, cream cheese, and sugar until well mixed.

2. Stir in banana, drained pineapple, drained maraschino cherries, pecans, and flaked coconut. Spoon into a 1½-quart glass bowl.

3. Cover and chill 1 to 2 hours before serving. If desired, garnish with the reserved whole maraschino cherry and the mint, putting the cherry in the center and arranging mint leaves around it to form a flower.

Makes 10 to 12 servings

Cook's Notes
This sweet and creamy salad makes a beautiful presentation for any party or event.

The pretzel crust in this salad is topped with a layer each of sweetened cream cheese, whipped topping, and strawberry gelatin. Serve it on the Fourth of July.

Pretzel Salad

Charidy—Ranchester, WY

+ · · · + · · · + · · · + · · · + · · · + · · · + · · · + · · · + · · · + · · · + · · · +

Prep: 30 minutes   **Bake:** 10 minutes   **Chill:** 4½ hours

Method

1. Preheat oven to 400°F. In a medium bowl beat together cream cheese and sugar; set aside.

2. In a small bowl combine crushed pretzels and melted butter; press into a 3-quart rectangular baking dish. Bake for 10 minutes. Cool.

3. Spread cream cheese mixture over pretzel mixture. Spread whipped topping over cream cheese mixture. Chill for 30 minutes.

4. In a small saucepan heat pineapple juice to boiling. Dissolve gelatin in hot pineapple juice. Add frozen strawberries; chill until partially set. Carefully pour gelatin mixture over layers in baking dish. Chill for 4 to 12 hours or until set.

Makes 10 servings

Cook's Notes
This is an excellent dish for any holiday!

Ingredients

12	ounces cream cheese
1½	cups sugar
2⅔	cups crushed pretzels
¾	cup butter or margarine, melted
½	of a 16-ounce container frozen whipped dessert topping, thawed
2	cups unsweetened pineapple juice
1	6-ounce package strawberry-flavor gelatin
1	16-ounce package frozen unsweetened whole strawberries

Easy and very popular, this old-fashioned molded salad combines red raspberry gelatin with applesauce.

Raspberry-Applesauce Gelatin

Janet —Nashville, TN

Ingredients

2 3-ounce packages raspberry-flavor gelatin

2½ cups boiling water

2 cups unsweetened applesauce

Prep: 10 minutes Chill: 4 hours

Method

1. In a medium bowl combine gelatin and boiling water, stirring to dissolve gelatin. Stir in applesauce.

2. Pour into a serving bowl or mold. Chill for 4 to 24 hours or until set.

Makes 8 to 10 servings

Cook's Notes
I call this recipe "my own" although it was actually my mother's. She brought it to many a potluck occasion.

Chapter 4
Poultry

These creamy enchiladas are filled with all kinds of treats—chicken, cheese, olives, veggies, salsa—and enchilada sauce rounds out the dish perfectly.

Simple Chicken Enchiladas

Valene—Eureka, MT

Ingredients

2 10-ounce cans enchilada sauce

½ of a green, red, orange, or yellow sweet pepper, chopped

½ of a large onion, chopped

1 tablespoon olive oil

1 cup purchased salsa

1 8-ounce package cream cheese, softened

1 cup sour cream, plus additional for serving

3 cups diced or shredded cooked chicken

1 2.25-ounce can sliced black olives, drained plus additional for serving

12 corn tortillas

2 cups shredded Mexican cheese blend

Guacamole

Prep: 35 minutes   Bake: 40 minutes

Method

1. Preheat oven to 350°F. Pour half of one can of the enchilada sauce into the bottom of a 13×9×2-inch baking pan. In a large skillet cook sweet pepper and onion in olive oil until tender. Add salsa. Stir in cream cheese until smooth. Gradually stir in the 1 cup sour cream until well mixed. Stir in chicken and the 2.25-ounce can of drained olives.

2. Divide chicken mixture among tortillas, spooning mixture down center of tortillas. Sprinkle with half of the Mexican cheese blend. Roll up tortillas to enclose chicken mixture and cheese. Arrange enchiladas in prepared baking pan. Pour the remaining enchilada sauce over the top.

3. Bake about 30 minutes or until bubbly. Sprinkle with remaining cheese blend. Bake for 10 minutes more. Serve with additional sour cream, guacamole, and additional olives.

Makes 12 servings

Cook's Notes
Flour tortillas may be used instead of corn tortillas, and you can add any mix of the sweet peppers you like (try jalapeño chile peppers too!). Onion can be added to taste, and the black olives can be omitted. Serve with Mexican or Spanish rice.

Chicken breast strips are stir-fried with green onions, ginger, and garlic and seasoned with bourbon and soy sauce.

quick Chinese Walnut Chicken

Lillian—Gainesville, FL

Start to finish: 25 minutes

Method

1. In a large bowl whisk together cold water, egg white, and cornstarch. Add chicken and toss to coat. In a small bowl combine soy sauce, bourbon, and sugar. Set aside.

2. Heat a wok or large heavy skillet over high heat until a drop of water dances across the surface and evaporates immediately. Add 2 tablespoons of the oil; swirl. Add chicken; stir-fry for 3 to 5 minutes or until no longer pink. Quickly remove from pan and set aside.

3. Reduce heat to medium-high; add the remaining 2 tablespoons oil to pan. Add green onion, ginger, and garlic; stir-fry for 1 minute. Return chicken to pan. Add soy sauce mixture; cook and stir for 1 minute. Stir in walnuts. Serve with hot cooked rice.

Makes 4 servings

Cook's Notes
One tablespoon of bourbon is the secret ingredient in this recipe. But since nobody in our family drinks alcohol I buy the smallest bottle of bourbon possible and keep it in my seasoning and flavoring cabinet with the vanilla extract, maple syrup, and spice blends. It keeps forever.

Ingredients

1 tablespoon cold water

1 egg white, beaten

1 teaspoon cornstarch

4 skinless boneless chicken breast halves, cut into 1-inch pieces

3 tablespoons soy sauce

1 tablespoon bourbon

½ teaspoon sugar

4 tablespoons cooking oil

3 green onions, cut into 2-inch slivers

2 slices fresh ginger, minced

1 medium clove garlic, minced

¾ cup coarsely chopped walnuts

Hot cooked rice

Poultry

83

This flavorful roasted chicken is rubbed with a savory mix of seasonings.

Chicken with Seasoned Rub

Melma—Horicon, WI

84

Ingredients

4   teaspoons salt

2   teaspoons paprika

1   teaspoon onion powder

1   teaspoon dried thyme, crushed

½   teaspoon garlic powder

½   teaspoon black pepper

1   4½- to 5-pound whole roasting chicken

Prep: 10 minutes   Chill: 2 hours   Roast: 1½ hours   Stand: 10 minutes

Method

1. In a small bowl combine salt, paprika, onion powder, thyme, garlic powder, and pepper.

2. Sprinkle salt mixture evenly over chicken; rub in with your fingers. Place chicken in a large resealable plastic bag. Seal bag. Refrigerate for 2 to 24 hours.

3. Preheat oven to 375°F. Remove chicken from plastic bag. Place chicken, breast side up, on rack in a shallow roasting pan. Roast, basting frequently with pan juices, for 1½ to 2 hours or until an instant-read thermometer inserted in inside thigh registers 180°F.

4. Let stand for 10 minutes before carving.

Makes 4 servings

Cook's Notes
I have a rotisserie when making this and I do not put my bird in a bag overnight. The chicken is fantastic and is done in 1½ hours when cooked on the rotisserie.

A large roasting chicken is brushed with olive oil and rubbed with a mixture of lemon zest, lemon-pepper seasoning, and herbs.

Roasted Lemon-Pepper Chicken

Leslie—Muenster, IN

✦ ✦

Prep: 15 minutes **Grill:** 1½ hours **Stand:** 10 minutes

Method

1. Brush outside and inside of the chicken with olive oil. In a small bowl combine lemon-pepper seasoning, lemon zest, thyme, salt, basil, black pepper, and garlic. Sprinkle lemon zest mixture evenly over chicken; rub in with your fingers. Place lemon slices in cavity of chicken. Using 100-percent-cotton kitchen string, tie chicken legs to tail.

2. Prepare grill for indirect grilling. Test for medium heat above drip pan. Place chicken on grill rack over drip pan. Cover and grill for 1¾ to 2 hours or until an instant-read meat thermometer inserted in inside thigh registers 180°F.

3. Let stand for 10 minutes before carving.

Makes 6 to 8 servings

Ingredients

1   4½- to 5-pound whole roasting chicken

2   tablespoons olive oil

4   teaspoons lemon-pepper seasoning

1   tablespoon finely shredded lemon zest

2   teaspoons dried thyme, crushed

1   teaspoon salt

1   teaspoon dried basil, crushed

½   teaspoon ground black pepper

4   large cloves garlic, minced

1   lemon, cut into ½-inch slices

The chicken is flavored with garlic and Italian seasonings and served with a rich tomato sauce and Parmesan cheese. See photo on page 212.

Chicken Parmesan

Craig—Tuscola, IL

Ingredients

4	skinless boneless chicken breast halves
1	8-ounce wedge Parmesan cheese
3	tablespoons dried Italian seasoning, crushed
3	tablespoons olive oil
3	cloves garlic, cut into slivers
1	6-ounce can tomato paste
1¼	cups chicken broth
1	pound dried spaghetti, cooked and drained
¼	cup chopped fresh flat-leaf parsley

Prep: 20 minutes Cook: 23 minutes

Method

1. Cut each chicken breast piece almost in half, leaving one side uncut to form a hinge. Cut four ¼-inch slices from the piece of Parmesan cheese. Nestle a slice of the Parmesan cheese inside each chicken breast half. Sprinkle 2 tablespoons of the Italian seasoning over chicken breasts.

2. In a large skillet heat olive oil over medium-low heat. Add chicken breasts and garlic; cook about 20 minutes or until brown, turning once. Transfer chicken breasts to a platter.

3. Add tomato paste and the remaining 1 tablespoon Italian seasoning to the skillet. Gradually stir in chicken broth; bring to boiling. Return chicken breasts to skillet. Heat chicken through, about 3 to 4 minutes.

4. Serve chicken and sauce with hot cooked spaghetti. Grate the remaining Parmesan cheese over chicken; sprinkle with parsley.

Makes 4 servings

Cook's Notes
I make this in a grill pan so the chicken has nice grill marks on it. If you'd like to melt the grated cheese on your chicken, cook the chicken in an ovenproof skillet. After returning chicken breasts to skillet with the sauce, grate the remaining Parmesan cheese over the chicken. Transfer skillet to a preheated 350°F oven; bake for 3 to 4 minutes or until the cheese is melted and slightly brown.

Salami imparts an Italian flair and a bit more spice to traditional cordon bleu. You could substitute provolone cheese for the mozzarella.

Italian Chicken Cordon Bleu

Jackie–Tewksbury, MA

Prep: 20 minutes **Bake:** 45 minutes

Method

1. Preheat oven to 350°F. Place each chicken piece between two sheets of plastic wrap. Using flat side of a meat mallet, lightly pound chicken to ¼-inch thickness.

2. Top each chicken piece with one of the ham slices, one of the mozzarella cheese slices, and one of the salami slices. Roll up chicken pieces to enclose meat and cheese. If necessary, secure with wooden picks.

3. In a shallow bowl beat egg with a fork. Place bread crumbs in another shallow bowl. Dip chicken roll-ups in egg, turning to coat; dip in bread crumbs, turning to coat.

4. Place chicken roll-ups on a greased baking sheet. Bake for 35 minutes.

5. Sprinkle with garlic powder, salt, and pepper. Sprinkle with shredded mozzarella cheese. Bake 10 minutes more.

Makes 4 servings

Cook's Notes
I like to serve this dish with salad and mashed potatoes.

Ingredients

- 4   skinless boneless chicken breast halves
- 4   slices cooked ham
- 4   slices mozzarella cheese
- 4   slices salami
- 1   egg
- ⅓   cup seasoned fine dry bread crumbs
-     Garlic powder
-     Salt
-     Ground black pepper
- ¼   cup shredded mozzarella cheese

Skinless and boneless chicken breast halves are marinated in a mixture of mayonnaise, Dijon-style mustard, and honey before grilling.

Grilled Honey-Mustard Chicken

Debbie—Lebanon, TN

88

Ingredients

- 1   cup mayonnaise or salad dressing
- ¼   cup Dijon-style mustard
- ¼   cup honey
- ½   teaspoon salt
- ½   teaspoon ground black pepper
- 4   skinless boneless chicken breast halves

Prep: 10 minutes Marinate: 2 hours Grill: 12 minutes

Method

1. In a medium bowl combine mayonnaise, mustard, honey, salt, and pepper. Reserve ½ cup of the mayonnaise mixture to use as a brush-on; chill until needed. Place chicken in a large resealable plastic bag. Pour remaining mayonnaise mixture over chicken. Seal bag; turn to coat chicken. Marinate in the refrigerator for 2 to 24 hours, turning bag occasionally.

2. Drain chicken, discarding marinade. Place chicken on rack of an uncovered grill directly over medium coals. Grill for 12 to 15 minutes or until chicken is tender and juices run clear (170°F), turning once and brushing with reserved mayonnaise mixture during the last 5 minutes of grilling.

Makes 4 servings

This baked chicken recipe pumps up the flavor by incorporating the unique tastes of Gouda cheese and honey.

Honey-Stuffed Chicken Breasts

Roya—San Pedro, CA

Prep: 20 minutes **Bake:** 30 minutes **Stand:** 5 minutes

Method

1. Preheat oven to 375°F. For stuffing, in a medium bowl stir together cream of chicken soup, Gouda cheese, drained mushrooms, bread crumbs, 3 tablespoons of the honey, the olives, green onion, salt, and garlic.

2. Divide stuffing among chicken pieces, spooning the mixture near one end of each piece. Roll up chicken pieces to enclose stuffing. If necessary, secure with wooden toothpicks. Place chicken roll-ups on a baking sheet. In a small bowl combine olive oil and the remaining 1 tablespoon honey; brush over chicken roll-ups.

3. Bake about 30 minutes or until chicken is no longer pink (170°F). Let stand for 5 minutes before serving.

Makes 8 servings

Ingredients

1 **10.75-ounce can condensed cream of chicken soup**

1 **cup shredded smoked Gouda cheese (4 ounces)**

1 **4-ounce can chopped mushrooms, drained**

½ **cup bread crumbs**

4 **tablespoons honey**

10 **green olives, pitted and finely chopped**

3 **or 4 green onions, finely chopped**

1 **teaspoon salt**

1 **teaspoon minced garlic**

4 **skinless boneless chicken breast halves, each halved lengthwise to form two thin pieces**

2 **tablespoons olive oil**

Here, chicken breasts ooze with a delicious mixture of cream cheese, dried chives, and minced dried onion.

Stuffed Chicken Breasts

Monica–Waco, TX

Best of Hometown Cooking

Ingredients

4 skinless boneless chicken breast halves

Salt

Ground black pepper

1 8-ounce package cream cheese, softened

1 ½ teaspoons dried chives

1 ½ teaspoons minced dried onion

4 teaspoons butter or margarine

4 slices bacon

Prep: 25 minutes **Bake:** 50 minutes **Broil:** 5 minutes

Method

1. Preheat oven to 350°F. Place each chicken breast half between two pieces of plastic wrap. Using the flat side of a meat mallet, lightly pound each to about ¼-inch thickness. Sprinkle chicken with salt and pepper. Set aside.

2. In a small bowl stir together cream cheese, dried chives, and minced dried onion, stirring until creamy. Divide cream cheese mixture among chicken pieces, spooning the mixture near one end of each piece. Top cream cheese mixture with butter. Fold in the sides to hold in the cheese mixture; roll up. Wrap each roll-up with a slice of bacon; if necessary secure with wooden picks. Place, seam sides down, in a 11×7×1½-inch baking pan.

3. Bake for 50 to 60 minutes or until chicken is tender and no longer pink. Turn oven to broil. Broil about 5 minutes or until bacon is brown.

Makes 4 servings

With a spicy marinade of ginger, garlic, yogurt, lemon juice, cumin, coriander, and chili powder, this tandoori chicken is tops.

Tandoori Chicken

Beth—Middleburg, VA

Prep: 15 minutes **Marinate:** 8 hours **Grill:** 12 minutes

Method

1. In a food processor combine onion, ginger, and garlic; process until finely chopped. Add yogurt, lemon juice, paprika, cumin, coriander, salt, chili powder, pepper, and nutmeg; pulse a few times until well mixed.

2. Using a sharp knife, make three ¼-inch-deep diagonal cuts across top of each chicken breast half. Place chicken in a large resealable plastic bag. Pour yogurt mixture over chicken. Seal bag; turn to coat chicken. Marinate in the refrigerator for 8 to 24 hours, turning bag occasionally.

3. Drain chicken, discarding marinade. Coat rack of an uncovered grill with nonstick cooking spray. Place chicken on rack directly over medium coals. Grill for 12 to 15 minutes or until chicken is tender and juices run clear (170°F).

Makes 4 servings

Ingredients

¾ cup coarsely chopped onion

1 teaspoon coarsely chopped fresh ginger

2 cloves garlic, peeled

½ cup plain low-fat yogurt

1 tablespoon lemon juice

1 teaspoon paprika

1 teaspoon ground cumin

1 teaspoon ground coriander

½ teaspoon salt

½ teaspoon chili powder

¼ teaspoon ground black pepper

Dash nutmeg

4 skinless boneless chicken breast halves (about 1 pound total)

Nonstick cooking spray

When you serve these delicious chicken rolls to your friends and family, you'd better be prepared to hand out seconds!

Buffalo-Style Cheesy Chicken

Marjorie—Skaneateles, NY

Best of Hometown Cooking

92

Ingredients

1   8-ounce package cream cheese, softened

1   cup bottled ranch salad dressing

8   ounces blue cheese, crumbled

¾   cup finely chopped celery

7   tablespoons butter, softened

2   pounds skinless boneless chicken breast halves

1   2-ounce bottle hot pepper sauce

1   clove garlic, minced

½   cup all-purpose flour

½   cup fine dry bread crumbs

3   tablespoons olive oil

Prep: 30 minutes   **Bake:** 45 minutes

Method

1. Preheat oven to 375°F. In a medium bowl combine cream cheese, ranch salad dressing, blue cheese, celery, and 5 tablespoons of the butter, stirring until well mixed. Set aside.

2. Place each chicken half between two pieces of plastic wrap. Using the flat side of a meat mallet, lightly pound chicken breast halves to ¼-inch thickness. Divide cream cheese mixture among chicken breast halves, spooning near one end of each chicken piece; roll up chicken pieces to enclose cream cheese mixture. Secure ends with wooden picks.

3. In a small saucepan melt the remaining 2 tablespoons butter; stir in hot pepper sauce and garlic. Dip chicken roll-ups in flour, turning to coat evenly. Dip flour-dusted chicken roll-ups in the butter mixture to coat. Dip in bread crumbs, turning to coat evenly.

4. In a large ovenproof skillet heat olive oil over medium heat. Brown chicken roll-ups in hot oil, turning to brown evenly. Place chicken in skillet in oven and bake about 45 minutes or until chicken is no longer pink (170°F).

Makes 6 servings

Tip

Flattening Chicken Breasts Any time you flatten a chicken breast (or veal or boneless pork chop), you are making what the Italians call a scaloppine and the French call a paillard—a flat piece of meat that can be pan fried and eaten as is or stuffed and rolled. The best way to do this is to place the chicken breasts—one at a time—between two pieces of plastic wrap and pound them with the flat side of a meat mallet.

A stuffing of feta cheese and spinach makes these baked chicken breasts irresistible. No need for a side dish—they're served with plenty of cooked veggies.

Veg-Out Chicken

Randy—Columbus, IN

✦ ✦✦ ✦✦ ✦✦ ✦✦ ✦✦ ✦✦ ✦✦ ✦✦ ✦✦ ✦✦ ✦✦ ✦✦ ✦✦ ✦✦ ✦✦ ✦

Prep: 25 minutes **Bake:** 40 minutes

Method

1. Preheat oven to 325°F. In a large saucepan steam spinach for 3 to 5 minutes or just until wilted. Set aside.

2. Cut a slit in the thickest part of each chicken breast half, cutting to but not through the other side. Stuff one-sixth of the spinach and 1 tablespoon of the feta cheese into each slit. Arrange chicken in a 13×9×2-inch baking dish. Brush chicken with some of the vinaigrette salad dressing.

3. Bake for 40 to 50 minutes or until chicken is tender and no longer pink (170°F), brushing with additional vinaigrette salad dressing every 10 minutes for the first 30 minutes of baking.

4. Meanwhile, in a large skillet combine ½ cup of the vinaigrette salad dressing and the peanut oil. Add zucchini, onion, mushrooms, cherry tomatoes, and garlic; cook until vegetables are tender.

5. To serve, using a slotted spoon, transfer chicken and vegetables to a serving platter. Sprinkle with remaining feta cheese.

Makes 6 servings

Cook's Notes
This is a great dish to serve with a tabbouleh (bulgur wheat) salad. Prepare packaged tabbouleh salad mix according to directions, adding 1 chopped tomato, some chopped fresh cilantro, 2 tablespoons lemon juice, and 2 tablespoons olive oil.

Ingredients

1   small bunch fresh spinach

6   large skinless boneless chicken breast halves

8   ounces feta cheese with basil and tomato, crumbled

1   14-ounce bottle vinaigrette salad dressing with dried tomatoes and roasted sweet peppers

2   teaspoons peanut oil

2   zucchini, cubed

2   sweet onions (such as Vidalia), finely chopped

1   pound fresh mushrooms, sliced

8   ounces red cherry tomatoes

8   ounces yellow cherry tomatoes

2   cloves garlic, thinly sliced

The chicken breasts are sprinkled with Creole seasoning, grilled, and served with a relish of corn, black beans, tomatoes, avocados, and cilantro. See photo on page 212.

Grilled Chicken with Sweet Corn Relish

Darby—Columbia, MD

Ingredients

- 2 large ears sweet corn, shucked
- 1 15-ounce can black beans, rinsed and drained
- 2 large tomatoes, finely chopped (about 2 cups)
- 2 avocados, pitted, peeled, and cut into ½-inch pieces
- ⅓ cup finely chopped red onion
- 2 tablespoons chopped fresh cilantro
- 3 tablespoons olive oil
- 1 tablespoon lemon juice
- 1 teaspoon salt
- ½ teaspoon freshly ground black pepper
- 4 skinless boneless chicken breast halves (about 6 ounces each)
- 1 teaspoon Creole seasoning

Prep: 25 minutes   Grill: 12 minutes

Method

1. For relish, in a medium saucepan cook corn in a large amount of boiling water for 4 to 5 minutes or until tender. Drain. When cool enough to handle, cut the kernels from the ears and place in a medium bowl. Stir black beans, tomato, avocado, onion, cilantro, 2 tablespoons of the olive oil, the lemon juice, ½ teaspoon of the salt, and ¼ teaspoon of the pepper into the corn. Toss to combine; set aside.

2. Lightly brush chicken with the remaining 1 tablespoon olive oil; sprinkle evenly with Creole seasoning, remaining ½ teaspoon salt, and remaining ¼ teaspoon pepper. Place chicken on rack of an uncovered grill directly over medium coals. Grill for 12 to 15 minutes or until chicken is tender and juices run clear (170°F), turning once. Serve chicken with the relish.

Makes 4 servings

Cook's Notes
You'll love this recipe! Contrasting flavors make for a very interesting meal to share with your family and friends.

Two cheeses plus mushrooms, onions, and sweet peppers make this quick and easy version of grilled chicken a winner!

Smothered Grilled Chicken Breasts

Stacey—Claremore, OK

Prep: 25 minutes **Grill:** 12 minutes

Method

1. Sprinkle chicken with seasoned salt. Place chicken on rack of an uncovered grill directly over medium coals. Grill for 12 to 15 minutes or until chicken is tender and juices run clear (170°F).

2. Meanwhile, in a large skillet cook bacon until crisp. Transfer bacon to paper towels and reserve 1 teaspoon of the drippings in skillet. Add mushrooms, onion, and sweet pepper to reserved drippings in skillet; cook about 15 minutes or until tender.

3. Line a baking sheet with heavy-duty foil. Place chicken on prepared baking sheet. Spoon barbecue sauce over chicken. Top chicken with mushroom mixture and mozzarella and American cheese slices.

4. Place baking sheet with chicken on the grill just until cheese melts.

Makes 4 servings

Cook's Notes
In a hurry? Cook the bacon first and then cook the mushrooms, onion, and pepper while the chicken breasts are grilling. As soon as the chicken is cooked, you are ready to put all the ingredients on top and then right back on the grill.

Ingredients

4 **skinless boneless chicken breast halves**

2 **tablespoons seasoned salt**

8 **ounces mesquite-smoked bacon**

2 **cups sliced fresh mushrooms**

½ **cup chopped onion**

½ **cup chopped green sweet pepper**

1 **cup bottled barbecue sauce**

4 **slices mozzarella cheese**

4 **slices American cheese**

Chicken breasts are grilled and then brushed with a mix of apple butter, ketchup, honey, and seasonings, and topped with cheese and grilled onion slices.

Sweet Barbecued Chicken

Melissa—Studio City, CA

Ingredients

6 skinless boneless chicken breast halves

Juice of 2 oranges

¼ cup olive oil

3 cloves garlic, minced

½ cup packed brown sugar

½ cup apple butter

½ cup ketchup

2 tablespoons honey

2 tablespoons Worcestershire sauce

½ teaspoon black pepper

½ teaspoon garlic powder

½ teaspoon dry mustard

½ teaspoon bottled hot pepper sauce

2 large white onions, cut into ½-inch slices

6 slices cheddar, American, or mozzarella cheese

Prep: 20 minutes Marinate: 30 minutes Grill: 12 minutes

Method

1. Place chicken in a large resealable plastic bag. In a small bowl combine orange juice, olive oil, and garlic; pour over chicken in bag. Marinate in the refrigerator for 30 minutes, turning bag occasionally.

2. Meanwhile, in a small saucepan combine brown sugar, apple butter, ketchup, honey, Worcestershire sauce, pepper, garlic powder, dry mustard, and hot pepper sauce; cook over low heat for 8 to 10 minutes or until thickened, stirring frequently.

3. Drain chicken, discarding marinade. Place chicken on rack of an uncovered grill directly over medium coals. Grill for 12 to 15 minutes or until chicken is tender and juices run clear (170°F), turning once, and brushing with the apple butter mixture during the last 2 minutes of cooking.

4. Meanwhile, brush onion slices with apple butter mixture. Grill 6 minutes or until onion starts to caramelize, turning once.

5. Top each chicken breast half with a slice of cheese. Top each with an onion slice.

Makes 6 servings

These breaded chicken strips are wrapped with bacon and baked. Complete the meal by serving them on rice or adding them to a garden salad.

Mom's Pinwheel Chicken

Jeanne—Winchester, IL

Prep: 30 minutes **Bake:** 20 minutes **Broil:** 4 minutes

Method

1. Place flour in a shallow bowl. In another shallow bowl stir together bread crumbs, half of the mozzarella cheese, the onion, and garlic. In another shallow bowl beat eggs with a fork; stir in Italian salad dressing, lemon juice, oregano, parsley flakes, pepper, and seasoned salt.

2. Cut chicken into 1-inch-wide strips. Place strips between pieces of plastic wrap. Using the flat side of a meat mallet, lightly pound chicken. Cut bacon slices in half crosswise.

3. Preheat oven to 350°F. Coat a baking sheet with nonstick cooking spray; set aside. Dip chicken strips into flour, turning to coat. Dip chicken strips into egg mixture, turning to coat. Dip chicken strips into bread crumb mixture, turning to coat.

4. Place a half slice of the bacon on each chicken strip. Roll up chicken and bacon in a spiral, rolling so the bacon is on the outside. If necessary, secure roll-ups with wooden toothpicks. Place roll-ups on prepared baking sheet. Sprinkle with remaining cheese.

5. Bake for 20 to 25 minutes or until chicken is no longer pink and bacon is nearly done. Turn oven to broil. Broil for 4 to 5 minutes or just until bacon is crisp.

Makes 8 to 10 servings

Cook's Notes
My family adores these, and they don't take much time. They are flavorful and a huge hit at reunions. My four teenage daughters also love them on top of salads.

Ingredients

1   **cup all-purpose flour**

3   **cups seasoned fine dry bread crumbs**

3   **cups shredded mozzarella cheese**

1   **sweet onion (such as Vidalia), finely chopped**

3   **cloves garlic, minced**

3   **eggs**

1   **cup bottled Italian salad dressing**

   Juice of 1 lemon

1   **teaspoon dried oregano**

1   **teaspoon dried parsley flakes, crushed**

1   **teaspoon crushed black pepper**

¼   **cup seasoned salt**

3   **pounds skinless boneless chicken breast halves**

1   **pound bacon or turkey bacon**

   Nonstick cooking spray

Sprinkle this Italian-style slow-cooked dish with plenty of freshly grated mozzarella and/or Parmesan cheese.

Slow-Cooker Chicken Cacciatore

Paula—Lenhartsville, PA

Ingredients

½   **cup all-purpose flour**

1   **teaspoon salt**

¼   **teaspoon crushed red pepper**

8   **skinless boneless chicken thighs**

1½   **pounds skinless boneless chicken breast halves**

3   **tablespoons olive oil**

1   **14.5-ounce can diced tomatoes with roasted garlic, undrained**

1   **14-ounce can chicken broth**

1   **14-ounce can artichoke hearts, drained and cut into quarters**

1   **cup sliced fresh mushrooms**

⅓   **cup chopped onion**

1   **3-ounce package thinly sliced prosciutto**

2   **tablespoons chopped pimiento-stuffed green olives**

1½   **teaspoons minced garlic**

¼   **teaspoon dried oregano, crushed**

¼   **teaspoon dried thyme, crushed**

Prep: 25 minutes   Cook: 4 hours on low-heat setting

Method

1. In a large resealable plastic bag combine the flour, salt, and red pepper. Add chicken, a few pieces at a time; shake to coat. In a large skillet brown chicken, in batches, in hot olive oil. Transfer chicken to a 5-quart slow cooker.

2. In a large bowl stir together undrained tomatoes, broth, drained artichoke hearts, mushrooms, onion, prosciutto, olives, garlic, oregano, and thyme. Cover and cook on low-heat setting for 4 to 4½ hours.

3. Serve with a slotted spoon.

Makes 6 to 8 servings

Cook's Notes
Take advantage of the slow cooker's convenience by making this meal on busy weeknights. You can use a mixture of other chicken such as drumsticks, etc. This chicken dish is great served over hot cooked linguine or rice.

Crisp crushed cornflakes and intriguing spices coat this Southern-style oven-fried chicken. You won't miss the fat!

Spicy Healthier Southern Fried Chicken

Heather—Twentynine Palms, CA

+ +

Prep: 20 minutes   **Bake:** 45 minutes

Method

1. Preheat oven to 375°F. In a shallow bowl combine cornflakes, onion powder, cumin, crushed red pepper, and pumpkin pie spice. In another shallow bowl beat eggs with a fork. Line a baking sheet with foil.

2. Dip the chicken in the eggs, then roll in the cornflake mixture until each piece is coated. Place chicken on the prepared baking sheet.

3. Bake for 45 to 55 minutes or until chicken is tender and no longer pink (180°F) and coating is golden brown.

Makes 8 servings

Cook's Notes
This recipe allows my family to enjoy a much healthier version of our traditional Southern-style food.

Ingredients

1   **cup finely crushed cornflakes**

1   **teaspoon onion powder**

1   **teaspoon ground cumin**

1   **teaspoon crushed red pepper**

½   **teaspoon pumpkin pie spice**

4   **eggs**

8   **chicken drumsticks**

8   **chicken thighs**

Chicken drumsticks are seasoned with a kickin' mixture of dry mustard, chili powder, black pepper, and brown sugar before grilling.

Spicy Grilled Chicken Drumsticks

Lillian—Gainesville, FL

100

Ingredients

Nonstick cooking spray

2 teaspoons dry mustard

1 teaspoon salt

1 teaspoon chili powder

1 teaspoon freshly ground black pepper

1 teaspoon packed brown sugar

2 tablespoons cooking oil

8 chicken drumsticks

Prep: 15 minutes Grill: 35 minutes

Method

1. Coat grill rack with nonstick cooking spray.

2. In a small bowl stir together dry mustard, salt, chili powder, pepper, and brown sugar. Brush drumsticks with the oil; pat about ¾ teaspoon of the mustard mixture onto each drumstick, leaving the bone bare.

3. Place drumsticks on the prepared rack of an uncovered grill directly over medium coals. Grill for 35 to 45 minutes or until chicken is tender and juices run clear (180°F).

4. To serve, wrap a sturdy paper napkin around the lower bone of each drumstick.

Makes 4 servings

Cook's Notes
I've used the same spice mixture on other grilled meats such as steaks and pork chops.

Here's fried chicken at its best! Dipped in buttermilk and a spicy flour mixture, the chicken fries up to a delicious golden perfection. See photo on front cover.

Grandma's Fried Chicken

Erika—Hanahan, SC

Prep: 30 minutes   **Cook:** 12 minutes per batch

Method

1. In a large bowl combine flour, salt, black pepper, cayenne pepper, and garlic powder. Place buttermilk in a shallow dish. Coat chicken with flour mixture. Dip in the buttermilk; coat again with flour mixture.

2. Meanwhile, in a deep, heavy Dutch oven or kettle or a deep-fat fryer, heat 1½ inches oil to 350°F. Using tongs carefully add a few pieces of chicken to Dutch oven. (Oil temperature will drop; maintain temperature at 325°F.) Fry chicken for 12 to 15 minutes or until chicken is no longer pink (170°F for breasts, 180°F for thighs and drumsticks) and coating is golden, turning once.

3. Drain on paper towels. Keep fried chicken warm in a 300°F oven while frying remaining chicken pieces.

Makes 6 servings

Cook's Notes
My husband's grandmother used to make this fried chicken for every family get-together—now the recipe has been passed on to me. In the summer we serve it with picnic favorites like potato salad and coleslaw; in the winter it goes great with mashed potatoes, gravy, and green beans. My husband, Steve, likes his chicken SPICY, so I usually add extra cayenne pepper just for him.

Ingredients

2	cups all-purpose flour
¼	teaspoon salt
¼	teaspoon ground black pepper
1½ to 2	teaspoons cayenne pepper
1	teaspoon garlic powder
¾	cup buttermilk
2½ to 3	pounds meaty chicken pieces (breast halves, thighs, and drumsticks)
	Cooking oil

These chicken breast tenderloins are spiked with tequila and lime juice, then cooked with ranch dressing and corn. Serve with tortilla chips, salsa, tomato, and sour cream.

Tequila Chicken quick

Deborah—Lilburn, GA

Ingredients

- 2 cloves garlic, minced
- 1 lime
- ½ cup tequila
- 1½ pounds skinless boneless chicken breast tenderloins
- 1½ cups tortilla chips, crumbled
- 1 tablespoon olive oil
- ⅔ cup bottled ranch dressing or Southwestern ranch dressing
- 1 11-ounce can whole kernel corn, drained
- 1½ cups shredded Mexican cheese blend (6 ounces)
- 1 cup purchased salsa
- 1 medium tomato, chopped
- ⅔ cup sour cream

Start to finish: 25 minutes

Method

1. Preheat oven to 325°F. Place garlic in a large resealable plastic bag. Grate the zest of the lime into the bag and squeeze the juice of the lime into the bag. Add the tequila and stir to mix. Add the chicken; turn to coat. Marinate at room temperature for 15 minutes.

2. Meanwhile, spread the chips in a small baking pan; bake about 5 minutes or until toasted.

3. In a large nonstick skillet heat olive oil over medium-low heat. Add chicken and marinade; cook about 6 minutes or until chicken is brown, turning once.

4. Add ranch dressing; cook for 2 minutes, turning the chicken once to coat. Sprinkle the drained corn over; cook for 1 minute more. Sprinkle with cheese; cook for 1 to 2 minutes more or until cheese melts.

5. To serve, top with the toasted tortilla chips, salsa, tomato, and sour cream.

Makes 5 servings

Chicken breast tenders are marinated in a flavorful mixture of pureed nectarine, toasted walnuts, honey, and spices, then grilled.

California Grilled Chicken

Teresa—Little Egg Harbor Township, NJ

+ · · ·+ · + · ·+ · + · ·+ · + · ·+ · + · ·+ · + · ·+ · + · ·+ · + · ·+ · + · ·+ · + · ·+ · +

Prep: 25 minutes **Marinate:** 1 hour **Grill:** 12 minutes

Method

1. In a small skillet toast walnuts over low heat for 3 to 5 minutes or until fragrant. Remove from heat and let cool. In a food processor or blender process walnuts until finely chopped. Set aside.

2. In food processor or blender process cut-up nectarine until smooth. Pour pureed nectarine into a medium saucepan. Stir in brown sugar, honey, lemon juice, cinnamon, and ginger. Bring to boiling; reduce heat to low. Cook for 8 to 12 minutes or until thickened, stirring constantly. Remove from heat and let cool.

3. Place chicken in a large resealable plastic bag; pour nectarine mixture over. Add walnuts. Seal bag; turn to coat chicken. Marinate in the refrigerator for 1 to 2 hours, turning bag occasionally.

4. Drain chicken, discarding marinade. Place chicken on the rack of an uncovered grill directly over medium coals. Grill for 12 to 15 minutes or until chicken is tender and juices run clear (170°F), turning once.

Makes 4 to 6 servings

Cook's Notes
The marinating mixture is also good with pork or shrimp.

Ingredients

½   **cup walnuts**

1   **large nectarine, pitted and cut up**

½   **cup packed light brown sugar**

¼   **cup honey**

3   **tablespoons lemon juice**

½   **teaspoon ground cinnamon**

¼   **teaspoon ground ginger**

1   **to 1½ pounds chicken breast tenderloins**

Poultry

103

Baked chicken tenderloins get a tasty coating of instant potato flakes, Parmesan cheese, Italian seasoning, and garlic salt.

Crispy Herb-Baked Chicken ◆quick◆

Dani—Poplar Bluff, MO

Ingredients

Nonstick cooking spray

½   **cup shredded Parmesan cheese**

½   **cup instant mashed potato flakes**

2   **tablespoons dried Italian seasoning**

1   **teaspoon garlic salt**

1½   **pounds chicken breast tenderloins**

¼   **cup olive oil**

Prep: 15 minutes   Bake: 12 minutes

Method

1. Preheat oven to 375°F. Coat a 13×9×2-inch baking pan with nonstick cooking spray. In a medium bowl combine Parmesan cheese, dry potato flakes, Italian seasoning, and garlic salt. Brush chicken tenderloins with olive oil; roll in potato flake mixture. (Chicken should be heavily coated with potato flake mixture.) Place chicken in single layer in prepared baking pan.

2. Bake for 12 to 15 minutes or until chicken is golden, juices run clear, and meat is no longer pink (170°F), turning once halfway through baking.

Makes 4 to 6 servings

Serve these crispy chicken fingers with salsa, ranch salad dressing, or even some honey-mustard.

Italian Club Chicken Tenderloins

Mary—Ada, OK

· + ·

Prep: 20 minutes **Marinate:** 1 hour **Bake:** 25 minutes

Method

1. Place chicken in a large resealable plastic bag. In a small bowl stir together egg, salad dressing, and ½ teaspoon of the Italian seasoning; pour over chicken in bag. Seal bag; turn to coat chicken. Marinate in the refrigerator for 1 to 2 hours, turning bag occasionally.

2. Preheat oven to 375°F. Coat a large baking sheet with nonstick cooking spray; set aside.

3. In a large bowl stir together crushed crackers, pecans, Parmesan cheese, parsley flakes, the remaining ½ teaspoon Italian seasoning, and garlic salt.

4. Drain chicken, discarding marinade. Dip chicken in cracker mixture, turning to coat. Place chicken on prepared baking sheet. Bake for 25 to 30 minutes or until chicken is no longer pink (170°F). Serve with your favorite dipping sauce.

Makes 4 to 6 servings

Cook's Notes
These chicken tenderloins have very little fat because they are baked in fat-free dressing and reduced-fat cracker crumbs. The delicious Italian flavor of these tenders ensures that the platter is emptied every time.

Ingredients

2 **pounds skinless boneless chicken breast tenderloins**

1 **egg**

¾ **cup bottled fat-free creamy Italian salad dressing**

1 **teaspoon dried Italian seasoning, crushed**

· **Nonstick cooking spray**

2 **cups crushed reduced-fat butter crackers**

⅓ **cup finely chopped pecans**

¼ **cup grated Parmesan cheese**

1 **teaspoon dried parsley flakes**

½ **teaspoon garlic salt**

Desired dipping sauce

These chicken and vegetable kabobs are marinated in a sweet-savory sauce and served on a bed of jasmine rice.

Tropical Macadamia Nut Chicken Kabobs

Tiffany—San Diego, CA

Ingredients

1   20-ounce can pineapple chunks (juice pack)

2   cups macadamia nuts, finely chopped

1   cup shredded coconut, toasted

½   teaspoon ground ginger

¼   teaspoon cayenne pepper

¼   cup honey

2   tablespoons Dijon-style mustard

1   tablespoon soy sauce

1   teaspoon minced garlic

1½ pounds skinless boneless chicken breast halves, cut into 1-inch cubes

1   red sweet pepper, cut into 1-inch pieces

1   green sweet pepper, cut into 1-inch pieces

1   sweet onion (such as Maui), cut into 1-inch pieces

     Jasmine rice

     Sweet-and-sour sauce

Prep: 25 minutes Bake: 15 minutes

Method

1. Drain pineapple chunks, reserving juice; set aside. Preheat oven to 400°F. In a large plastic bag combine macadamia nuts, coconut, ginger, and cayenne pepper; shake bag to mix well and set aside. In a medium bowl whisk together reserved pineapple juice, honey, mustard, soy sauce, and garlic.

2. Add chicken cubes to pineapple juice mixture; stir to coat well. Place chicken in the bag with the macadamia nut mixture; shake to coat chicken.

3. On long metal skewers, alternately thread chicken, pineapple, sweet pepper, and onion, leaving a ¼-inch space between pieces. Place skewers on a foil-lined baking pan. Bake for 15 to 20 minutes or until the chicken is no longer pink.

4. Arrange skewers on a platter over hot cooked jasmine rice. Serve with sweet-and-sour sauce for dipping.

Makes 4 servings

Cook's Notes
This is such an easy and fun recipe. If you like, serve with 2 cups of hot cooked jasmine rice and sweet-and-sour sauce for dipping the kabobs.

Tip

Soak Your Skewers! Anytime you are using wooden skewers on the grill, it's important to soak them in water for at least 30 minutes first so they don't catch on fire and burn up, torching your dinner along with them!

You get a triple dose of citrus—orange, lemon, and lime—in these chicken and vegetable kabobs, which make a great appetizer or main dish.

Citrus Chicken Kabobs

Pamela—Parkersburg, WV

+ · +

Prep: 25 minutes Marinate: 2 hours Grill: 12 minutes

Method

1. Drain pineapple, reserving juice. In a small bowl whisk together the reserved pineapple juice, the orange juice, lemon juice, lime juice, olive oil, salt, and black pepper. Reserve ½ cup of the juice mixture to use as a brush-on.

2. Place chicken in a large resealable bag; pour remaining juice mixture over chicken. Seal bag; turn to coat chicken. Marinate in the refrigerator for 2 hours, turning bag occasionally. Meanwhile, soak eight long wooden skewers in water for at least 30 minutes (see tip, page 106).

3. Drain chicken, discarding marinade. Cut chicken into 1-inch pieces. On the skewers, alternately thread fruit pieces, vegetable pieces, and chicken, leaving a ¼-inch space between pieces.

4. Place skewers on rack of an uncovered grill directly over medium coals. Grill for 12 to 14 minutes or until chicken is no longer pink, basting occasionally with reserved juice mixture and turning frequently.

Makes 8 servings

Cook's Notes
These are so colorful and really make an attractive dish for a party. The fruits make the chicken so moist and tender. It can help to parboil (preboil) the pepper and onion pieces for 2 to 3 minutes prior to adding them to the skewers. This process helps to ensure they will finish cooking with the rest of the food and it helps prevent cracking when you thread them onto the skewers.

Ingredients

1   8-ounce can pineapple chunks (juice pack)

½   cup orange juice

¼   cup lemon juice

¼   cup lime juice

¼   cup olive oil

½   teaspoon salt

½   teaspoon black pepper

4   skinless boneless chicken breast halves

1   lemon cut into 1½-inch pieces

1   lime cut into 1½-inch pieces

1   small orange cut into 1½-inch pieces

½   of a green sweet pepper cut into 1-inch pieces

½   of a red sweet pepper cut into 1-inch pieces

1   cup whole mushrooms, halved

1   small red onion cut into 1-inch pieces

Chunks of chicken team up with shrimp, mushrooms, water chestnuts, and Szechwan vegetables for a killer stir-fry.

Szechwan Chicken Stir-Fry

Colleen –Lake Orion, MI

Ingredients

1 **pound skinless boneless chicken breast halves, cubed**

1 **12-ounce bottle lemon-pepper marinade**

1 **tablespoon cooking oil**

½ **to 1 pound uncooked peeled and deveined medium shrimp**

1 **21-ounce package frozen Szechwan-style stir-fry mixed vegetables (with sauce packet)**

¼ **cup water**

1 **8-ounce can sliced water chestnuts, drained**

½ **cup small whole fresh or drained canned mushrooms**

Hot cooked basmati rice

Prep: 20 minutes **Marinate:** 1 hour **Cook:** 8 minutes

Method

1. Place chicken in a large resealable plastic bag. Pour lemon-pepper marinade over chicken. Seal bag; turn to coat chicken. Marinate in the refrigerator for 1 to 4 hours, turning bag occasionally.

2. Drain chicken, discarding marinade. In a large skillet or wok heat oil over medium heat. Add chicken; cook and stir for 3 to 4 minutes or until chicken is no longer pink. Add shrimp; cook and stir for 2 minutes more. Transfer chicken and shrimp to a plate.

3. Add stir-fry vegetables, sauce packet, and water to the skillet or wok; cook and stir 2 to 3 minutes or until vegetables are just tender. Stir in water chestnuts and mushrooms. Stir in chicken and shrimp. Cook about 1 minute more or until heated through. Serve over hot cooked basmati rice.

Makes 4 generous servings

Cook's Notes
Allow at least 1 hour for marinating. The lemon-pepper flavor complements the other ingredients in this recipe. Jasmine rice makes a great substitute for the basmati.

Tip

Rice Is Nice Although you could certainly use plain white rice in this dish, basmati rice adds an extra dimension of flavor and elegance. Basmati rice, jasmine rice, and Texmati rice are all considered aromatic rices. They have a nutty flavor and a perfumey scent as they cook.

This Florentine dish features two hallmarks of such recipes: plenty of spinach and a cheese topping that is lightly browned in the oven.

Chicken Florentine Casserole

Jennifer—Merrillville, IN

Prep: 20 minutes **Bake:** 45 minutes

Method

1. Preheat oven to 350°F. Place each chicken breast half between two pieces of plastic wrap. Using the flat side of a meat mallet, pound each to about half its original thickness.

2. In a large bowl toss together cooked pasta shells, olive oil, and 1 teaspoon of the basil. Spread in a 3-quart rectangular baking dish. Arrange half of the chicken evenly over the pasta.

3. Spread cottage cheese over chicken; spread spinach on top. Sprinkle with half of the shredded Italian cheese. Spoon half of the Alfredo sauce over; sprinkle with remaining 1 teaspoon basil. Place the remaining chicken on top; spoon the remaining Alfredo sauce over. Sprinkle with the remaining shredded Italian cheese. Bake for 45 minutes.

Makes 6 servings

Cook's Notes
This goes well with a tossed salad and garlic bread.

Ingredients

- 2 **to 3 pounds skinless boneless chicken breast halves**
- 8 **ounces dried medium pasta shells, cooked and drained**
- 2 **tablespoons olive oil**
- 2 **teaspoons dried basil, crushed**
- 1 **16-ounce container small curd cottage cheese**
- 1 **10-ounce package frozen chopped spinach, thawed and well drained**
- 16 **ounces shredded Italian-blend cheese**
- 1 **1.25-ounce envelope Alfredo sauce mix, prepared according to package directions**

If you like fettuccine Alfredo, you'll love this lasagna with chicken, spinach, and cheese layered with roasted garlic Alfredo sauce.

Chicken Alfredo Lasagna

Erin—Titusville, FL

Ingredients

6   **skinless boneless chicken breast halves**

1   **cup balsamic vinegar**

⅓   **cup olive oil**

1   **0.7-ounce envelope dry Italian salad dressing mix**

1   **10-ounce package frozen chopped spinach**

    Garlic salt

1   **8-ounce container ricotta cheese**

¼   **cup grated Parmesan cheese**

¼   **teaspoon dried Italian seasoning, crushed**

2   **16-ounce jars roasted garlic Alfredo spaghetti sauce**

1   **cup milk**

1   **8-ounce package oven-ready lasagna noodles**

3   **plum tomatoes, finely chopped**

1   **medium onion, finely chopped**

4   **cups shredded mozzarella cheese**

Prep: 40 minutes   **Marinate:** 1 hour   **Grill:** 12 minutes   **Bake:** 45 minutes

Method

1. Place chicken in a large resealable plastic bag. In a small bowl combine balsamic vinegar, olive oil, and dry salad dressing mix; pour over chicken in bag. Seal bag; turn to coat. Marinate in the refrigerator for 1 hour, turning occasionally.

2. Drain chicken, discarding marinade. Place chicken on the rack of an uncovered grill directly over medium coals. Grill for 12 to 15 minutes or until chicken is tender and juices run clear (170°F), turning once. Remove from heat and let cool. Cut chicken into bite-size pieces. Set aside.

3. Meanwhile, defrost spinach in microwave oven according to package directions. Drain well. In a small bowl combine spinach and garlic salt and *ground black pepper* to taste. In a medium bowl stir together ricotta cheese, Parmesan cheese, and Italian seasoning. Set aside.

4. Preheat oven to 400°F. Whisk together Alfredo sauce and milk. Spoon a thin layer of the sauce mixture into the bottom of a 3-quart rectangular baking dish. Layer one-fourth of the lasagna noodles over the sauce. Top noodles with ricotta cheese mixture and tomato. Spoon another layer of the sauce mixture over the tomato; top with another one-fourth of the lasagna noodles. Spread spinach mixture over; sprinkle with onion.

5. Sprinkle one-third of the mozzarella cheese over onion. Top with another layer of the sauce mixture and another one-fourth of the noodles. Scatter chicken over; top with another layer of the sauce mixture. Sprinkle with another one-third of the mozzarella cheese. Cover with remaining noodles. Pour remaining sauce mixture over; top with remaining mozzarella cheese. Bake about 45 minutes or until noodles are tender and center is hot.

Makes 8 servings

First coated with taco seasoning mix, these chicken tenderloins are grilled beside a packet of veggies. Everything can be packed into tortillas for sensational fajitas.

Spice-Crusted Chicken Fajitas

Heather—Austin, TX

Prep: 25 minutes   **Grill:** 8 minutes

Method

1. Pour 4 tablespoons of the olive oil onto a large plate. Pour dry taco seasoning mix on another large plate. Dip chicken breast tenderloins into olive oil, turning to coat. Dip tenderloins into taco seasoning mix, turning to coat. Thread tenderloins, accordion-style, onto long metal skewers.

2. Place onion and sweet pepper in the center of a 12-inch square of heavy-duty foil. Drizzle with the remaining 2 tablespoons olive oil. Sprinkle with any remaining taco seasoning mix. Top with another 12-inch square of heavy-duty foil. Seal foil on all sides by folding over each edge twice. Shake gently to coat vegetables with oil and seasoning mix.

3. Place foil packet on rack of an uncovered grill directly over medium-hot coals. Grill for 5 minutes. Turn foil packet over. Place skewers on grill. Grill for 3 to 5 minutes or until chicken is cooked through.

4. Serve grilled chicken and vegetables with tortillas, cheese, sour cream, tomato, avocado, and salsa.

Makes 4 servings

Cook's Notes
I sometimes serve these with heated canned black beans that are seasoned with dried cilantro, garlic powder, and onion powder.

Ingredients

6 tablespoons olive oil

1 1.21-ounce envelope taco seasoning mix

1 pound chicken breast tenderloins

1 medium onion, thinly sliced

1 medium red or green sweet pepper, thinly sliced

8 to 12 fajita-size tortillas

2½ cups shredded cheddar and Monterey Jack cheese blend

1 cup sour cream

1 tomato, chopped

1 avocado, chopped

Purchased salsa

Corn tortillas are filled with a mixture of shredded chicken, enchilada sauce, Mexican-blend cheese, green chiles, and onion, then rolled up and baked until crisp.

Easy Chicken Taquitos

Awilda—New York, NY

Ingredients

2	cups shredded cooked chicken
1	10-ounce can mild enchilada sauce
1	cup shredded Mexican cheese blend
½	cup finely chopped onion
1	4-ounce can diced green chile peppers
½	teaspoon garlic salt
¾	cup cooking oil
24	corn tortillas
	Nonstick cooking spray

Prep: 30 minutes Bake: 15 minutes

Method

1. Preheat oven to 400°F. In a large bowl combine chicken, enchilada sauce, cheese, onion, chile peppers, and garlic salt. Set aside.

2. In a small skillet heat oil over medium heat. Using tongs, dip tortillas in oil for 5 seconds on each side; drain on paper towels. Keep warm.

3. Coat baking sheet with nonstick cooking spray. Place 2 tablespoons of the chicken mixture onto each tortilla; roll up. Place roll-ups, seam sides down, on prepared baking sheet. Bake about 15 minutes or until taquitos are as crisp as desired.

Makes 6 servings (24 taquitos)

The list of ingredients may be lengthy, but most of the fixings come from the package chopped and ready to use.

Chicken-Pesto Pot Pie

Barbara–Lodi, CA

Prep: 25 minutes   Bake: 15 minutes   Stand: 10 minutes

Method

1. Preheat oven to 425°F. Grease a 3-quart rectangular baking dish with 1 tablespoon of the butter; set aside.

2. In a very large skillet melt the remaining 3 tablespoons butter over medium heat. Add sweet pepper, mushrooms, onion powder, and garlic powder; stir to combine. Reduce the heat to medium-low. Sprinkle flour over mushroom mixture; cook for 1 minute, stirring constantly. Add vegetables and chicken broth; cook and stir about 5 minutes or until mixture is thickened and has just come to a boil. Remove from heat. Stir in chicken, Parmesan cheese, whipping cream, pesto, and black pepper. Pour the mixture into the baking dish and spread evenly.

3. Unroll the breadstick dough and separate the long sides, leaving the short ends connected. (You will have 5 long strips of dough.) Place the long dough strips lengthwise on top of the chicken mixture spacing evenly in the baking dish. Using a pastry brush, brush the garlic butter that is included with the dough evenly over the strips.

4. Bake about 15 minutes or until the bread is golden and the sauce is bubbling. Remove from oven. Let stand for 10 minutes before serving.

Makes 8 servings

Cook's Notes
Since there is no chopping and not much cooking, you can easily have this on the table in less than an hour. I prefer to use pesto found in the refrigerated section with the fresh pastas.

Ingredients

4   tablespoons butter

½   cup bottled roasted red sweet pepper strips

1   7-ounce can portobello mushrooms

1   teaspoon onion powder

½   teaspoon garlic powder

¼   cup all-purpose flour

2   16-ounce packages frozen mixed vegetables, thawed

1   14-ounce can reduced-sodium chicken broth

2   6-ounce packages diced cooked chicken

½   cup grated Parmesan cheese

⅓   cup whipping cream

⅓   cup purchased pesto

½   teaspoon freshly ground black pepper

1   10.6-ounce package refrigerated garlic breadstick dough (it will include a small container of garlic butter)

Try this simple recipe that contains tender chicken, crunchy celery, and water chestnuts. It is sure to impress your guests.

Company's Coming Chicken Casserole

Jill—Dublin, OH

114

Ingredients

1	10.75-ounce can cream of chicken soup
1	cup sour cream
1	15-ounce can sliced water chestnuts, drained and chopped
1	stalk celery, chopped
2	pounds cubed cooked chicken
	Dash black pepper
36	rich round crackers, crushed
¼	cup butter, melted

Prep: 25 minutes Bake: 30 minutes Stand: 10 minutes

Method

1. Preheat oven to 350°F. In a large saucepan combine cream of chicken soup and sour cream; cook and stir over medium heat just until boiling.

2. Stir in chopped water chestnuts and celery. Turn off the heat.

3. Stir chicken and pepper into the soup mixture. Spoon into a 3-quart casserole. Set aside.

4. Stir together crushed crackers and melted butter; sprinkle over casserole.

5. Bake for 30 to 35 minutes or until golden brown. Let stand for 10 minutes before serving.

Makes 6 to 8 servings

Olives and strips of marinated and grilled chicken breast are placed on a pizza crust that's spread with pesto. Shredded cheddar cheese tops it all before baking.

Chicken Pesto Pizza

Kim—Bellefontaine, OH

Prep: 15 minutes **Marinate:** 1 hours **Grill:** 12 minutes **Bake:** 10 minute

Method

1. Place chicken in a large resealable plastic bag; pour Italian salad dressing over chicken. Seal bag; turn to coat chicken. Marinate in the refrigerator for 1 hour, turning bag occasionally.

2. Drain, discarding marinade. Place chicken on the rack of an uncovered grill directly over medium coals. Grill for 12 to 15 minutes or until chicken is tender and juices run clear (170°F). Let chicken cool slightly; slice chicken into thin strips.

3. Preheat oven to 425°F. Spread pizza crust evenly with pesto. Sprinkle with drained olives. Arrange chicken on pizza. Sprinkle cheddar cheese evenly over pizza.

4. Place pizza on pizza stone or baking sheet. Bake for 10 to 12 minutes or just until cheese melts.

Makes 4 servings

Cook's Notes
This is one of our family favorites. My husband and children go crazy when I tell them that Chicken Pesto Pizza is on the menu for supper. It's a definite winner every time (and healthy too)!

Ingredients

10 ounces skinless boneless chicken breast halves

½ cup bottled Italian salad dressing

1 12-inch baked pizza crust

6 ounces purchased pesto

2 2.25-ounce cans sliced black olives, drained

1½ cups shredded mild cheddar cheese

Poultry

115

This spicy hot skillet meal combines Mexican-style rice and pasta with cubes of chicken, corn, tomatoes, and canned jalapeño chile peppers.

Zippy Tex-Mex Chicken quick

Linda—St. Paul, MN

Ingredients

2   **6.4-ounce packages Mexican-flavor rice and vermicelli mix**

¼   **cup butter**

3   **to 4 cups cubed cooked chicken breast**

1   **cup frozen whole kernel corn**

1   **to 2 tomatoes, cut up**

½   **cup bottled sliced jalapeño chile peppers, drained**

    Sour cream

Start to finish: 20 minutes

Method

1. Prepare rice and vermicelli mix according to package directions, using the ¼ cup butter and the amount of water directed on package.

2. Stir in cooked chicken, corn, tomato, and drained chile peppers. Cook until heated through. Serve with sour cream.

Makes 6 to 8 servings

Cook's Notes
To save time and make it really easy, I usually cook the chicken in the microwave oven and then cut it into pieces. Also, this makes a rather large amount. You can easily cut the recipe in half.

All the flavor of a margarita—infused in one sassy bird! Add some kick to your holiday meal with this margarita mix, tequila, and Triple Sec-spiked turkey.

Margarita Turkey with Sauce

Kelly—Whiteland, IN

+ · · · · + + · · · · · + + + · · · · + + + · · · · · + + + · · · · + + + · · · · · + + + · · · · · + +

Prep: 20 minutes **Roast:** 2 hours **Stand:** 20 minutes

Method

1. Preheat oven to 325°F. In a small bowl combine ½ cup of the margarita mix, 1 ounce of the tequila, and ½ ounce of the Triple Sec; set aside.

2. Place turkey breast in a medium roasting pan. Rub salt and pepper over the outside and in the cavities. Carefully loosen the skin from the breast. Pour lime juice over the breast and into the cavities. Replace the skin. Using a pastry brush, baste the turkey with the tequila mixture.

3. Roast turkey for 2 to 2½ hours or until an instant-read thermometer inserted in center of turkey breast (not touching bone) registers 170°F; baste with the tequila mixture every 30 minutes.

4. Remove turkey from oven and let stand for 20 minutes before carving.

5. Meanwhile, in a medium saucepan combine any remaining tequila mixture, the remaining margarita mix, the remaining 1 ounce tequila, the remaining ½ ounce Triple Sec, the cornstarch, and the lime zest. Cook and stir until thickened. Serve over the carved turkey.

Makes 8 servings

Cook's Notes
This makes an extremely moist turkey with flavors that you probably haven't had before. This is a great way to add a twist to your holidays.

Ingredients

1 ¼ cups frozen margarita mix concentrate, thawed

2 ounces tequila

1 ounce Triple Sec liqueur

1 6½- to 7-pound bone-in turkey breast, thawed if frozen

1 teaspoon salt

½ teaspoon freshly ground black pepper

Juice from 1 lime

Finely shredded zest from 1 lime (set aside)

1 ½ teaspoons cornstarch

Poultry

117

For this simple yet stunning dish, brown thin slices of turkey breast and drizzle with a luscious apple-cream sauce. See photo on page 213.

Turkey Scallop Skillet

Scott—Trumbull, CT

Ingredients

- 2 pounds ¼- to ⅜-inch turkey breast slices or cutlets
- 1 teaspoon kosher salt
- 1 teaspoon coarsely ground black pepper
- 4 tablespoons olive oil
- 2 shallots, finely chopped
- 2 tablespoons apple brandy
- ½ cup canned turkey or chicken broth
- 1½ cups diced apples
- 3 tablespoons butter
- 1 cup whipping cream
- 1 tablespoon chopped fresh flat-leaf parsley

Start to finish: 35 minutes

Method

1. Sprinkle turkey with salt and pepper. In an extra-large skillet heat 2 tablespoons of the olive oil over medium-high heat. Add half of the turkey slices; cook about 5 minutes or until light brown, turning once. Transfer turkey to a plate. Repeat with remaining olive oil and turkey.

2. Add shallot to hot skillet; cook until tender. Add apple brandy; cook for 1 minute. Add broth; cook until reduced by half.

3. Add apples and butter to skillet; reduce heat to medium. Cook for 2 minutes, stirring occasionally. Add whipping cream; cook for 3 to 4 minutes more or until sauce thickens. Reduce heat. Add turkey; simmer for 5 minutes, turning once.

4. Transfer turkey to serving platter; spoon apple mixture over turkey. Sprinkle with parsley.

Makes 6 servings

Cook's Notes
This recipe also works well with veal, chicken, and even filet mignon.

Savor classic Thanksgiving turkey and stuffing any day of the week with this quick-to-assemble casserole.

One-Dish Turkey and Stuffing

Mary—Henderson, NC

Prep: 15 minutes **Bake:** 35 minutes

Method

1. Preheat oven to 350°F. Coat a 3-quart rectangular baking dish with nonstick cooking spray. Place turkey in single layer in the dish; sprinkle with salt and pepper.

2. Prepare stuffing mix according to package directions. In a medium bowl combine cream of mushroom soup, milk, and sour cream. Pour soup mixture over turkey. Top with stuffing mixture.

3. Bake about 35 minutes or until turkey is tender and no longer pink (170°F).

Makes 4 servings

Cook's Notes
This recipe goes great with cranberry sauce, macaroni and cheese, or mashed potatoes.

Ingredients

Nonstick cooking spray

4   ¼- to ⅜-inch turkey breast slices

Salt

Ground black pepper

1   6-ounce package chicken-flavor stuffing mix

1   10.75-ounce can condensed cream of mushroom soup

1¼   cups milk

½   cup sour cream

Here's everything you love about this enduring casserole with the hearty addition of ground turkey breast. A sprinkle of cheddar cheese completes the dish nicely.

Turkey Tot Casserole

Correna—Birmingham, AL

Ingredients

1   pound uncooked ground turkey breast

1   10.75-ounce can reduced-fat and reduced-sodium condensed cream of mushroom soup

1   tablespoon salt-free seasoning blend

⅛   teaspoon seasoned salt (optional)

1   8-ounce package reduced-fat cheddar cheese

1   32-ounce package frozen fried potato nuggets

Prep: 15 minutes Bake: 20 minutes

Method

1. Preheat oven to 350°F. In a large skillet cook ground turkey breast until brown. Stir in cream of mushroom soup, salt-free seasoning blend, and, if desired, seasoned salt.

2. Spoon turkey mixture into a 3-quart rectangular baking dish. Sprinkle with cheddar cheese. Top with potato nuggets.

3. Bake about 20 to 30 minutes or until potato nuggets are golden brown.

Makes 6 servings

Crescent roll dough encases a savory filling of ground turkey, onion, and cabbage to make mini meat pies. Serve with your favorite style of mustard.

Weeknight Magic Pouches

Jen –Shrewsbury, MA

+ +

Prep: 30 minutes   **Bake:** 8 minutes

Method

1. Preheat oven to 350°F. In a large skillet heat oil over medium heat. Add ground turkey and onion; cook until turkey is brown. Add cabbage, salt, and pepper. Cook and stir about 2 minutes or until cabbage is wilted. Remove skillet from heat.

2. Coat 16 muffin cups with nonstick cooking spray.

3. Place the wide side of each crescent triangle over muffin cup, allowing the wide part of the dough triangle to drape into the muffin cup. Place ¼ cup of the meat mixture in the center of the dough in each muffin cup; fold the points of the dough triangle over each other to enclose. Pinch shut.

4. Bake for 8 to 10 minutes or until the pouches are golden brown. Serve hot with mustard.

Makes 8 servings

Cook's Notes
This recipe is so quick to make we serve it on busy weeknights.

Ingredients

2   **teaspoons cooking oil**

1   **pound uncooked ground turkey**

1   **large onion, finely chopped**

3   **cups thinly sliced cabbage**

½   **teaspoon salt**

¼   **teaspoon black pepper**

   Nonstick cooking spray

2   **8-ounce cans refrigerated crescent roll dough**

   Mustard

This homemade pizza with turkey and a white sauce has lots of fresh flavor. It starts with a precooked crust so it can be made quickly and easily.

Turkey Pizza quick

Anita—Michigan City, IN

Ingredients

1 **cup chopped cooked turkey or chicken**

1 **cup frozen chopped spinach, thawed and well drained**

2 **teaspoons lemon juice**

½ **teaspoon salt**

¼ **teaspoon ground black pepper**

1 **clove garlic, halved**

1 **12-inch Italian bread shell (such as Boboli brand)**

½ **cup bottled Alfredo spaghetti sauce**

¾ **cup shredded fontina cheese**

½ **teaspoon red pepper flakes**

Prep: 15 minutes **Bake:** 15 minutes

Method

1. Preheat oven to 450°F. In a medium bowl combine turkey, spinach, lemon juice, salt, and black pepper. Rub cut sides of garlic over bread shell; discard garlic.

2. Spread Alfredo sauce over bread shell; top with turkey mixture. Sprinkle fontina cheese over. Sprinkle with red pepper flakes.

3. Bake about 15 minutes or until crust is crisp.

Makes 4 servings

Cook's Notes
You can lighten this up by using light Alfredo sauce—any brand works well.

Refried beans, ground turkey flavored with taco seasoning, and cheese make up the toppings for this tasty twist on pizza. See photo on page 213.

Mexican Pizza

Tammy—Ward, AR

✦ ✦

Prep: 25 minutes **Bake:** 25 minutes **Stand:** 10 minutes

Method

1. Preheat oven to 375°F. Place pizza dough on a 12- to 14-inch pizza stone; spread out dough but do not shape. Let dough stand at room temperature while you prepare turkey topping.

2. In a medium skillet brown ground turkey; drain off fat, if necessary. Stir taco seasoning mix into ground turkey in skillet. Set aside.

3. Using a lightly floured rolling pin, shape pizza dough on pizza stone. Spread refried beans over dough. Spoon ground turkey mixture over beans. Sprinkle with co-jack cheese.

4. Bake for 25 minutes. Turn off oven; let pizza stand in oven for 10 minutes (this allows the cheese to become crusty). Top pizza with lettuce, tomato, olives, sour cream, and taco sauce.

Makes 4 servings

Cook's Notes
You can substitute ground beef for turkey. To start your meal, serve tortilla chips and salsa.

Ingredients

1 **13.8-ounce package refrigerated pizza dough**

1 **pound uncooked ground turkey**

1 **1.25-ounce envelope taco seasoning mix**

1 **16-ounce can refried beans**

1 **8-ounce package finely shredded co-jack cheese**

Shredded lettuce

Chopped tomato

Sliced black olives

Sour cream

Bottled taco sauce

These cute cups, made from refrigerated biscuit dough, are filled with ground turkey, onion, and sweet pepper and topped with a mixture of egg, milk, and cheese.

Easy and Healthful Turkey Cups

Tom—San Diego, CA

Ingredients

1   pound uncooked ground turkey

½   cup chopped onion

¼   cup finely chopped green sweet pepper

1   clove garlic, minced

1   tomato, chopped

¼   teaspoon dried basil, crushed

2   4.5-ounce cans refrigerated biscuits (12)

3   eggs, beaten

3   tablespoons regular or soy milk

⅔   cup shredded Monterey Jack cheese

Prep: 30 minutes   Bake: 18 minutes

Method

1. Preheat oven to 400°F. In a large nonstick skillet combine ground turkey, onion, sweet pepper, and garlic. Cook over medium-high heat until turkey is evenly brown and onion is tender, stirring often. Remove from heat; stir in tomato and basil and set aside.

2. Separate biscuit dough into 12 individual biscuits. Flatten each biscuit. Line the bottom and sides of 12 muffin cups with the flattened biscuits.

3. Drain the turkey mixture. Evenly divide the turkey mixture among the muffin cups.

4. In a small bowl beat together eggs and milk. Pour egg mixture into the muffin cups. Sprinkle tops with shredded Monterey Jack cheese.

5. Bake for 18 to 20 minutes or until filling sets.

Makes 12 servings

Chapter 5
Beef, Pork & Lamb

A jar of spaghetti sauce and lots of mozzarella and Parmesan make this a hassle-free version of everybody's favorite Italian recipe: beef lasagna.

Quick Lasagna

Lisa—Austin, TX

Ingredients

1 **pound ground beef**

½ **cup salad dressing or light salad dressing**

½ **cup grated Parmesan cheese**

6 **lasagna noodles, cooked and drained**

1 **14-ounce jar spaghetti sauce**

2 **cups shredded mozzarella cheese (8 ounces)**

Prep: 20 minutes   Bake: 30 minutes

Method

1. Preheat oven to 350°F. In a large skillet brown meat; drain off fat. Stir in salad dressing and Parmesan cheese.

2. In a 12×8×2-inch baking dish layer half of the lasagna noodles, half of the meat mixture, half of the spaghetti sauce, and half of the mozzarella cheese. Repeat layers. Bake about 30 minutes or until heated through.

Makes 4 servings

These beef-and-cheese-stuffed peppers are cooked in a slow cooker. Use a purchased rice and vermicelli mix to cut down prep time.

Slow-Cooker Stuffed Peppers

Rayma—Nepi, UT

Prep: 25 minutes **Cook:** 6 to 8 hours on low-heat setting or 3 to 4 hours on high-heat setting

Method

1. Wash sweet peppers and cut off tops. Clean out seeds from insides of the peppers. Chop the tops of the peppers and set aside.

2. In a large skillet cook ground beef until light brown. Drain off fat. In same skillet combine cooked ground beef, onion, and chopped pepper tops; cook until peppers start to soften.

3. In medium bowl combine beef mixture, vermicelli mix, corn, Worcestershire sauce, salt, and black pepper. Stir in mozzarella cheese. Mix well. Scoop mixture evenly into the six peppers.

4. Lightly coat the inside of a 5- to 6-quart slow cooker with nonstick cooking spray. Place the filled peppers in the slow cooker. Pour the tomato sauce evenly over the peppers. Cook for 6 to 8 hours on low-heat setting or 3 to 4 hours on high-heat setting.

Makes 6 servings

Cook's Notes
This great-tasting autumn recipe makes a colorful presentation.

Ingredients

6	green sweet peppers
1	pound lean ground beef
½	of a medium onion, chopped
1	6.9-ounce package chicken-flavor rice and vermicelli mix
1	cup frozen whole kernel corn
1½	teaspoons Worcestershire sauce
1	teaspoon salt
¼	teaspoon ground black pepper
1	cup shredded mozzarella cheese
	Nonstick cooking spray
1	8-ounce can tomato sauce

A beef eye of round roast is cooked in a mixture of coffee, herbs, and garlic. The flavorful pan juices are thickened with flour to make the savory gravy.

Mom's Roast Beef

Lisa—Austin, TX

Ingredients

1 tablespoon cooking oil

1 beef eye of round roast (about 2½ pounds)

1 medium onion, chopped

1 cup brewed coffee

1 cup water

1 beef bouillon cube

2 teaspoons dried basil, crushed

1 teaspoon dried rosemary, crushed

1 clove garlic, minced

1 teaspoon salt

½ teaspoon ground black pepper

¼ cup all-purpose flour

Prep: 20 minutes   Cook: 2½ hours

Method

1. In a Dutch oven heat oil over medium heat; brown roast on all sides in hot oil. Add onion and cook until tender. Add coffee, ½ cup of the water, the bouillon cube, basil, rosemary, garlic, salt, and pepper. Cover and simmer about 2½ hours or until meat is tender. Remove roast.

2. For gravy, in a small bowl stir together the remaining ½ cup water and the flour, stirring until smooth; stir into pan juices. Cook and stir until thickened and bubbly. Slice roast; serve with gravy.

Makes 8 servings

Add vegetables and tomatoes with green chile peppers to a beef roast and slow cook until the meat is fall-apart tender.

Texas Pot Roast

Jennifer–Dickinson, TX

Prep: 20 minutes   **Cook:** 12 hours on low-heat setting

Method

1. Rub steak seasoning into roast and allow to rest while you prepare the remaining ingredients. Cut onion into large pieces. Cut out core of cabbage and chop cabbage loosely.

2. Place meat in 5- to 7-quart slow cooker. Layer onion, cabbage, carrots, and potatoes over meat, distributing vegetables evenly. Sprinkle garlic and crushed bouillon cubes on top. Pour undrained tomatoes and water over all.

3. Cook on low-heat setting for 12 hours.

Makes 12 servings

Ingredients

2   teaspoons steak seasoning

1   4- to 5-pound beef eye of round roast

1   large yellow onion

½   of a head cabbage

8   ounces baby carrots

1   5-pound bag small red potatoes

2   cloves garlic, minced

4   beef bouillon cubes, crushed

3   10-ounce cans tomatoes and green chile peppers, undrained

3¼   cups water

The spices and cocoa powder give this recipe its name. The beef is sprinkled with the spice mixture, then cooked with tomatoes, vinegar, and graham cracker crumbs.

Slow-Cooker Beef in Red Mole Sauce

Kathryn—Ashland, MA

Ingredients

2   tablespoons cooking oil

2   tablespoons unsweetened cocoa powder

1   tablespoon Mexican-style chili powder

2   teaspoons dried oregano

1   teaspoon salt

1   teaspoon ground cumin

½   teaspoon black pepper

½   teaspoon ground cloves

½   teaspoon ground cinnamon

    Nonstick cooking spray

2½ to 3 pounds beef bottom round roast, trimmed and cut into 1- to 2-inch cubes

1   medium onion, chopped

1   28-ounce can whole peeled tomatoes

3   tablespoons cider vinegar

1½ cups finely crushed graham crackers

8   to 10 cloves garlic, peeled

1   tablespoon sugar

2   to 4 tablespoons sesame seeds, toasted

Prep: 20 minutes   **Cook:** 6 hours on low-heat setting

Method

1. In a small bowl stir together oil, cocoa powder, chili powder, oregano, salt, cumin, pepper, cloves, and cinnamon.

2. Lightly coat inside of a 3½- or 4-quart slow cooker with nonstick cooking spray. Place beef and onion in slow cooker. Pour oil mixture into cooker; stir to coat beef and onion.

3. Pour undrained tomatoes over beef mixture. Sprinkle vinegar over tomatoes. Sprinkle finely crushed graham crackers in an even layer over top. Scatter garlic cloves over. Cover and cook for 6 to 8 hours on low-heat setting.

4. Before serving, add sugar; stir until graham crackers and sugar are evenly mixed in. Sprinkle servings with sesame seeds.

Makes 10 to 12 servings

Cook's Notes
This is delicious with warm corn tortillas, corn bread, or a loaf of crusty bread. Leftovers freeze and reheat well.

To toast sesame seeds, stir in a dry skillet over medium heat until light brown.

Long, slow cooking is the key to great flank steak. Tomato paste, veggies, and beef broth add rich, delicious flavor.

Slow-Cooker Braised Flank Steak

Paul—Des Moines, IA

Prep: 25 minutes **Cook:** 8 hours on low-heat setting or 4 hours on high-heat setting

Method

1. Cut meat as necessary to fit into a 3½- or 4-quart slow cooker. Rub meat with flour. In a heavy large skillet heat oil over medium heat. Add meat; cook until brown, turning to brown evenly. Remove meat and place in slow cooker. Add onion, carrot, and sweet pepper to skillet; cook about 5 minutes or until tender. Stir beef broth into tomato paste; add to vegetables and bring to boiling. Pour vegetable mixture over meat.

2. Cook for 8 to 12 hours on low-heat setting or 4 to 6 hours on high-heat setting. Remove meat from slow cooker and slice across the grain into thin strips. Spoon vegetables and sauce over meat.

Makes 6 to 8 servings

Cook's Notes
To make a "gravy" after cooking, pour the vegetables and liquid into a food processor and process until smooth.

Ingredients

1½ to 2 pounds beef flank steak

1 tablespoon all-purpose flour

1 tablespoon cooking oil

1 medium onion, finely chopped

1 medium carrot, finely chopped

1 green sweet pepper, finely chopped

1 10.5-ounce can condensed beef broth

1 tablespoon tomato paste

Tip

Cutting Across the Grain Roasts and steaks should always be cut or sliced across, not parallel to, the grain of the fibers to avoid shredding the meat and to create the best texture in each bite. You can see which way they run by looking at the top of the fibers of the meat.

This classic dish features pan-seared beef flavored with mustard, Worcestershire sauce, and dry sherry.

Steak Diane ◀quick▶

Gail—Covina, CA

Ingredients

1½	pounds boneless beef top sirloin steak, cut ½ inch thick
	Salt
	Ground black pepper
4	tablespoons butter
½	teaspoon dry mustard
¼	cup chopped green onion
3	tablespoons dry sherry
1	tablespoon Worcestershire sauce
¼	teaspoon garlic powder
1	tablespoon chopped fresh parsley

Start to Finish: 25 minutes

Method

1. Cut steak into four serving-size portions; using a meat mallet pound steak portions to ¼-inch thickness. Sprinkle lightly with salt and pepper.

2. In a large heavy skillet melt 2 tablespoons of the butter; stir in mustard. Add green onion and as many of the steaks as will fit in the skillet. Quickly brown steaks; transfer to heated serving platter. Repeat with remaining steaks.

3. Add sherry, the remaining 2 tablespoons butter, the Worcestershire sauce, and garlic powder to pan drippings in skillet. Cook over high heat until slightly thickened. Stir in fresh parsley. Serve sherry mixture over steaks.

Makes 4 servings

Cook's Notes
Serve these steaks with new potatoes, Bibb lettuce salad, and broiled tomatoes.

Peppercorn-rubbed rib eye steaks are cooked and served with a rich cream sauce studded with green onion. See photo on page 214.

quick Peppercorn Steaks

Janet—Keller, TX

Start to finish: 30 minutes

Method

1. Crush peppercorns with a mallet or heavy saucepan. Press crushed peppercorns evenly over both sides of each steak. In a large skillet heat oil over medium-high heat until almost smoking

2. Add steaks to skillet. Cook for 3 minutes per side for medium doneness. Remove steaks to a serving platter; keep warm. Drain fat from skillet. Add 2 teaspoons of the butter and the green onion to skillet.

3. Cook and stir green onions over medium heat about 4 minutes or until tender. Add wine. Simmer over low heat about 5 minutes or until liquid is evaporated, stirring frequently.

4. Stir whipping cream into skillet. Simmer for 1 minute, whisking constantly. Add remaining 1 teaspoon butter; whisk until melted. Pour sauce over steaks. Serve immediately.

Makes 4 servings

Ingredients

5   teaspoons whole
    black peppercorns

4   beef rib eye steaks
    (6 ounces each)

3   tablespoons cooking oil

3   teaspoons butter

2   tablespoons chopped
    green onion

½   cup dry white wine or
    chicken broth

½   cup whipping cream

The simple marinade for these beef steaks is teriyaki sauce, garlic, and freshly ground black pepper. After marinating, the steaks are grilled until done as desired.

Teriyaki Garlic Rib Eyes

Marika—Crown Point, IN

Best of Hometown Cooking

Ingredients

4 beef rib eye steaks

1 20-ounce bottle teriyaki sauce

3 cloves garlic, sliced

2 teaspoons freshly ground black pepper

Prep: 10 minutes Marinate: 4 hours Grill: 10 minutes

Method

1. Place steaks in large resealable plastic bag. For marinade, in a medium bowl combine teriyaki sauce, garlic, and pepper. Pour marinade over steaks in bag. Seal bag; turn to coat steaks. Marinate in refrigerator for 4 hours to overnight.

2. Drain steaks, discarding marinade. Place steaks on rack of an uncovered grill over medium-hot coals. Grill for 5 to 6 minutes per side for medium doneness.

Makes 4 servings

These steaks are smothered in flavor! Besides being generously seasoned before grilling, they're also served with a sensational pesto.

Cumin-Grilled Steaks

Greg—The Woodlands, TX

Prep: 30 minutes **Grill:** 10 minutes **Stand:** 10 minutes

Method

1. For the pesto, place sweet pepper and chile peppers on rack of an uncovered grill directly over medium coals. Grill until pepper skins are charred, turning to char evenly. Remove peppers from grill and place in a paper bag. Close bag; let stand for 5 minutes.

2. Carefully peel peppers; discard seeds. Chop peppers. In a food processor combine cilantro, the ½ cup olive oil, the garlic, lime juice, and ½ teaspoon of the salt; cover and process until smooth. Spoon cilantro mixture into a small bowl. Fold chopped peppers, Parmesan cheese, and pecans into cilantro mixture. Set aside.

3. Rub steaks with the 2 tablespoons olive oil. In a small bowl stir together cumin, the remaining 1 teaspoon salt, the chili powder, black pepper, and white pepper. Sprinkle cumin mixture over all sides of steaks; rub in with your fingers. Place steaks on oiled rack of an uncovered grill directly over medium coals.

4. Grill until desired doneness, allowing 10 to 12 minutes for medium-rare (145°F) or 12 to 15 minutes for medium (160°F). Let stand for 5 minutes before serving. Serve with the pesto.

Makes 4 servings

Ingredients

1   red sweet pepper

1   fresh jalapeño chile pepper (or to taste)

1   poblano chile pepper

1   cup fresh cilantro

½   cup olive oil

2   cloves garlic

2   teaspoons lime juice

1½   teaspoons salt

¼   cup freshly grated Parmesan cheese

¼   cup pecans, toasted and coarsely chopped

4   1-inch-thick beef rib eye steaks (8 to 10 ounces each)

2   tablespoons olive oil

4   teaspoons ground cumin

½   teaspoon chili powder

¼   teaspoon ground black pepper

⅛   teaspoon white pepper

At your next dinner party, feature filet mignons marinated with rum, soy sauce, garlic, and shallots and broiled until medium rare.

Filet Mignons Steeped in Rum Glaze

Donna–Gray, ME

Ingredients

4	1½-inch-thick beef filet mignons
⅔	cup 80-proof amber rum
⅔	cup soy sauce
1	clove garlic, minced
1	small shallot, minced
1 ½	teaspoons crushed red pepper
2	tablespoons cooking oil
	Watercress
	Sliced radishes
	Cucumber spears

Prep: 10 minutes Marinate 2 hours Broil: 18 minutes

Method

1. Place steaks in a large resealable bag. For marinade, in a medium bowl combine rum, soy sauce, garlic, shallot, and crushed red pepper. Pour marinade over steaks in bag. Seal bag; turn to coat steaks. Marinate in refrigerator for 2 hours, turning occasionally.

2. Preheat broiler. Remove steaks from marinade; discard marinade. Brush steaks lightly with oil. Broil 6 inches from heat for 1 minute on each side. Turn and broil about 16 minutes or until medium-rare (145°F). Arrange filets on serving platter; garnish with watercress, sliced radishes, and cucumber spears.

Makes 4 to 6 servings

Cook's Notes
This recipe is worthy fare for even the most elegant dinner parties.

To make them supertender, beef short ribs are cooked slowly in a flavorful sauce and then baked with sliced onions.

Sweet and Spicy Short Ribs

Hazel—Courtenay, BC

Prep: 15 minutes **Cook:** 2 hours **Chill:** several hours **Bake:** 30 minutes

Method

1. In a large Dutch oven combine short ribs, ketchup, the water, sugar, dry mustard, vinegar, Worcestershire sauce, horseradish, salt, pepper, and bay leaf. Bring to a boil; reduce heat. Cover and simmer for 2 to 3 hours or until very tender. Cool. Chill several hours; skim off fat.

2. Preheat oven to 350°F. Transfer short ribs to a large baking dish, reserving sauce in Dutch oven. Discard loose bones and bay leaf. Arrange sliced onion over short ribs; pour sauce over all. Cover with foil; bake for 30 minutes.

Makes 4 servings

Cook's Notes
These short ribs are great with mashed potatoes and a vegetable of your choice. Beef ribs should be simmered until the meat is very tender.

Ingredients

3 to 4 pounds beef chuck
    short ribs

1 cup ketchup

1 cup water

1 tablespoon sugar

1 tablespoon dry mustard

1 tablespoon cider vinegar

1 tablespoon Worcestershire
    sauce

1 tablespoon prepared
    horseradish

1 teaspoon salt

½ teaspoon ground
    black pepper

1 bay leaf

2 medium onions, sliced

Have a taco party! The beef steak for this recipe is marinated in a mojo mixture for supreme flavor. It is then cooked, sliced, and served in tortillas with all the extras.

Tacos Carne Asada

Alexa—Seattle, WA

Ingredients

2 **pounds beef flank or skirt steak, trimmed of fat**

1 **recipe Mojo Marinade**

  Kosher salt

  Freshly ground black pepper

16 **7-inch corn tortillas**

  Shredded romaine or iceberg lettuce

  Chopped onion

  Shredded Monterey Jack cheese

½ **cup purchased pico de gallo**

2 **limes, cut in wedges**

Prep: 25 minutes   Marinate: 1 hour   Grill: 14 minutes   Stand: 5 minutes

Method

1. Lay the flank steak in a large baking dish; pour the Mojo Marinade over the steak. Cover with plastic wrap; marinate in the refrigerator for at least 1 hour or up to 8 hours. (Don't marinate the steak for more than 8 hours or the fibers break down too much and the meat gets mushy.)

2. Drain steak, discarding marinade. Season steak on both sides with salt and pepper. Place steak on oiled rack of an uncovered grill directly over medium-hot coals. Grill for 14 to 20 minutes or until medium-rare (145°F), turning once.

3. Remove the steak to a cutting board and let it stand for 5 minutes. Thinly slice the steak across the grain on a diagonal. In a dry skillet or on the grill, warm the tortillas for 30 seconds on each side until pliable.

4. For each taco, stack two of the warm tortillas; lay about 4 ounces of the beef down the center and sprinkle with some lettuce, onion, and Monterey Jack cheese. Top each taco with a spoonful of the pico de gallo; garnish with lime wedges.

Makes 4 servings

Mojo Marinade: With a mortar and pestle or in a bowl mash together 1 large handful fresh cilantro leaves, finely chopped; 4 cloves garlic, minced; 1 fresh jalapeño chile pepper, minced; dash kosher salt; and dash freshly ground black pepper until a paste forms. Transfer the paste to a screw-top jar. Add ½ cup olive oil, the juice from 2 limes, the juice from 1 orange, and 2 tablespoons white vinegar. Cover and shake well until combined. Makes about 1¼ cups.

Need a fast meal but don't want to skimp on flavor? This pepper steak dish is loaded with onion, sweet pepper, and mushrooms in a rich tomato sauce.

Pepper Steak Stir-Fry

Jackie—Tewksbury, MA

Prep: 25 minutes   Cook: 30 minutes

Method

1. Slice steak into thin strips.

2. In a large skillet cook steak strips in hot olive oil until brown. Add mushrooms, onion, sweet pepper strips, and garlic; cook for 10 minutes, stirring occasionally.

3. Stir in tomato sauce, Worcestershire sauce, and sugar. Season to taste with salt and black pepper. Cover and simmer on low heat for 20 minutes.

Makes 4 servings

Cook's Notes
Serve over white rice.

Ingredients

1¼ to 1½ pounds boneless
    beef sirloin steak

1   tablespoon olive oil

2   cups sliced fresh
    mushrooms

1   large onion, sliced

1   large green sweet pepper,
    cut into strips

1   clove garlic, minced

1   8-ounce can tomato sauce

3   drops Worcestershire sauce

    Pinch of sugar

    Salt

    Ground black pepper

All the comforting goodness of beef stew—wrapped up in flour tortillas! This recipe uses packaged and canned ingredients to make it supereasy.

Easy Beef Stew Enchiladas

Patricia—Baden, PA

140

✦ ✦ · ✦

Ingredients

Nonstick cooking spray

2 tablespoons cooking oil

1 medium onion, chopped

1 clove garlic, minced

1 17-ounce package fully cooked beef pot roast with gravy

1 15-ounce can mixed vegetables, drained

1 10-ounce can mild enchilada sauce

1½ cups finely shredded 4-cheese Mexican blend

8 8-inch flour tortillas

1 10.75-ounce can condensed cream of celery soup

1 4.5-ounce can chopped green chile peppers, drained

¼ cup milk

½ cup sour cream

¼ cup thinly sliced green onion

Prep: 30 minutes Bake: 35 minutes

Method

1. Preheat oven to 350°F. Coat a 13×9×2-inch baking dish with nonstick cooking spray. In a large skillet heat oil over medium heat. Add onion and garlic; cook for several minutes or until tender. Drain pot roast, reserving gravy. Chop meat into ½-inch pieces. Add meat and drained mixed vegetables to skillet.

2. Stir ½ cup of the enchilada sauce into the reserved gravy. Add gravy mixture to skillet along with ½ cup of the cheese. Evenly spoon meat mixture down center of each tortillas (about a generous ½ cup for each). Roll up tortillas and place, seam sides down, in prepared baking dish.

3. In a medium bowl combine cream of celery soup, drained chile peppers, the remaining enchilada sauce, and the milk; pour over tortillas in pan. Sprinkle with remaining 1 cup cheese.

4. Cover with foil. Bake for 35 to 40 minutes. To serve, garnish with sour cream and sprinkle with green onion.

Makes 8 servings

Cook's Notes
This dish combines the taste of beef stew with Mexican flavors for a great easy-to-make casserole that the whole family will love.

This easy dish will become a family favorite in no time. It tastes just like pizza, but it has the heartiness of a casserole.

Easy Pizza Casserole

Marjorie—Skaneateles, NY

· ·

Prep: 30 minutes   **Bake:** 25 minutes

Method

1. Preheat oven to 400°F. In a large skillet brown ground beef; drain off fat. Stir spaghetti sauce, onion, sweet pepper, and garlic into beef. Simmer for 10 minutes.

2. In small bowl mix milk, eggs, and oil. Beat with an electric mixer on medium speed for 1 minute. Add flour and salt; beat for 2 minutes.

3. Pour hot meat mixture into ungreased 13x9x2-inch baking pan. Top with mozzarella cheese. Pour batter over cheese, covering completely. Sprinkle with Parmesan cheese.

4. Bake for 25 to 30 minutes or until puffed and deep golden brown. Serve immediately.

Makes 10 servings

Ingredients

1½ pounds ground beef

16 ounces bottled spaghetti sauce

1 cup chopped onion

1 cup chopped green sweet pepper

2 cloves garlic, minced

1 cup milk

2 eggs

1 tablespoon cooking oil

1 cup all-purpose flour

½ teaspoon salt

8 ounces mozzarella cheese, shredded

½ cup grated Parmesan cheese

Casseroles are always a hit—this zesty one is no different. For hectic days, prep it ahead of time and put it into the oven when you get home.

Mexicole Casserole

Renee—Hodgenville, KY

Ingredients

1   **pound ground beef**

1   **1.5-ounce package taco seasoning mix**

1   **14.5-ounce can whole tomatoes, drained and chopped**

1   **8.5-ounce can whole kernel corn, drained**

1   **6.5-ounce package Mexican corn bread mix**

Prep: 25 minutes   **Bake:** 15 minutes   **Cool:** 10 minutes

Method

1. Preheat oven to 400°F. Grease a shallow 2-quart baking dish; set aside.

2. In a large skillet brown ground beef; drain fat. Stir taco seasoning mix into ground beef; stir in drained tomatoes and corn. Pour into prepared dish.

3. Prepare corn bread batter according to package directions; pour over ground beef mixture. Bake for 15 to 20 minutes or until a toothpick inserted in center of corn bread comes out clean. Cool for 10 minutes before serving.

Makes 4 to 6 servings

Nothing satisfies hunger like spaghetti and meatballs! This version uses purchased marinara and cheese sauces to get it on the table quickly. See photo on page 214.

Homemade Meatballs and Spaghetti

Pamela—Parkersburg, WV

Prep: 30 minutes **Cook:** 30 minutes

Method

1. In a large bowl combine ground beef, eggs, bread crumbs, milk, salt, and pepper. Using your hands, mix in cheese blend. Shape into small balls. In a large skillet heat 3 tablespoons of the olive oil over medium heat. Add meatballs and cook until brown, turning to brown all sides. Remove from skillet.

2. In a large saucepan brown onion and garlic in remaining 1 tablespoon olive oil. Add 5-cheese pasta sauce, marinara sauce, and undrained tomatoes. Add meatballs to sauce and simmer over low heat for 30 minutes, stirring occasionally.

3. Meanwhile, cook spaghetti according to package directions; drain. Serve spaghetti with meatballs and sauce on plate; top with shredded mozzarella cheese.

Makes 8 servings

Ingredients

1 **pound ground beef**

2 **eggs, beaten**

¼ **cup seasoned fine dry bread crumbs**

2 **tablespoons milk**

½ **teaspoon kosher salt**

¼ **teaspoon ground black pepper**

¾ **cup shredded 4-cheese blend**

¼ **cup olive oil**

1 **small onion, chopped**

1 **teaspoon minced garlic**

1 **26-ounce jar 5-cheese pasta sauce**

1 **26-ounce jar marinara sauce**

1 **14.5-ounce can Italian-style tomatoes, diced and undrained**

1 **pound dried spaghetti**

2 **cups shredded mozzarella or Parmesan cheese**

Shaping Meatballs Hand-rolling meatballs can be a messy proposition—but here's a trick. Keep a shallow bowl of cool water next to you on the counter and frequently wet your hands as you roll, changing the water occasionally. The meat mixture won't stick to your wet hands—and you'll have smooth-surface meatballs to boot!

This flavorful Sicilian-style meat loaf looks and tastes delicious. A spiral of ham and cheese add interest to the well-seasoned ground beef mixture.

Sicilian Meat Roll

Joann—Mobile, AL

144

Ingredients

- **2** eggs, beaten
- **¾** cup fine dry bread crumbs
- **½** cup tomato juice
- **2** teaspoons chopped fresh parsley
- **½** teaspoon salt
- **½** teaspoon dried oregano, crushed
- **½** teaspoon ground black pepper
- **1** clove garlic, minced
- **2** pounds ground beef
- **8** slices ham (thinly sliced lunch meat)
- **1½** cups shredded mozzarella or cheddar cheese
- **3** slices mozzarella or cheddar cheese

Prep: 25 minutes Bake: 1 hour 20 minutes

Method

1. Preheat oven to 350°F. In a large bowl combine eggs, bread crumbs, tomato juice, parsley, salt, oregano, pepper, and garlic. Stir in ground beef, mixing thoroughly.

2. Place beef mixture on a large sheet of foil; pat into a 12×10-inch rectangle. Arrange ham slices on top of beef mixture, leaving a small margin along the sides. Sprinkle shredded cheese over ham.

3. Starting from a short end, carefully roll up meat, using the foil to lift. Seal seam and ends. Place roll, seam side down, in a greased 13×9×2-inch baking pan. Bake for 1¼ hours (center of roll will look pink from the ham). Remove from oven; place cheese slices over top of roll. Bake about 5 minutes more or until cheese melts.

Makes 8 servings

This meat loaf shines with a combination of ground beef with kalamata olives and roasted red sweet peppers.

Mediterranean Meat Loaf

Melissa—Studio City, CA

Prep: 20 minutes   **Bake:** 45 minutes

Method

1. Preheat oven to 375°F. In a large bowl combine ground beef, roasted pepper, onion, olives, bread crumbs, egg, the 1 teaspoon salt, garlic powder, oregano, and the ½ teaspoon black pepper; mix well with hands.

2. In a large baking dish shape meat mixture into a long loaf about 4 inches wide. Bake for 45 to 55 minutes or until cooked through (160°F).

3. Meanwhile, in small bowl mix tomato, lemon zest, lemon juice, and olive oil. Season to taste with salt and black pepper. Slice meat loaf and top with tomato mixture and crumbled feta.

Makes 8 servings

Cook's Notes
For a lighter meal replace beef with ground turkey.

Ingredients

2   **pounds lean ground beef**

½   **cup roasted red sweet peppers, finely chopped**

½   **of a small red onion, diced**

½   **cup chopped kalamata olives**

½   **cup fine dry bread crumbs**

1   **egg, beaten**

1   **teaspoon salt**

1   **teaspoon garlic powder**

1   **teaspoon dried oregano, crushed**

½   **teaspoon ground black pepper**

1   **large tomato, finely chopped**

½   **of a lemon, zested and juiced**

½   **teaspoon olive oil**

½   **cup crumbled feta cheese**

A tasty version of an old family favorite—meat loaf gets a flavor boost from Italian bread crumbs plus steak and Worcestershire sauce.

Easy Tangy Meat Loaf

Pamela—Woodbury, MN

146

Ingredients

1 egg

½ cup milk

½ cup seasoned fine dry bread crumbs

1½ pounds beef-pork meat loaf mix

¼ cup chopped onion

1 tablespoon bottled steak sauce

1 tablespoon Worcestershire sauce

1 teaspoon salt

½ teaspoon black pepper

½ cup bottled steak sauce or favorite barbecue sauce for glaze

Prep: 15 minutes   Bake: 1½ hours

Method

1. Preheat oven to 350°F. In a large bowl beat together egg and milk. Add bread crumbs to egg mixture and mix lightly. Allow bread crumb mixture to stand for 2 to 3 minutes so crumbs absorb liquid.

2. Add meat, onion, the 1 tablespoon steak sauce, the Worcestershire sauce, salt, and pepper; mix well with hands.

3. Transfer meat mixture to a 8×4×2-inch loaf pan and pat down. Bake for 1 hour. Drain fat from pan.

4. Spoon the ½ cup steak sauce over meat loaf to glaze, spreading sauce with a spoon to cover entire meat loaf. Bake for another 30 minutes. Slice and serve.

Makes 4 to 6 servings

Cook's Notes
The steak sauce, seasoned bread crumbs, and Worcestershire sauce really boost the flavor of the meat loaf.

Try this recipe for stuffed pork loin as your main dish for a special dinner. It's easy to make, and it's delicious. See photo on page 215.

Stuffed Pork Loin Roast

Patsy—Kamloops, BC

Prep: 25 minutes **Bake:** 1½ hours **Stand:** 15 minutes

Method

1. Preheat oven to 350°F. For stuffing, in a medium bowl combine sausage, bread crumbs, onion, parsley, garlic, and desired seasonings to taste.

2. Cut a spiral into the pork loin allowing you to spread it out flat on a cutting board.

3. Using a meat mallet, pound pork lightly until flat enough to roll. Spread stuffing across entire piece of meat. Roll up carefully; tie meat roll with 100-percent-cotton kitchen string to secure.

4. Brush meat roll with oil; place in shallow roasting pan. Bake about 1½ hours or until cooked through (150°F).

5. Cover with foil and let stand for 15 minutes. The temperature of the meat should reach 160°F.

Makes 4 servings

Cook's Notes
Gravy can be made in the pan when meat is cooked. This is truly a very lovely recipe with easy preparation.

Ingredients

4 breakfast sausages, finely chopped

1 cup soft bread crumbs

1 medium onion, chopped

2 teaspoons chopped fresh parsley

1 to 2 cloves garlic, finely chopped

Seasonings of choice (such as rosemary, thyme, sage, salt, and black pepper)

1 4- to 5-pound pork loin roast

Cooking oil

Pork roast gets a double coating of flavor, first with Dijon-style mustard, then later with apple butter. During baking, the apple butter forms a tasty crust on the pork.

Apple Butter-Crusted Dijon Pork Loin

Rhonda—Glasgow, KY

Ingredients

1	3- to 4-pound boneless pork loin
	Olive oil
	Salt
	Ground black pepper
½	cup Dijon-style mustard
½	cup water
1½	cups apple butter

Prep: 10 minutes Chill: 1 hour Bake: 65 minutes

Method

1. Rub pork with olive oil, then salt and pepper.

2. Coat the pork loin with a generous layer of mustard; refrigerate for at least 1 hour or overnight.

3. Preheat oven to 375°F. Place pork loin in an oiled Dutch oven. Add the water to Dutch oven. Spread all sides of pork with apple butter.

4. Bake pork loin, covered, for 45 minutes. After 45 minutes, remove cover and bake an additional 20 to 30 minutes or until an instant-read thermometer inserted in meat registers 160°F.

Makes 8 servings

Cook's Notes
The Dijon-style mustard and complementary apple butter add a unique flavor to the pork. This is a great low-fat and healthy main dish, and it goes well with a variety of vegetables—my family especially likes it with Brussels sprouts.

A pork loin roast with raisins, slices of apple, potato, and onion is seasoned with brown sugar, allspice, and nutmeg.

Autumn Pork and Apples

Molly—Atlanta, GA

+ · + · · + · · + · + · + · · + · + · + · + + · + · + · · + · + · + · + · + · + · + · + + · + · + · + · + · + · + · + · + + · +

Prep: 25 minutes   **Roast:** 1¼ hours   **Stand:** 15 minutes

Method

1. Preheat oven to 325°F. Brush pork with mustard and place in a baking dish. Arrange apples, onion, sweet potato, and raisins around pork. Pour apple juice in bottom of baking dish. Sprinkle all with brown sugar, nutmeg, allspice, salt, and pepper.

2. Cover with foil. Roast for 1¼ to 1½ hours or until instant-read thermometer inserted in center of pork registers 150°F. Remove from oven. Cover with foil; let stand for 15 minutes. The temperature of the pork after standing should be 160°F.

Makes 6 servings

Ingredients

1   2- to 2½-pound boneless pork top loin roast (single loin)

    Dijon-style mustard

2   or 3 Granny Smith or Golden Delicious apples, peeled and sliced

1   onion, sliced

1   large sweet potato, peeled and sliced

½   cup golden raisins

1   to 1½ cups apple juice

    Brown sugar

2   teaspoons ground nutmeg

2   teaspoons ground allspice

    Salt

    Ground black pepper

Pork tenderloin stuffed with blue cheese, spinach, walnuts, and thyme makes a tasty main dish, especially when served with balsamic gravy.

Elegant Rolled Pork Tenderloin

Lisa—Kansas City, MO

Ingredients

2   1-pound pork tenderloins

1   teaspoon salt

1   10-ounce package frozen spinach, thawed and squeezed dry

4   ounces blue cheese, crumbled

½   cup walnuts, toasted and chopped

1   tablespoon chopped fresh thyme

2   tablespoons all-purpose flour

1   cup chicken broth

1   shallot, minced

2   tablespoons balsamic vinegar

Prep: 25 minutes   Roast: 25 minutes   Stand: 15 minutes

Method

1. Preheat oven to 425°F. Place tenderloins on work surface; cut a lengthwise slit in each, cutting to but not through the other side. Place each tenderloin between two pieces of plastic wrap. Using the flat side of a meat mallet, pound each to about ¼-inch thickness. Remove plastic wrap. Season with salt. Top tenderloins with spinach, blue cheese, walnuts, and thyme, spreading to within one inch of edges. Roll up, starting with long edge. Tie up with 100-percent-cotton string at equal intervals. Place on rack in roasting pan.

2. Roast for 25 to 35 minutes or until an instant-read thermometer inserted in center registers 155°F. Remove from oven. Place tenderloins on a platter; cover and let stand for 15 minutes. The temperature of the pork after standing should be 160°F.

3. Meanwhile, sprinkle flour in bottom of roasting pan; place over medium-high heat. Cook and stir for 2 minutes. Whisk in broth and shallot and bring to boiling. Cook and stir for 2 minutes. Remove from heat and stir in balsamic vinegar. Serve over pork.

Makes 8 servings

Cook's Notes
This is certainly elegant enough when you want to impress, yet it's easy enough for a casual weekend meal.

Make this blend of spices to rub over pork tenderloin. Store the remaining spice mixture in an airtight container in a cool, dark place.

Latin-Spiced Pork Tenderloin

Lyle—Ponca City, OK

Prep: 15 minutes **Grill:** 20 minutes

Method

1. For spice rub, in a small bowl combine cumin, chili powder, salt, coriander, black pepper, cinnamon, brown sugar, and crushed red pepper.

2. Rub 2 tablespoons of the spice rub over each tenderloin.

3. Place tenderloins on rack of an uncovered grill directly over medium-slow coals. Grill for 20 to 30 minutes or until an instant-read thermometer inserted in thickest part of each tenderloin registers 160°F, turning occasionally. If desired, garnish with lime wedges.

Makes 6 to 8 servings

Cook's Notes
The spice mixture will keep for about 6 weeks covered and stored in a cool, dark place.

Ingredients

2   tablespoons ground cumin

2   tablespoons chili powder

1   tablespoon salt

1   tablespoon ground coriander

1   tablespoon ground black pepper

1½ teaspoons ground cinnamon

1½ teaspoons packed brown sugar

1½ teaspoons crushed red pepper

2   10- to 12-ounce pork tenderloins, trimmed

Lime wedges (optional)

Pork chops smothered in a rich mushroom and onion sauce and served over warm egg noodles make easy and delicious dinnertime fare.

French Onion Pork Chops

Lara—Cape Coral, FL

Ingredients

2 1-inch-thick pork chops

1 10.5-ounce can condensed French onion soup

1 teaspoon garlic powder

1 4-ounce can mushroom stems and pieces, drained

1 cup cold water

1 tablespoon all-purpose flour

8 ounces dried wide egg noodles

Prep: 20 minutes Cook: 30 minutes

Method

1. In a large skillet brown pork chops over medium heat. Add French onion soup and garlic powder. Cook about 30 minutes or until chops are cooked through and tender. Remove chops.

2. Add drained mushrooms to skillet. Whisk together the water and flour; stir into skillet. Cook and stir until thickened and bubbly; cook and stir for 1 minute more.

3. Meanwhile, cook noodles according to package directions.

4. Serve noodles with pork chops and cover with onion-mushroom sauce.

Makes 2 servings

These elegant pork chops have a colorful, flavorful sauce of cranberries, pomegranate, Gorgonzola cheese, and pecans.

Cranberry-Pomegranate Pork Chops

Marie—Austin, TX

Prep: 20 minutes **Cook:** 32 minutes

Method

1. Sprinkle pork chops evenly with salt and pepper. In a large nonstick skillet heat 1 tablespoon of the olive oil over medium-high heat. Add four of the chops; cook for 6 to 8 minutes or until brown and cooked through (160°F).

2. Remove and keep warm. Repeat with the remaining four chops and the remaining 1 tablespoon olive oil. Transfer pork chops to a serving platter and drizzle evenly with Cranberry-Pomegranate Sauce.

3. Sprinkle with Gorgonzola cheese and pecans. If desired, garnish with parsley.

Cranberry-Pomegranate Sauce: In a small saucepan combine one 16-ounce can whole cranberry sauce, ⅓ cup pomegranate juice, ⅓ cup reduced-sodium chicken broth, and ½ teaspoon lemon juice. Bring to boil; reduce heat to low. Simmer, uncovered, about 20 minutes or until reduced to 1½ cups.

Makes 8 servings

Cook's Notes
You can prepare the cranberry-pomegranate sauce up to two days ahead and refrigerate. Warm the sauce in the microwave or on the range top while searing the pork chops.

Ingredients

8 boneless pork loin chops (about 5 ounces each)

1 teaspoon kosher salt

1 teaspoon ground black pepper

2 tablespoons olive oil

1 recipe Cranberry-Pomegranate Sauce

4 ounces Gorgonzola cheese, crumbled

½ cup chopped pecans, toasted

Fresh parsley sprig (optional)

Adding pears and ginger to deglazed pork juices makes a very flavorful sauce for these pork chops.

Pork Chops with Pear and Ginger Sauce quick

James—Neligh, NE

Ingredients

4 **4-ounce boneless pork chops (½ inch thick)**

   Salt

   Ground black pepper

2 **teaspoons canola oil**

3 **tablespoons cider vinegar**

2 **tablespoons sugar**

⅔ **cup dry white wine**

1 **cup chicken broth**

1 **firm ripe pear (Bosc or Anjou), peeled, cored, and cut lengthwise into eighths**

1 **1½-inch-long piece fresh ginger, peeled and cut into thin julienne strips**

6 **green onions sliced into ½-inch strips**

2 **teaspoons cornstarch mixed with 2 teaspoons cold water**

Start to finish: 30 minutes

Method

1. Season pork chops with salt and pepper. In a large nonstick skillet heat canola oil over medium-high heat. Add chops and cook for 2 to 3 minutes per side or until brown and just cooked through. Transfer chops to a plate and keep warm.

2. Add vinegar and sugar to the skillet; stir to dissolve the sugar. Cook over medium-high heat for 10 to 20 seconds or until the syrup turns dark amber. Pour in wine (stand back because the hot syrup may splatter); bring to a simmer, stirring constantly.

3. Add chicken broth, pear, and ginger; bring to a simmer. Cook for 5 minutes, turning the pear slices occasionally. Add green onion; cook about 2 minutes more or until the pear is tender. Add the cornstarch mixture; cook and stir until sauce is slightly thickened.

4. Reduce heat to low. Return the chops and any accumulated juices to the skillet; turn to coat with the sauce. Heat through. Serve immediately.

Makes 4 servings

Cook's Notes
A must-have recipe!!

Spiral-cut ham is made even tastier with this cranberry glaze. Mustard, apple brandy, and lemon juice are stirred into cranberry sauce to make the shiny glaze.

Ham with Cranberry-Mustard Glaze

Athena—Florence, SC

+ · + · + · + · + · ++ · + · ++ · + · + · + · + · + · + · + · + · + · + · + · + · + · ++ · + · +

Prep: 20 minutes Bake: 1 hour 5 minutes Stand: 10 minutes

Method

1. In a small saucepan heat cranberry sauce over medium heat until melted, stirring frequently. Remove from the heat. Whisk in mustard, brandy, and lemon juice. Cool to room temperature.

2. Preheat oven to 350°F.

3. Place the ham, cut side down, in a roasting pan. Bake about 1 hour (8 minutes per pound). Remove the ham from the oven. Increase the oven temperature to 450°F.

4. Brush the ham with the cranberry mixture. Bake for 5 to 7 minutes more or until glazed. Remove from the oven; let stand for 10 minutes before serving.

5. To serve, place the ham on a serving plate cut side up. Gently fan the slices out from the bone. If desired, garnish with fresh cranberries.

Makes 12 to 14 servings

Ingredients

1 16-ounce can jellied cranberry sauce

3 tablespoons spicy brown mustard

2 tablespoons apple brandy

2 tablespoons lemon juice

1 8-pound spiral-cut ham with bone

   Fresh cranberries (optional)

Beef, Pork & Lamb

155

Pork loin is coated with a dry rub and oven-roasted until tender. It's then carved, brushed with a sweet barbecue sauce, and grilled.

Boneless Barbecued Pork Ribs

Pamela–Parkersburg, WV

156

Ingredients

- 3 tablespoons coarse salt
- 3 tablespoons paprika
- 1 tablespoon garlic powder
- 1 tablespoon packed brown sugar
- 2 tablespoons black pepper
- 2 3- to 4-pound boneless pork loin roasts
- 1 36-ounce bottle ketchup
- 1 cup packed brown sugar
- ¾ cup bottled honey barbecue sauce
- ½ teaspoon lemon juice

Prep: 20 minutes **Roast:** 1½ hours **Stand:** 10 minutes **Grill:** 20 minutes

Method

1. Preheat oven to 325°F. In a small bowl combine salt, paprika, garlic powder, the 1 tablespoon brown sugar, and the pepper. Rub this mixture on all sides of the pork loins. Place pork roasts on a rack in a roasting pan with about 1 inch of water in the bottom.

2. Roast for 1½ to 2¼ hours or until an instant-read thermometer inserted in center registers 160°F. Let roasts stand for 10 minutes.

3. Meanwhile, in a saucepan combine ketchup, the 1 cup brown sugar, the barbecue sauce, and lemon juice. Simmer over low heat about 10 minutes; remove from heat.

4. Place meat on cutting board and cut into 1½-inch slices. Cut in half vertically.

5. Preheat grill or ridged grill pan to medium. Place meat on grill and brush with the sauce. Turn meat frequently and brush with sauce each time. Grill about 20 minutes total.

Makes 12 to 16 servings

Cook's Notes
The pork can be prepared a day ahead of time. Just warm it up on the grill, brushing with the barbecue sauce before serving.

This dish of sweet Italian sausage and sliced sweet peppers with onion, garlic, basil, and crushed tomatoes is made in a slow cooker.

Italian Sausage and Peppers

Debbie—Albuquerque, NM

Prep: 25 minutes **Cook:** 7 hours on low-heat setting

Method

1. Turn an empty 4- to 5-quart slow cooker on high-heat setting; pour the olive oil into the bottom. Stir the garlic into the oil; cover the slow cooker. Let the garlic heat up while you prepare the other ingredients.

2. Slice the onion and add to the oil in the slow cooker. Cut each sausage link in two; add to the slow cooker. Cut sweet peppers into strips; add to sausage. Stir all ingredients well. Add undrained tomatoes. Stir again; add basil leaves, salt, and black pepper.

3. Cover and cook for 7 to 8 hours on low-heat setting. Serve over pasta.

Makes 6 to 8 servings

Cook's Notes
This meal will taste even better as leftovers. If there seems to be too much liquid, turn the slow cooker to high-heat setting and cook uncovered while you prepare the rest of the meal.

Ingredients

1   tablespoon olive oil

1   tablespoon chopped garlic

1   medium yellow onion

2   pounds sweet Italian sausage links

6   green sweet peppers

1   28-ounce can crushed tomatoes, undrained

3   or 4 fresh basil leaves

    Salt

    Ground black pepper

    Cooked pasta

Pizza is great any way you slice it, but when topped with barbecued pork, pineapple, peppers, and cheese, it's second to none!

Barbecued Pork Pizza quick

Gina—Baltimore, MD

Ingredients

1   12-inch gourmet pizza crust

    Olive oil spray

1   cup bottled barbecue sauce

1   cup cooked shredded pork

½   cup canned diced pineapple

½   cup finely chopped red sweet pepper

¼   cup sliced green onions

1   cup shredded Swiss cheese

1   cup shredded smoked Gouda cheese

½   teaspoon garlic powder

    Salt and ground black pepper to taste

Prep: 20 minutes   Bake: 10 minutes

Method

1. Preheat oven to 425°F. Place pizza crust on work surface and mist the edges with olive oil. Spread barbecue sauce on the pizza crust; top with pork, pineapple, sweet pepper, and green onion. Top with the Swiss cheese and smoked Gouda cheese, distributing evenly. Sprinkle the top with garlic powder and salt and black pepper to taste.

2. Place pizza directly on top rack of oven. Bake for 10 to 12 minutes or until cheese is melted and bubbly. (If desired, you may also broil for an additional 1 to 2 minutes to brown cheese.) Cool a few minutes before slicing.

Makes 8 servings

Cook's Notes
For a softer crust, cook on a pizza pan or stone.

Rosemary, thyme, white wine, and red currant jelly season this roast lamb.

Elegant Roast Lamb

Linda—Almonte, ON

· + · ·

Prep: 20 minutes **Roast:** 2½ hours

Method

1. Preheat oven to 325°F. Score fat on leg of lamb. In a small bowl combine ½ teaspoon of the rosemary, the thyme, and the ⅛ teaspoon pepper; rub into cuts in fat. Place lamb in roasting pan. Pour wine into pan. Insert ovenproof meat thermometer into thickest part of lamb (do not touch bone). Roast about 2½ hours or until thermometer registers 150°F.

2. While lamb is roasting, in a small saucepan combine red currant jelly, the remaining ½ teaspoon rosemary, and the mustard. Heat and stir over low heat until jelly is melted. During last hour of roasting time, baste lamb frequently with jelly mixture.

3. When lamb is cooked, remove to serving platter and keep warm. Pour drippings into measuring cup. Skim off fat; measure 1 cup of the drippings and pour into a small saucepan. In a screw-top jar combine the water and flour; shake well. Stir into drippings. Cook over medium heat until thickened. Season to taste with salt and additional pepper. Serve with roast.

Makes 6 to 8 servings

Ingredients

1   7- to 8-pound leg of lamb

1   teaspoons dried rosemary, crushed

½   teaspoon dried thyme, crushed

⅛   teaspoon ground black pepper

1   cup dry white wine

1   8-ounce jar red currant jelly

½   teaspoon Dijon-style mustard

3   tablespoons cold water

1   tablespoon all-purpose flour

Salt

Ground black pepper

These two herbed racks of lamb are roasted, sliced, and served with a rich, savory mushroom sauce.

Rack of Lamb with Porcini Sauce

Tom—Somerset, NJ

Ingredients

2	8-rib racks of lamb
3	tablespoons olive oil
3	teaspoons chopped fresh rosemary
3	teaspoons chopped fresh marjoram
¼	cup finely chopped shallot
1	tablespoon butter
1½	cups reduced-sodium beef broth
1	tablespoon tomato paste
4	ounces fresh porcini mushrooms, chopped
3	tablespoons red currant jelly

Prep: 30 minutes Roast: 16 minutes Stand: 15 minutes

Method

1. Preheat oven to 450°F. Brush lamb with 1 tablespoon of the olive oil; press rosemary and marjoram onto each rack. In a large skillet heat another 1 tablespoon olive oil over high heat; cook one rack about 5 minutes or until brown on all sides. Remove to roasting pan, placing meaty sides up. Repeat with second rack and remaining 1 tablespoon olive oil.

2. Roast about 16 minutes or until instant-read thermometer inserted in center (not touching bone) registers 130°F for medium-rare. Let stand for 15 minutes.

3. In a saucepan cook shallot in butter over medium heat for 3 minutes. Add broth and tomato paste; cook for 5 minutes. Add mushrooms and currant jelly; cook for 7 minutes.

4. Slice racks into separate chops and place on 4 dinner plates; serve with sauce.

Makes 4 servings

Cook's Notes
If fresh porcini mushrooms are not available, use 2 ounces dried porcini mushrooms soaked in ½ cup of hot beef broth for 15 minutes.

Lamb chops are coated with fresh rosemary, panko bread crumbs, pine nuts, and garlic, then cooked in a skillet and served with goat cheese salsa.

Lamb Chops with Goat Cheese Salsa

Elaine—Dallas, TX

Stand: 30 minutes **Prep:** 20 minutes **Cook:** 16 minutes

Method

1. Allow goat cheese to stand at room temperature for 30 minutes; crumble cheese. For salsa, in a medium bowl combine plum tomato, goat cheese, olives, toasted pine nuts, basil, green onion, lime juice, honey, dried oregano, ½ teaspoon of the sea salt, and ½ teaspoon of the black pepper. Cover and set aside while cooking lamb.

2. Rub 2 tablespoons of the olive oil over all sides of the lamb chops. In a shallow bowl combine fresh rosemary, panko bread crumbs, chopped pine nuts, garlic, the remaining ½ teaspoon sea salt, and the remaining ½ teaspoon black pepper. Coat lamb chops with rosemary mixture, turning to coat evenly.

3. In a large skillet heat another 1 tablespoon of the olive oil over medium heat. Cook half of the lamb chops in hot oil for 4 minutes per side; remove from skillet and keep warm. Cook remaining lamb chops in the remaining 1 tablespoon olive oil.

4. To serve, place two chops on each of four dinner plates. Top chops with salsa.

Makes 4 servings

Ingredients

4   ounces goat cheese

6   plum tomatoes, seeded and chopped

½   cup pitted and sliced kalamata olives

⅓   cup pine nuts, toasted

3   tablespoons chopped fresh basil

2   green onions, chopped

1   tablespoon lime juice

1   tablespoon honey

1   teaspoon dried oregano, crushed

1   teaspoon sea salt

1   teaspoon freshly ground black pepper

¼   cup olive oil

8   4-ounce lamb chops (about 1 inch thick)

⅓   cup chopped fresh rosemary

⅓   cup panko bread crumbs

3½ tablespoons chopped pine nuts

2   cloves garlic, finely minced

Lamb chops are served with a topping of tart apple and sweet onion seasoned with brown sugar, lemon juice, garlic, and mint.

Grilled Lamb with Apple-Onion Chutney

Tom—Somerset, NJ

Best of Hometown Cooking

Ingredients

1 cup peeled and chopped Granny Smith apples

1 cup chopped sweet onion (such as Vidalia)

2 tablespoons butter

1 tablespoon packed dark brown sugar

1 tablespoon lemon juice

2 cloves garlic, minced

1 teaspoon chopped fresh mint

8 4-ounce lamb rib chops

2 tablespoons olive oil

Salt

Ground black pepper

Prep: 20 minutes **Cook:** 10 minutes **Grill:** 12 minutes

Method

1. In a medium saucepan combine apples, onion, butter, brown sugar, lemon juice, garlic, and mint. Cook over medium heat about 10 minutes or until thick and syrupy; remove from heat and set aside.

2. Brush lamb chops with olive oil; season with salt and pepper. Place chops on rack of uncovered grill directly over medium-hot coals. Grill for 12 to 14 minutes or until medium-rare (145°F). (Or cook chops on grill pan over medium-high heat for 12 to 14 minutes or until medium-rare doneness [145°F].) Place two lamb chops on each of 4 plates; spoon apple-onion mixture over.

Makes 4 servings

Cook's Notes
Serve with roasted red potatoes and roasted asparagus.

This lamb meat loaf gets spiciness from the Italian sausage and extra flavor from fresh mint. Add a mint and garlic sauce to the top.

Mint Lamb Meat Loaf

Terasa—Watertown, MA

Prep: 25 minutes **Bake:** 1 hour

Method

1. Preheat oven to 425°F. With clean hands, in a large bowl combine ground lamb, sausage, eggs, cracker crumbs, chopped green onion, chopped mint, dash salt, and dash pepper. Line two 8×4×2-inch loaf pans with foil and press meat loaf into pans.

2. For mint sauce, in food processor combine mint leaves, green onion pieces, and garlic; process until pureed, adding olive oil and vinegar gradually while processing. Season to taste with salt and pepper.

3. Spoon mint sauce over meat loaves. Bake for 30 minutes. Reduce oven temperature to 350°F. Bake for 30 minutes more or until an instant-read thermometer inserted in center of loaf registers 160°F.

Makes 8 servings

Ingredients

2 pounds lean ground lamb

3 links hot Italian sausage (removed from casings)

4 eggs, lightly beaten

1 cup dry cracker crumbs (rosemary-flavor crackers are best)

1 cup finely chopped green onion

½ cup finely chopped fresh mint

Salt

Ground black pepper

½ cup fresh mint leaves

½ cup green onion pieces

4 cloves garlic, peeled

1 tablespoon olive oil

1 tablespoon cider vinegar

This hot appetizer with a tangy sauce is a great way to use venison.

Sweet-and-Sour Venison Meatballs

Melissa—Buffalo, WV

Ingredients

1 **pound uncooked ground venison or ground beef**

1 **cup rolled oats**

1 **small onion, chopped**

1 **egg, beaten**

4 **tablespoons ketchup**

1 **teaspoon cayenne pepper**

¼ **teaspoon salt**

½ **cup apple jelly**

½ **cup grape jelly**

2 **tablespoons Worcestershire sauce**

Prep: 20 minutes Bake: 15 minutes

Method

1. Preheat oven to 350°F. In a large bowl combine ground meat, oats, onion, egg, 2 tablespoons of the ketchup, cayenne pepper, and salt; mix well. Shape into 32 meatballs. Arrange meatballs in a 15×10×1-inch baking pan. Bake for 15 to 20 minutes or until cooked through (160°F); drain.

2. Meanwhile, for sauce, in a small saucepan combine apple jelly, grape jelly, Worcestershire sauce, and remaining 2 tablespoons ketchup; cook over low heat until jelly melts, stirring frequently. Pour sauce over meatballs.

Makes 4 to 6 servings

Cook's Notes
You can also use uncooked ground turkey in place of the venison.

Best of Hometown Cooking

Chapter 6
Fish & Seafood

The salmon fillet is brushed with a mixture of bottled barbecue sauce, lemon juice and zest, cilantro, soy sauce, and cumin before grilling.

Lemon Barbecue Grilled Salmon

Jill—Des Moines, IA

Ingredients

⅓ cup bottled tangy barbecue sauce

¼ cup chopped fresh cilantro

Zest of 1 lemon, finely shredded

Juice of 1 lemon

1 tablespoon soy sauce

½ teaspoon ground cumin

1 1½- to 2-pound salmon fillet (skin on)

Prep: 15 minutes Stand: 10 minutes Grill: 9 minutes

Method

1. In a small bowl combine barbecue sauce, cilantro, lemon zest, lemon juice, soy sauce, and cumin. Rinse salmon; pat dry with paper towels. Brush salmon with just enough of the soy mixture to coat, reserving the rest for basting during grilling. Allow salmon to stand for 10 minutes.

2. Place salmon on oiled rack of an uncovered grill directly over medium coals. Grill for 4 minutes. Carefully turn salmon.

3. Brush with remaining soy mixture; grill for 5 to 7 minutes more or until salmon flakes easily when tested with a fork.

Makes 4 to 6 servings

Cook's Notes
If you are not comfortable flipping the salmon over during cooking, it may be cooked skin-side down. In that case cook the fish with the grill lid on for the first 4 to 5 minutes.

Salmon steaks are marinated in lime and garlic, grilled, and brushed with a honey-chipotle glaze. They're served with a mango-onion-cilantro salsa.

Chipotle-Glazed Salmon with Mango Salsa

Joni—Rocklin, CA

Prep: 20 minutes Marinate: 20 minutes Grill: 5 minutes

Method

1. In a small bowl combine olive oil, lime juice, and garlic. Rinse salmon; pat dry with paper towels. Place salmon in a shallow baking dish. Pour oil mixture over; turn to coat salmon. Marinate at room temperature for 20 minutes.

2. Meanwhile, for salsa, in a medium bowl combine mango, onion, and cilantro.

3. Drain salmon, discarding marinade. Place salmon on oiled rack of an uncovered grill directly over medium-hot coals. Grill for 5 to 6 minutes or until salmon flakes easily when tested with a fork, turning once.

4. In a small bowl stir together honey and chipotle chile pepper with adobo sauce; brush over both sides of each salmon steak. Serve salmon with salsa.

Makes 4 servings

Cook's Notes
This dish is a knockout. It's easy enough for weeknights yet impressive enough for company. The honey-chipotle mixture gives the salmon a bright, shiny glaze, and the flavors are delicious!

Ingredients

¼ cup olive oil

2 tablespoons lime juice

1 tablespoon minced garlic

4 salmon steaks,
cut 1 inch thick

1 mango, peeled, seeded,
pitted, and chopped

¼ of a red onion, chopped

2 tablespoons chopped
fresh cilantro

3 tablespoons honey

1 tablespoon canned chipotle
chile pepper with adobo
sauce, minced

167

A nutty crunch paired with a slightly sweet honey-mustard glaze brings out the rich flavor of salmon in this dish. See photo on page 216.

Pecan-Crusted Salmon with Glaze ⟨quick⟩

Carolyn—Corona, CA

Ingredients

6 **6-ounce salmon fillets (about 2¼ pounds total), boned and skinned**

¾ **cup honey**

¾ **cup Dijon-style mustard**

2 **tablespoons lemon juice**

½ **cup olive oil (or as needed to thin glaze)**

4 **cups pecans, finely ground**

1 **tablespoon olive oil**

   Salt

   Ground black pepper

Prep: 15 minutes Cook: 4 minutes Bake: 5 minutes

Method

1. Preheat oven to 350°F. Rinse salmon; pat dry with paper towels. For glaze, in a small bowl combine honey, mustard, and lemon juice. Add ½ cup olive oil, or just enough to keep glaze from getting too thick. Reserve ¼ cup glaze; coat salmon lightly with remaining glaze. Coat salmon with ground pecans. Set aside.

2. In a large ovenproof skillet heat the 1 tablespoon olive oil over medium heat. Add salmon; cook for 4 to 6 minutes or until light brown, turning once.

3. Transfer skillet to oven; bake about 5 minutes or until salmon flakes easily when tested with a fork. Drizzle with reserved glaze. Season to taste with salt and black pepper.

Makes 6 servings

Tuna steaks are coated with cracked black pepper, grilled, and served with a colorful salsa of mango, corn, roasted pepper, jalapeño, and green onion.

quick Peppered Tuna with Mango Salsa

Jennifer—Oak Hill, VA

Prep: 20 minutes **Grill:** 8 minutes

Method

1. Rinse tuna; pat dry with paper towels. Completely coat both sides of the tuna steaks with cracked black pepper. Place tuna steaks on an oiled rack of an uncovered grill directly over medium coals. Grill for 8 to 12 minutes or until tuna flakes easily when tested with a fork, turning once.

2. Meanwhile, for salsa, in a small bowl combine mango, green onion, corn, roasted red pepper, jalapeño chile pepper, parsley, and lime juice.

3. Serve tuna steaks topped with salsa.

Makes 4 servings

Ingredients

4   **tuna steaks, cut 1 inch thick**

    Freshly cracked black pepper

1   **mango, peeled, seeded, and chopped**

½   **cup chopped green onion**

½   **cup frozen whole kernel corn, thawed**

½   **cup chopped roasted red sweet pepper**

1   **fresh jalapeño chile pepper, minced**

2   **tablespoons fresh flat-leaf parsley, chopped**

    Juice of 1 lime

Fresh bass fillets, grilled in foil with butter, onion, lemon, and almonds, taste great and are easy to clean up!

Grilled Bass

Davontae—Cleveland Heights, OH

170

Ingredients

2 6-ounce largemouth bass fillets, skin removed

1 tablespoon butter or margarine, softened

4 thin slices red onion

4 thin slices lemon

2 tablespoons sliced almonds

¼ cup sliced green onion

⅛ teaspoon salt

⅛ teaspoon white pepper or lemon pepper

⅛ teaspoon paprika

Prep: 20 minutes Grill: 11 minutes

Method

1. Rinse fish; pat dry with paper towels. Grease the center of a 20×18-inch sheet of heavy foil with butter. Arrange two slices red onion and two slices lemon over the butter. Sprinkle with 1 tablespoon of the almonds and half of the green onion. Arrange the fillets in a single layer over the onion, lemon, and almonds. Top with remaining red onion, lemon, almonds, and green onion.

2. Season with salt, white pepper, and paprika. Fold the long sides of the foil together to seal. Fold and crimp short ends to seal tightly.

3. Place foil packet on rack of uncovered grill directly over medium coals. Cover and grill for 11 to 15 minutes or until fish flakes easily when tested with a fork.

Makes 2 servings

This easy-to-prepare fish recipe is baked in individual foil packets with lemon and a tasty rice pilaf.

Cod with Lemon Rice Pilaf

Ltlphyl—Alexandria, NH

+ · +

Prep: 20 minutes   **Bake:** 12 minutes

Method

1. Preheat oven to 450°F or a grill to medium-high. Prepare rice mix according to package directions.

2. Rinse cod; pat dry with paper towels. Place one cod fillet in the center of an 18×12-inch sheet of heavy foil. Repeat with remaining fish, using a separate sheet of foil for each. Coat with nonstick cooking spray. Sprinkle with lemon and herb seasoning.

3. Add lemon zest and juice to cooked rice; spoon some of the rice beside each cod fillet. Sprinkle sweet pepper over top.

4. Bring up sides of foil; double-fold tops and ends to seal packets, leaving room for heat circulation inside.

5. Place on baking sheet; bake for 12 to 14 minutes or until fish flakes easily when tested with a fork. (Or place on a grill rack directly over medium-hot coals. Cover grill and grill for 10 to 12 minutes or until fish flakes easily when tested with a fork.) Open packets and sprinkle with almonds.

Makes 4 servings

Ingredients

2   4.2-ounce packages desired rice and sauce mix

4   skinless cod, flounder, or sole fillets (4 to 5 ounces each)

Butter-flavored nonstick cooking spray

1½   teaspoons lemon and herb seasoning or lemon-pepper seasoning

Grated zest and juice of 1 lemon

½   of a medium red sweet pepper, chopped

¼   cup slivered almonds, toasted

A savory herb breading makes grouper fillets swim with flavor. This is one dish that can be made in less than 30 minutes—perfect for weeknight suppers!

Herbed Grouper quick

Betty—Atlanta, GA

Ingredients

1   1½-pound grouper fillet

2   teaspoons olive oil

¼   teaspoon salt

¼   teaspoon ground black pepper

¾   cup fine dry bread crumbs

½   cup chopped fresh parsley

1   tablespoon chopped fresh basil

1   teaspoon dried thyme, crushed

    Nonstick cooking spray

    Fresh parsley sprigs

    Fresh basil sprigs

    Lemon slices

Prep: 15 minutes   **Grill:** 14 minutes

Method

1. Rinse fish; pat dry with paper towels. Brush fillet with olive oil; sprinkle with salt and pepper. In a small bowl combine bread crumbs, parsley, basil, and thyme. Press mixture onto all sides of fish fillet.

2. Generously coat a grill basket with nonstick cooking spray. Place grill basket on rack of uncovered grill directly over medium coals. Cover and grill for 14 to 16 minutes or until fish flakes easily when tested with a fork, turning once. Garnish with parsley sprigs, basil sprigs, and lemon slices. Serve immediately.

Makes 4 servings

This quick-and-easy combination of tilapia and red curry is a new twist on traditional Thai cuisine.

quick Thai-Style Tilapia for Two

Tracie—West Peoria, IL

Start to finish: 25 minutes

Method

1. Rinse fish; pat dry with paper towels.

2. Lightly coat fish with seasoned flour; shake off excess.

3. In a shallow bowl whisk together egg and the water; set aside.

4. In a nonstick skillet combine butter, wine, yogurt, red curry paste, and lemon juice; cook over low heat until everything is well combined.

5. Dip the floured fillets in the egg mixture; place fillets in the skillet with the butter mixture.

6. Cook for 4 to 6 minutes per ½ inch or until fish flakes easily when tested with a fork, turning once. Garnish with chopped green onion.

Makes 2 servings

Ingredients

2   tilapia fillets

1   cup seasoned flour (season with salt, black pepper, and garlic or with lemon-pepper seasoning)

1   egg

3   tablespoons water

3   tablespoons butter

2   tablespoons dry white wine

1   tablespoon plain yogurt

1   teaspoon red curry paste

1   teaspoon lemon juice

2   green onions or chives, chopped

Fish kabobs like these are easier to grill than you could ever imagine. Dillweed and lemon juice add refreshing flavor to the marinade while pepper sauce adds zip.

Fish Kabobs

Lucy—Cypress, CA

Ingredients

- 2 **pounds halibut, salmon, or swordfish steaks, cut 1 inch thick**
- ½ **cup lemon juice**
- ⅓ **cup olive oil**
- 1 **bay leaf**
- 1 **tablespoon chopped fresh dillweed**
- ¼ **teaspoon coarsely ground black pepper**

  Several drops bottled hot pepper sauce

- 1 **large cucumber or zucchini, halved lengthwise and cut into ¾-inch-thick slices**
- ½ **of a 12-ounce jar roasted red sweet peppers, drained and cut into 1-inch pieces**
- 12 **small to medium mushrooms**
- 12 **pimiento-stuffed green olives**

  Hot cooked rice (optional)

Prep: 20 minutes **Marinate:** 30 minutes **Grill:** 8 minutes

Method

1. Rinse fish; pat dry with paper towels. If necessary, remove skin and bones. Cut fish into 1-inch cubes. Place fish in a resealable plastic bag set into a shallow dish.

2. For marinade, in small bowl combine lemon juice, olive oil, bay leaf, dillweed, black pepper, and hot pepper sauce. Pour over fish; seal bag. Marinate at room temperature for 30 minutes, turning bag occasionally.

3. Drain fish, reserving marinade. On six long metal skewers, alternately thread fish, cucumber, red pepper, mushrooms, and olives. Brush with marinade.

4. Place kabobs on the greased rack of an uncovered grill directly over medium coals. Grill for 8 to 12 minutes or until fish flakes easily when tested with a fork, turning once and brushing with reserved marinade halfway through grilling time. Discard any remaining marinade. If desired, serve kabobs over hot cooked rice.

Makes 6 servings

Cook's Notes
Whole brown or white mushrooms work great for these kabobs. However, if you like, you can cut portobello mushrooms into 1-inch pieces to thread on the skewers.

In this recipe, a colorful and healthful collection of fresh vegetables complements your choice of pasta and fish.

Santa Fe Pasta
Robyn—Easton, PA

Start to finish: 40 minutes

Method

1. In a large skillet heat ¼ cup olive oil over medium heat. Add butternut squash and onion; cook for 3 to 5 minutes or until squash is tender. Add carrot; cook for 3 minutes. Add pumpkin seeds and 2 tablespoons of the chili powder; cook for 2 minutes. Add zucchini and yellow summer squash; cook until tender. Stir in cooked pasta and the remaining 2 tablespoons chili powder; heat through. Season to taste with sea salt.

2. Meanwhile, rinse fish; pat dry with paper towels. Coat fish with 1 tablespoon olive oil; sprinkle with sea salt and pepper. In a large nonstick skillet cook fish for 4 to 6 minutes or until fish flakes easily when tested with a fork, turning once.

3. Top pasta mixture with fish; drizzle with additional olive oil and the lemon juice. Garnish with lime wedges.

Makes 6 to 8 servings

Cook's Notes
This dish is healthy and bursting with flavor. Try a flavored artisan salt for an added taste bonus.

Ingredients

Olive oil

1   **butternut squash, peeled and cut into ½-inch cubes**

1   **medium red onion, thinly sliced**

2   **carrots, peeled and cut into long thin strips**

½   **cup pumpkin seeds, lightly toasted**

¼   **cup chili powder**

2   **zucchini, cut into long, thin strips**

2   **yellow summer squash, cut into long, thin strips**

1   **pound dried pasta, cooked according to package directions**

    Sea salt

8   **4- to 6-ounce portions haddock or other white fish**

    Ground black pepper

1   **tablespoon lemon juice**

1   **lime, sliced into 6 wedges**

Ragoût is a hearty stewlike dish—and packed with seafood as it is here, it is simply divine. Serve in large soup bowls and garnish with sliced green onion.

Seafood Ragoût

Patsy—Kamloops, BC

176

Ingredients

1	**pound fish (such as halibut or monkfish)**
1	**pound shrimp**
1	**onion, chopped**
1	**tablespoon minced garlic**
1	**tablespoon butter**
1 ½	**cups dry white wine**
1 ¼	**cups chicken broth**
4	**large plum tomatoes, chopped**
½	**cup vermouth or 3 tablespoons Pernod (optional)**
2	**tablespoons dried dillweed, crushed**
	Zest from ½ of a large orange
¼	**teaspoon salt**
2	**pounds mussels, debearded, scrubbed, and rinsed**
3	**green onions, sliced**

Start to finish: 50 minutes

Method

1. Rinse fish. Peel and devein shrimp. Rinse shrimp. Pat fish and shrimp dry with paper towels. Set aside.

2. In a large saucepan cook onion and garlic in hot butter for 3 minutes. Add wine, chicken broth, tomatoes, vermouth (if desired), dillweed, orange zest, and salt. Bring to boiling over high heat; reduce heat to medium. Simmer, uncovered, for 10 minutes. Stir in mussels and shrimp.

3. Bring to boiling. Cover and cook about 4 minutes or just until mussels open. (Discard any mussels that do not open.) Add fish. Cover and cook for 2 to 3 minutes or until fish flakes easily when tested with a fork. Spoon ragoût into large soup bowls and sprinkle with green onion.

Makes 4 to 6 servings

Tip

Debearding Mussels If your fresh mussels have a dark, wiry tuft sticking out from the shell (called the beard), it's easy to remove. Just grasp it between your fingers and pull the fibers out, tugging toward the hinge of the shell. Then scrub the whole shell well with a stiff brush under cold running water to avoid getting any sand or grit in your dinner.

It's no wonder lobster is a favorite to many—it's brimming with such delicious flavor, it hardly needs any seasoning. Simple recipes such as this allow the lobster to shine.

quick Broiled Lobster Tails

Lori—Feeding Hills, MA

Prep: 10 minutes   **Broil:** 5 minutes

Method

1. Preheat broiler. Rinse lobster and pat dry with paper towels. Place lobster tails on a medium baking sheet. With a sharp knife or kitchen scissors, carefully cut top side of lobster shells lengthwise. Pull shells apart slightly. Brush meat with butter and sprinkle with paprika, salt, and white pepper.

2. Broil lobster tails for 5 to 10 minutes or until lobster meat is opaque. Garnish with lemon wedges.

Makes 2 servings

Ingredients

2   whole lobster tails

½   cup butter, melted

½   teaspoon paprika

    Salt

    White pepper

1   lemon, cut into wedges

Here's a New England staple that's sure to please: hoagies with a mixture of mayo, celery, and succulent lobster meat.

Lobster Rolls ◆quick◆

Lori–Feeding Hills, MA

Ingredients

6	tablespoons mayonnaise
¼	cup finely chopped celery
2	tablespoons finely chopped red onion
1 ½	tablespoons lemon juice
1	tablespoon finely chopped fresh parsley
1	tablespoon salt
1	tablespoon bottled hot pepper sauce
	White pepper
1	pound cooked lobster, cut up
6	hot dog buns, toasted
	Melted butter

Start to finish: 20 minutes

Method

1. In a medium bowl combine mayonnaise, celery, onion, lemon juice, parsley, salt, hot pepper sauce, and white pepper to taste. Stir in lobster meat until coated.

2. Brush toasted buns with melted butter. Divide lobster mixture among buns. Serve immediately.

Makes 6 servings

These fried shrimp have a slightly sweet and crunchy breading that goes great with the accompanying mustard-and-marmalade sauce. See photo on page 216.

Coconut Shrimp

Jo Ann—Conroe, TX

Prep: 25 minutes   **Cook:** 4 minutes   **Bake:** 5 minutes

Method

1. Preheat oven to 300°F. Peel and devein shrimp. Rinse shrimp; pat dry with paper towels. Set aside.

2. In a medium bowl combine flour, cornstarch, and salt. Add ice water and the 2 tablespoons oil; stir until well mixed.

3. In deep-fat fryer or electric skillet heat oil for frying to 350°F. Spread coconut on a flat pan, a little at a time, adding more as needed. Dip shrimp in flour mixture, then roll in coconut. Fry shrimp in hot oil about 4 minutes or until light brown.

4. Transfer shrimp to a baking pan and bake shrimp about 5 minutes or until shrimp are opaque.

5. For sauce, in a small bowl combine orange marmalade, mustard, honey, and hot pepper sauce. Serve sauce with shrimp.

Makes 4 servings

Ingredients

- 1 ½ pounds large shrimp
- ½ cup all-purpose flour
- ½ cup cornstarch
- 1 tablespoon salt
- 1 cup ice water
- 2 tablespoons cooking oil

  Cooking oil for deep-fat frying
- 2 cups shredded coconut
- ½ cup orange marmalade
- ¼ cup Dijon-style mustard
- ¼ cup honey
- 3 to 4 drops bottled hot pepper sauce

Fish & Seafood

179

Tip

Preparing Shrimp Getting fresh shrimp ready for cooking is a bit tedious but worth it when you're enjoying every tender, succulent bite. To peel and devein shrimp, begin peeling the shell at the thickest part of the shrimp and move down toward the thinner end. In most cases you can leave the tail on. To devein the shrimp, make a shallow cut down the length of the back with a small pair of kitchen scissors or the tip of a paring knife. With the tip of a paring knife, scrape out the vein and then rinse the shrimp in cool running water and pat dry.

Marinated shrimp are grilled or broiled, then served with a creamy sauce enriched with butter and flavored with garlic and rosemary.

Shrimp with Rosemary Cream Sauce

Rosalin–Waterford, TN

Ingredients

1 ½	pounds extra-large shrimp
2	sprigs fresh rosemary
4	cloves garlic, crushed
¼	cup olive oil
½	cup dry white wine
¼	cup water
½	cup whipping cream
¼	cup butter or margarine
	White pepper

Prep: 30 minutes Marinate: 4 hours Broil: 10 minutes

Method

1. Peel and devein shrimp, reserving shells. Rinse shrimp; pat dry with paper towels. Chop rosemary from 1 sprig.

2. For marinade, in a food processor or blender combine the chopped rosemary, half of the crushed garlic, and olive oil; cover and process or blend until spices are mixed with the oil. Place shrimp in a resealable plastic bag and pour marinade over. Seal bag; turn to coat shrimp. Marinate in the refrigerator for 4 hours to overnight.

3. For sauce, in a small saucepan combine wine and the water. Add reserved shrimp shells. Bring to boiling; reduce heat. Simmer, uncovered, for 10 minutes. Remove and discard shrimp shells. Continue to boil until liquid is reduced to ¼ cup. Stir in whipping cream, butter, the remaining rosemary sprig, and the remaining crushed garlic. Simmer until thickened. Strain; add white pepper to taste.

4. Preheat broiler. Drain shrimp, discarding marinade. Thread shrimp on skewers, leaving ¼-inch space between shrimp. Place skewers on the rack of an unheated broiler pan. Broil 4 to 5 inches from heat about 10 minutes or until shrimp are opaque, turning once. Spoon sauce on plate and top with cooked shrimp.

Makes 4 servings

Shrimp are marinated in a bourbon-maple glaze, wrapped in prosciutto, and broiled. This dish is sure to get requests for a repeat.

Prosciutto-Wrapped Shrimp

Kathi—Austin, TX

Prep: 30 minutes   **Broil:** 6 minutes

Method

1. Preheat broiler. Peel and devein shrimp, leaving tails intact. Rinse shrimp; pat dry with paper towels.

2. In a small bowl whisk together maple syrup, bourbon, teriyaki sauce, mustard, and chili powder. Add the shrimp to maple syrup mixture, tossing to coat. Drain shrimp, discarding maple mixture.

3. Cut each prosciutto slice lengthwise into four strips. Wrap one prosciutto strip around each shrimp. Thread shrimp onto four 8-inch skewers, leaving ¼-inch space between shrimp. Coat an unheated broiler pan with nonstick cooking spray. Place skewers on prepared broiler pan. Broil about 6 minutes or until shrimp are opaque, turning once.

Makes 4 servings

Ingredients

24 jumbo shrimp (about 1½ pounds total)

3 tablespoons maple syrup

2 tablespoons bourbon

1 tablespoon teriyaki sauce

2 teaspoons Dijon-style mustard

1 teaspoon chili powder

6 very thin slices prosciutto or ham (about 3 ounces total)

Nonstick cooking spray

The sauce—made with parsley, garlic, jalapeño chile pepper, oregano, vinegar, and oil—goes a long way in flavoring grilled shrimp kabobs.

Island Shrimp with Chimichurri Sauce 〈quick〉

Alexa—Seattle, WA

Ingredients

2 pounds large shrimp (tails on)

4 cloves garlic, coarsely chopped

1 fresh red jalapeño chile pepper, seeded and coarsely chopped

1 cup fresh parsley leaves

¼ cup fresh oregano leaves

½ cup olive oil

¼ cup red wine vinegar

¼ teaspoon salt

Prep: 20 minutes Grill: 7 minutes

Method

1. Peel and devein shrimp. Rinse shrimp; pat dry with paper towels. In a food processor combine garlic and chile pepper; mince finely. Add parsley and oregano; pulse until finely chopped. Add olive oil, vinegar, and salt, processing until smooth and emulsified. (The sauce can be used immediately, or pour it into a jar, cover, and refrigerate until ready to use.) Remove about ⅓ cup of the sauce to use to baste the shrimp. Set the remainder aside.

2. Thread the shrimp on skewers (if using wooden skewers, be sure to soak in water for 30 minutes), leaving a ¼-inch space between shrimp. Baste shrimp with the ⅓ cup sauce. Discard any remaining basting sauce. Place shrimp on oiled rack of an uncovered grill directly over medium coals. Grill for 7 to 9 minutes or until shrimp are opaque, turning once. Remove from skewers. Serve with the remaining sauce.

Makes 4 to 6 servings

This version of the traditional Thai dish has shrimp, peanuts, and tofu tossed with noodles in a flavorful broth.

 **Pad Thai**

Marjorie–Skaneateles, NY

Start to finish: 30 minutes

Method

1. Peel and devein shrimp. Rinse shrimp; pat dry with paper towels. Set aside. Soften rice noodles in cold water.

2. In a large wok or skillet heat oil over high heat. Add shrimp, garlic, and egg; stir slowly for about 1 minute. Add chicken broth, tomato sauce, sugar, fish sauce, and pickled radish. Stir in bean sprouts and tofu. Heat through. Add rice noodles; stir to coat noodles with sauce.

3. Cook and stir until sauce is slightly reduced. Noodles should be slightly moist but not wet. Top with chopped peanuts; toss to mix lightly. Garnish with lime wedges.

Makes 1 to 2 servings

Ingredients

4 to 8 large shrimp

8 ounces Thai rice noodles

¼ cup cooking oil

2 tablespoons minced garlic or onion

1 egg, lightly beaten

½ cup chicken broth or water

¼ cup tomato sauce

3 tablespoons sugar

2 tablespoons fish sauce or 1 tablespoon salt

1 tablespoon pickled radish

1 cup bean sprouts

1¼ ounces tofu, cubed

3 tablespoons chopped peanuts

Lime wedges

183

Arborio rice is traditionally used in risottos because of its high starch content. The starch gives the dish its classic creamy texture.

Seafood Risotto

Lori—Feeding Hills, MA

Ingredients

8	ounces shrimp
8	ounces scallops
1	tablespoon olive oil
½	cup chopped onion
1	clove garlic, minced
1	cup Arborio rice
2	cups chicken broth
½	cup chopped zucchini
8	ounces cooked lobster meat, coarsely chopped
½	cup frozen peas
¼	cup chopped fresh flat-leaf parsley
3	tablespoons freshly grated Parmesan cheese

Start to finish: 50 minutes

Method

1. Peel and devein shrimp. Halve any large scallops. Rinse shrimp and scallops; pat dry with paper towels.

2. In a heavy large skillet heat olive oil over medium heat. Add onion and garlic; cook until onion is tender. Add uncooked Arborio rice; cook for 3 minutes, stirring frequently. Add half of the chicken broth; bring to boiling; reduce heat. Cover and simmer about 10 minutes or until the liquid is absorbed.

3. Add remaining chicken broth and zucchini; cover and simmer for 5 minutes more. Add shrimp, scallops, lobster, and frozen peas. Cover and simmer for 5 minutes more, stirring once. Stir in parsley; cook about 2 minutes or until liquid is absorbed and rice is tender. Stir in grated Parmesan cheese.

Makes 4 to 5 servings

Tip

Scallop Types There are two kinds of scallops: bay scallops and sea scallops. Bay scallops are harder to find; they're generally available only on the East Coast. They're tiny—usually about ½ inch in diameter—and are slightly sweeter and more tender than the larger and more plentiful sea scallops. Sea scallops average about 1 ½ inches in diameter. Both types are best when briefly cooked; overcooking causes them to become rubbery.

Depending on what you like best, you can make this creamy rice dish with shrimp, crawfish, or crabmeat.

Seafood Étouffée

Stacy—Gueydan, LA

+ · + · + · + · + · + · + · + · + · + · + · + · + · + · + · + · + · + · + · +

Prep: 20 minutes **Cook:** 30 minutes

Method

1. Rinse seafood; pat dry with paper towels. Set aside. In a large saucepan melt butter over medium heat. Add onion, sweet pepper, garlic, and, if desired, jalapeño chile pepper; cook about 5 minutes or until onion is tender.

2. Stir in cream of shrimp soup and the water. Bring to boiling; reduce heat. Simmer, uncovered, for 20 minutes.

3. Sprinkle seafood with your favorite seasoning blend. Stir seafood into mixture in saucepan. Cook about 5 minutes or until seafood is opaque, stirring occasionally. Serve over hot cooked rice.

Makes 4 to 6 servings

Cook's Notes
Chicken étouffée is becoming a popular entrée. To make it, substitute a pound of cubed boneless skinless chicken for the seafood and one can of cream of celery soup instead of cream of shrimp soup.

Ingredients

1   **pound peeled, deveined shrimp, crawfish, or crabmeat**

½   **cup butter**

1   **chopped onion**

1   **chopped green sweet pepper**

1   **teaspoon minced garlic**

1   **teaspoon chopped fresh jalapeño chile pepper (optional)**

1   **10.75-ounce can condensed cream of shrimp soup**

½   **cup water**

   Seafood seasoning blend

   Hot cooked rice

Small shell pasta is combined with green onion, scallops, and chipotle spice to make this Southwestern treat!

Southwestern Scallops and Pasta

Susan—Winona, MN

186

Ingredients

8 **ounces bay scallops**

16 **ounces dried small shell pasta**

¼ **cup olive oil**

2 **bunches green onions, chopped**

1 **cup vegetable broth**

3 **tablespoons Southwestern chipotle spice blend**

1 **cup half-and-half or light cream**

Salt

Start to finish: 35 minutes

Method

1. Rinse scallops; pat dry with paper towels. Set aside. Cook pasta to barely al dente according to package directions; drain.

2. In a medium skillet heat olive oil over medium-high heat. Add green onion; cook for 1 minute. Add scallops; cook for 3 to 5 minutes or until scallops begin to lose their translucence.

3. Add cooked pasta, vegetable broth, and Southwestern spice; cook for 1 minute. Reduce heat to medium. Add half-and-half; simmer for 1 minute more (do not boil). Remove skillet from heat. Season to taste with salt. Serve immediately, or chill and serve cold.

Makes 8 servings

Cook's Notes
Any larger scallops may be cut in half for faster cooking.

Creole cooking combines French, Spanish, and African cuisines and is often flavored with the same trio of ingredients—onion, celery, and green pepper—as in this dish.

Scallops Creole

Karrie—West Des Moines, IA

Prep: 25 minutes **Cook:** 50 minutes

Method

1. Rinse scallops; pat dry with paper towels. Set scallops aside.

2. In a large saucepan cook onion, celery, and garlic in hot oil until tender. Add tomato sauce, tomatoes, sugar, Worcestershire sauce, salt, chili powder, and hot pepper sauce. Bring to boiling; reduce heat. Simmer, uncovered, for 45 minutes.

3. In a small bowl combine the cold water and cornstarch; stir into saucepan and cook until slightly thickened. Add scallops and sweet pepper; simmer, covered, for 5 minutes. Serve over hot cooked rice.

Makes 4 to 6 servings

Ingredients

1½   pounds scallops or peeled and deveined shrimp

½   cup chopped onion

½   cup chopped celery

3   cloves garlic

3   tablespoons cooking oil

2   8-ounce cans tomato sauce

1   14-ounce can tomatoes, undrained

1   tablespoon sugar

1   tablespoon Worcestershire sauce

1½   teaspoons salt

1   teaspoon chili powder

  Dash bottled hot pepper sauce

2   teaspoons cold water

1   teaspoon cornstarch

½   cup sliced green sweet pepper

  Hot cooked rice

This is a specialty dish using baked oysters topped with a savory, spinach-flecked breading and cheddar cheese.

Oysters Rockefeller  quick

Nancy–Bemus Point, NY

Ingredients

12	oysters, removed from shells
2	tablespoons finely chopped onion
2	tablespoons finely chopped celery
2	tablespoons chopped fresh parsley
¼	cup butter
½	cup chopped fresh spinach
⅓	cup fine dry bread crumbs
	Juice of ½ lemon
¼	teaspoon salt
7	drops bottled hot pepper sauce
	Shredded sharp cheddar cheese

Prep: 20 minutes **Bake:** 10 minutes

Method

1. Preheat oven to 400°F. Rinse oysters; pat dry with paper towels. Set aside.

2. In a small saucepan cook and stir onion, celery, and parsley in hot butter until onion is tender. Stir in spinach, bread crumbs, lemon juice, salt, and hot pepper sauce.

3. Arrange oysters in an 8×8×2-inch baking dish. Spoon about 1 tablespoon of the spinach mixture over each oyster. Sprinkle with cheddar cheese.

4. Bake about 10 minutes or until edges of oysters curl. Serve immediately.

Makes 4 servings

Cook's Notes
I always double the recipe. The spinach mixture is also good stuffed in mushrooms and baked.

Rich, velvety Alfredo sauce is made with butter, Parmesan cheese, and heavy cream. If you like, top each serving with lots of freshly ground black pepper.

quick Heavenly Crab Alfredo

Maureen—Deptford, NJ

Start to finish: 20 minutes

Method

1. In a medium saucepan melt butter over medium-high heat. Add crabmeat and parsley. Cook for 1 minute, stirring occasionally. Slowly stir in cream, Parmesan cheese, and cream cheese. Cook and stir about 3 minutes or until thickened. Fold in Monterey Jack cheese; heat about 1 minute more or until cheese is combined. Fold in the crumbled bacon.

2. Serve immediately over pasta. If desired, garnish with parsley sprigs.

Makes 4 servings

Cook's Notes
Serve with a salad and a warm crusty bread.

Ingredients

½ cup butter

2 6-ounce cans crabmeat, drained and flaked

⅓ cup chopped fresh parsley

1 cup whipping cream

½ cup grated Parmesan cheese

2 ounces cream cheese, softened and cut into cubes

1 cup shredded Monterey Jack cheese

8 slices bacon, crisp-cooked, drained, and crumbled

1 pound dried angel hair pasta, cooked and drained

Fresh parsley sprigs (optional)

Fish & Seafood

189

Make this healthy quiche for dinner, lunch, or brunch. It's full of yummy crab and good-for-you vegetables.

Crab Quiche

Doreen—Rochester, NY

Ingredients

Nonstick cooking spray

3 tablespoons diet margarine

1 medium carrot, grated

1 medium zucchini, thinly sliced

½ of a medium onion, finely chopped

½ of a medium red sweet pepper, finely chopped

½ cup chopped fresh parsley

8 ounces cooked crabmeat

¾ cup crushed saltine crackers

1 teaspoon baking powder

½ teaspoon white pepper

1 cup refrigerated or frozen egg product, thawed

1½ cups nonfat milk

Prep: 35 minutes **Bake:** 35 minutes **Stand:** 5 minutes

Method

1. Preheat oven to 375°F. Generously coat a 9-inch pie plate with nonstick cooking spray; set aside.

2. Coat an unheated large nonstick skillet with nonstick cooking spray. Add 1 tablespoon of the diet margarine; melt over medium heat. Add carrot, zucchini, onion, sweet pepper, and parsley; cook for 5 to 6 minutes or just until vegetables are tender. Stir in crabmeat. Transfer mixture to prepared pie plate.

3. In a medium bowl combine crackers, baking powder, and white pepper. Using a pastry cutter or two knives, cut in the remaining 2 tablespoons diet margarine. Add egg substitute and milk; mix well. Pour over crab mixture in pie plate.

4. Bake about 35 minutes or until golden brown and puffed. Let stand for 5 minutes before serving.

Makes 6 servings

Lump crabmeat is combined with egg, mayonnaise, sweet pepper, onion, pimiento, mustard, and seafood seasoning, then shaped into patties and panfried until golden.

quick Chesapeake Bay Crab Cakes

Janice—Ocean City, MD

Prep: 25 minutes **Cook:** 4 minutes

Method

1. Rinse crabmeat; pat dry with paper towels. In large bowl combine egg, mayonnaise, sweet pepper, pimiento, red onion, lemon juice, mustard, and seafood seasoning. Gently fold in crabmeat and bread crumbs, being careful not to break up lumps of crabmeat. Shape into 12 patties.

2. Coat an unheated large skillet with nonstick cooking spray. Preheat skillet over medium-high heat. Add crab patties to skillet; cook about 4 minutes or until golden and heated through, turning once.

Makes 4 to 6 servings

Ingredients

1 **pound lump crabmeat**

1 **egg, lightly beaten**

2 **tablespoons mayonnaise**

2 **tablespoons chopped green sweet pepper**

1 **2-ounce jar diced pimientos**

1 ½ **tablespoons chopped red onion**

1 ½ **teaspoons lemon juice**

1 **teaspoon Dijon-style mustard**

1 **teaspoon seafood seasoning**

½ **cup soft bread crumbs**

Nonstick cooking spray

Instead of a pastry crust, this quiche has a bottom layer of Swiss cheese and almonds.
The traditional egg filling—packed with crabmeat and shrimp—goes on top.

Cheesy Almond-Crusted Seafood Quiche

Zan–Jasper, AL

Ingredients

⅔	cup sliced almonds
1½	cups shredded Swiss cheese
8	ounces cooked crabmeat, flaked
8	ounces cooked shrimp, chopped
½	cup sliced green onion
4	eggs, beaten
1¼	cups whipping cream
½	teaspoon celery salt
⅛	teaspoon white pepper
	Paprika

Prep: 25 minutes Bake: 45 minutes Stand: 10 minutes

Method

1. Preheat oven to 350°F. Spread almonds in a 9-inch pie plate. Sprinkle evenly with 1 cup of the Swiss cheese. Bake about 10 minutes or until cheese melts. Remove from oven; top with crabmeat, shrimp, and green onion.

2. In a medium bowl beat together eggs, whipping cream, celery salt, and white pepper. Pour over seafood. Sprinkle with the remaining ½ cup cheese. Sprinkle lightly with paprika.

3. Bake about 45 minutes or until set in center. Let stand for 10 minutes before serving.

Makes 6 servings

Cook's Notes
This makes a wonderful brunch or luncheon main dish.

This seafood quiche showcases a combo of crabmeat and shrimp, plus lots of extras. Give it a try at your next brunch or Saturday luncheon.

San Francisco Seafood Quiche

Saunie—North Las Vegas, NV

Prep: 25 minutes **Bake:** 30 minutes **Stand:** 5 minutes

Method

1. Preheat oven to 350°F. In a medium bowl combine crabmeat, shrimp, Swiss cheese, celery, and green onion. Divide the seafood mixture between the two pie shells.

2. In another bowl combine mayonnaise, wine, eggs, and flour; whisk lightly and pour evenly into the pie shells.

3. Bake for 30 to 40 minutes or until set in the center. Let stand for 5 minutes before serving.

Makes 8 to 10 servings

Cook's Notes
Serve with vodka gimlets, tossed green salad to which you can add canned artichoke hearts and red onion rings, and breadsticks with butter. I've served this many times and it's always a hit.

Ingredients

6	ounces cooked crabmeat
1½	cups chopped cooked shrimp
8	ounces Swiss cheese, chopped
½	cup finely chopped celery
½	cup finely chopped green onion
2	9-inch unbaked pie shells
1	cup mayonnaise
1	cup dry white wine
4	eggs, lightly beaten
2	tablespoons all-purpose flour

Tuna noodle casserole is always a hit with kids and adults alike! This version is seasoned with hot sauce and plenty of Mexican cheese.

Gordon Family's Tuna Casserole

Jolene—Tarawa Terrace, NC

194

Ingredients

1   16-ounce package dried egg noodles

2   6-ounce cans tuna (water pack), drained

1   14.5-ounce can peas, drained

1   14.5-ounce can mixed vegetables, drained

¾   cup milk

½   cup mayonnaise

4   teaspoons bottled hot pepper sauce

2   teaspoons ground black pepper

    Dash salt

2   10.75-ounce cans condensed cream of mushroom soup

1½ cups shredded Mexican cheese blend

Prep: 25 minutes Bake: 35 minutes Stand: 10 minutes

Method

1. Preheat oven to 375°F. Cook egg noodles according to package directions.

2. While noodles are cooking, in a large saucepan combine tuna, peas, drained mixed vegetables, milk, mayonnaise, hot pepper sauce, black pepper, and salt. Stir in cream of mushroom soup and 1 cup of the cheese. Cook over medium heat until cheese melts.

3. Drain noodles; add to tuna mixture, stirring until well combined. Cook for 10 minutes.

4. Spoon into greased 3-quart casserole; top with remaining ½ cup cheese. Bake for 35 minutes. Let stand for 10 minutes before serving.

Makes 8 servings

Chapter 7
Meatless

Try this casserole recipe that's teeming with vegetables and topped with a nice smoky cheese. This is one that any cowgirl can make.

Cowgirl Casserole

Laurie—Thompson, ND

Best of Hometown Cooking

Ingredients

1   medium onion, chopped

1   cup finely chopped carrot

1   red sweet pepper, finely chopped

1   tablespoon cooking oil

1   cup fresh or frozen green beans, cut in ½-inch-long pieces

1   15- or 16-ounce can vegetarian baked beans

1   cup canned or frozen corn

1   tablespoon ketchup or tomato paste

1   teaspoon barbecue seasoning

3   ounces smoked cheddar or smoked Edam cheese, diced or shredded

Prep: 25 minutes   Bake: 30 minutes

Method

1. Preheat oven to 375°F. In a nonstick skillet cook onion, carrot, and sweet pepper in hot oil until tender. Add green beans; cook for 5 minutes. Stir in undrained baked beans, corn, ketchup, and barbecue seasoning; cook about 2 minutes or until heated through. Pour into a 2-quart casserole. Sprinkle with smoked cheese.

2. Cover and bake about 30 minutes or until casserole is bubbling and the cheese melts.

Makes 6 servings

This flavorful dish is based on an Eastern European favorite. It features layers of noodles, mashed potatoes, sauerkraut, and cheese.

Pierogi Casserole

Marjorie—Skaneateles, NY

Prep: 25 minutes **Bake:** 45 minutes

Method

1. Preheat oven to 400°F. In small saucepan cook onion in hot butter until tender.

2. Spread one-third of the onion mixture over the bottom of a 3-quart rectangular baking dish. Cover with one-third of the lasagna noodles. Spread 2 cups of the potatoes over noodle layer. Place ⅓ cup of the cheese on the potatoes. Place one-third of the sauerkraut on cheese. Repeat layers two more times. Sprinkle with paprika, salt, and pepper. Bake for 45 minutes.

Makes 6 to 8 servings

Cook's Notes
Pierogi are Polish noodle dumplings. This recipe turns them into a delicious layered casserole with the traditional ingredients.

Ingredients

1	**large yellow onion, chopped**
1¼	**sticks melted butter (¾ cup)**
1	**12-ounce package dried lasagna noodles, cooked according to package directions and drained**
6	**cups mashed potatoes**
1	**cup cubed pasteurized prepared cheese product**
4	**ounces sauerkraut, drained**
	Paprika
	Salt
	Ground black pepper

Meatless

197

This vegetarian lasagna layers eggplant, zucchini, portobello mushrooms, artichokes, and ricotta cheese with noodles, pasta sauce, and mozzarella.

Veggie Lovers' Lasagna

Melissa—Robbinsville, NJ

Ingredients

3   tablespoons olive oil

2   cloves garlic, crushed

1   large eggplant, chopped

2   zucchini, thinly sliced

1   cup sliced portobello mushrooms

1   8-ounce jar artichoke hearts, drained

1   12-ounce container ricotta cheese

1   tablespoon dried Italian seasoning, crushed

2   26-ounce jars spaghetti sauce (any flavor)

1   8-ounce package oven-ready lasagna noodles

8   ounces fresh mozzarella cheese, sliced

Prep: 30 minutes   Bake: 45 minutes

Method

1. Preheat oven to 375°F. In a large saucepan heat olive oil over medium heat. Add garlic; cook for 1 minute. Add eggplant; cook for 3 minutes (you may need to add more olive oil). Stir in zucchini, mushrooms, and drained artichoke hearts; cook for 10 minutes more, stirring often. Stir in ricotta cheese and Italian seasoning. Remove from heat.

2. Spread a thin layer of spaghetti sauce in the bottom of a 3-quart rectangular baking dish. Alternate layers of noodles, ricotta mixture, and remaining sauce to fill baking dish, ending with sauce. Top with sliced mozzarella cheese.

3. Bake for 45 minutes. Cool slightly; cut into squares to serve.

Makes 4 to 6 servings

Cook's Notes
I suggest a garden veggie or tomato-basil pasta sauce for this recipe.

These cheesy pasta roll-ups with a tomato sauce and Parmesan topping will become one of your family's favorites! See photo on page 217.

Family Manicotti

Sandie—Freeland, MI

+ +

Prep: 30 minutes   **Bake:** 35 minutes

Method

1. Preheat oven to 375°F. For sauce, in a medium bowl stir together spaghetti sauce, sugar, basil, oregano, and garlic salt. Spoon one-quarter of the sauce on the bottom of a 3-quart rectangular baking dish.

2. Cut each lasagna noodle in half crosswise. In another medium bowl stir together ricotta cheese, 2 cups of the mozzarella cheese, ½ cup of the Parmesan cheese, the egg, bread crumbs, and parsley. Spoon a heaping tablespoon of the cheese mixture onto one end of a lasagna noodle half; roll up, starting at the cheese end. Place roll-up, seam side down, on sauce in baking dish. Repeat with remaining cheese mixture and lasagna noodles.

3. Pour remaining sauce evenly over roll-ups. Top with the remaining 2 cups mozzarella cheese and the remaining ¼ cup Parmesan cheese. Cover with foil.

4. Bake for 20 minutes. Uncover and bake about 15 minutes more or until hot in center.

Makes 6 servings

Cook's Notes
This is my family's favorite of all time! Serve it with salad and bread or rolls.

Ingredients

1	**28-ounce jar spaghetti sauce (any flavor)**
2	**tablespoons sugar**
1	**teaspoon chopped fresh basil**
1	**teaspoon dried oregano, crushed**
⅛	**teaspoon garlic salt**
8	**ounces dried lasagna noodles, cooked, drained, and rinsed**
1	**pound ricotta cheese**
4	**cups shredded mozzarella cheese**
¾	**cup grated Parmesan cheese**
1	**egg, lightly beaten**
½	**cup seasoned fine dry bread crumbs**
2	**tablespoons chopped fresh parsley or 1 teaspoon dried parsley flakes, crushed**

Tip

Prepping Fresh Herbs When using woody-stem herbs, such as oregano, rosemary, and thyme, from which you only want the leaves, you don't have to pick each individual leaf. Here's a trick: Grasp the top of the stem with the thumb and forefinger of one hand; then, with the other hand, strip the leaves off the stem starting at the top and moving down the stem.

In this classic pasta dish that everyone will love, ziti is mixed with ricotta, mozzarella, and Parmesan cheeses and spaghetti sauce.

Three-Cheese Baked Ziti

Timi—Rainbow City, AL

Ingredients

1 15-ounce container ricotta cheese

2 eggs, beaten

¼ cup grated Parmesan cheese

1 16-ounce package dried ziti pasta, cooked and drained

1 28-ounce jar spaghetti sauce

1 cup shredded mozzarella cheese

Prep: 25 minutes **Bake:** 30 minutes

Method

1. Preheat oven to 350°F. In large bowl combine ricotta cheese, eggs, and Parmesan cheese; set aside. In another large bowl stir together hot pasta and pasta sauce.

2. Spread half of the pasta mixture in a 3-quart rectangular baking dish; evenly top with ricotta cheese mixture, then remaining pasta mixture. Sprinkle with mozzarella cheese. Bake, uncovered, about 30 minutes or until heated through.

Makes 8 servings

This yummy eggplant dish includes lots of other veggies—red onion, sweet peppers, green beans, tomatoes, and mushrooms.

Eggplant Italiano
Barbara—Rhinelander, WI

Prep: 25 minutes **Bake:** 1¼ hours **Stand:** 5 minutes

Method

1. Cut eggplant crosswise into ¼-inch slices; sprinkle with salt. Layer slices in a colander with a plate underneath to catch juice. Let stand for 45 minutes.

2. Preheat oven to 350°F. Pat both sides of eggplant slices dry with a paper towel. Cut slices into small wedges or cubes; place in a 3-quart rectangular baking dish. Top with red onion and sweet pepper. Drizzle with olive oil; toss to coat.

3. In a small bowl combine ricotta cheese and garlic; drop by teaspoonfuls evenly over eggplant mixture. Top with drained green beans and undrained tomatoes. Pour wine over the top; sprinkle with basil. Top with olives, mushrooms, Asiago cheese, and bread crumbs.

4. Cover with foil; bake for 45 minutes. Uncover; bake for 30 minutes more. Let stand for 5 minutes before serving.

Makes 6 servings

Cook's Notes
This recipe is nutritious and low in fat. You can further reduce the fat by using only 1 tablespoon oil and low-fat or reduced-fat ricotta. Leftovers are great for lunch served in warm whole wheat 'n' honey pita pocket halves. I also mash leftovers and spread on toasted bread rounds as an appetizer. To serve the rounds warm, sprinkle them with grated Asiago or Romano cheese and place under broiler.

Ingredients

- 1 1¼- to 1½-pound eggplant
  Salt
- ⅓ of a medium red onion, thinly sliced
- ⅓ of a medium red sweet pepper, thinly sliced
- ⅓ of a medium green sweet pepper, thinly sliced
- 2 tablespoons olive oil
- ½ cup ricotta cheese
- 1½ tablespoons bottled roasted garlic
- 1 14.5-ounce can Italian-style green beans, drained
- 1 14.5-ounce can diced tomatoes with green pepper, celery, and onion undrained
- ¼ cup dry white wine
- 2 tablespoons chopped fresh basil
- ½ cup sliced pitted ripe olives
- 4 large fresh mushrooms, sliced
- ¼ cup freshly grated Asiago cheese
- 3 tablespoons seasoned fine dry bread crumbs

Scrambled eggs, seasoned with chili powder and cumin, are sprinkled over corn bread batter in a baking dish. Onion, salsa, and two cheeses top it all before baking.

Southwest Corn Bread and Egg Casserole

Autumn—North Bend, OR

Ingredients

1 **8-ounce package corn muffin mix**

2 **tablespoons butter**

1 **teaspoon chili powder**

1 **teaspoon ground cumin**

4 **eggs, beaten**

¼ **cup chopped onion**

½ **cup purchased salsa**

½ **cup shredded Monterey Jack cheese**

½ **cup shredded cheddar cheese**

Sour cream

Prep: 20 minutes **Bake:** 20 minutes **Stand:** 5 minutes

Method

1. Preheat oven to 400°F. Prepare corn muffin mix according to package directions. Spread in a greased 11×7×1½-inch baking dish.

2. In a medium skillet melt butter over medium heat; stir in chili powder and cumin. Pour in eggs. Cook over medium heat, without stirring, until mixture begins to set on the bottom and around edges. Remove from heat; cool slightly.

3. Spoon the scrambled eggs evenly over the unbaked corn bread, breaking up any large clumps. Sprinkle the onion evenly over the eggs. Drizzle salsa over the eggs; use the back side of a spoon to spread it out. Sprinkle with Monterey Jack and cheddar cheeses.

4. Bake for 20 to 30 minutes or until a knife inserted in the center comes out clean. Let stand for 5 to 10 minutes before cutting into squares. Serve with sour cream.

Makes 4 servings

The healthful crust in this recipe is made of egg substitute and biscuit mix and topped with cheese, tomato, and basil.

quick Low-Carb Pizza Frittata

Britt—Santa Barbara, CA

Start to finish: 20 minutes

Method

1. In a small bowl whisk together egg product, biscuit mix, and garlic salt. Coat a small nonstick omelet pan with nonstick cooking spray. Preheat over medium heat. Pour egg mixture into pan; cook over medium heat for 4 to 5 minutes or until egg is nearly set.

2. Using a wide spatula, flip egg (like a pancake) and immediately put pizza sauce and cheese slices on top. Cook about 2 minutes more or until cheese slices begin to melt and egg is set.

3. Transfer to a microwave-safe plate and microwave on 100% power (high) about 30 seconds or until cheese melts and is bubbly. Top pizza with tomato slices and fresh basil; sprinkle with Parmesan cheese.

Makes 1 serving

Cook's Notes
This recipe is high in protein and low in carbs. It works best in a small nonstick omelet pan.

Ingredients

½ cup refrigerated or thawed frozen egg product

¼ cup packaged biscuit mix

1 teaspoon garlic salt

Nonstick cooking spray

2 tablespoons purchased pizza sauce

1 slice cheddar cheese

1 slice mozzarella cheese

3 slices tomato

1 tablespoon chopped fresh basil

Grated Parmesan cheese to taste

This delicious spinach and cheese soufflé is made by cooking and draining frozen spinach, then folding it into a sauce made with Parmesan and Swiss cheese.

Spinach-Cheese Soufflé

Ruth—Fort Worth, TX

204

Ingredients

1½	**cups milk**
3	**eggs, separated**
2	**tablespoons tapioca flour**
½	**teaspoon salt**
½	**teaspoon freshly ground black pepper**
1	**10-ounce package frozen spinach, cooked and well drained**
⅔	**cup finely shredded Swiss cheese**
⅓	**cup freshly grated Parmesan or Pecorino-Romano cheese**
	Nonstick cooking spray

Prep: 15 minutes   **Bake:** 35 minutes

Method

1. Preheat oven to 350°F. In a large bowl beat together milk, egg yolks, tapioca flour, salt, and pepper. Stir in cooked spinach and cheeses.

2. In a small bowl beat egg whites until stiff peaks form. Fold egg whites into spinach mixture.

3. Coat a 10-inch pie plate with nonstick cooking spray. Spoon egg and spinach mixture into pie plate. Bake for 35 to 40 minutes or until set in center.

Makes 4 servings

Who says meat lovers have all the fun? This veggie burger loaf has all the flavor of meat loaf with the addition of cheese and a glaze of brown sugar and ketchup.

Burger Loaf with Sweet-and-Sour Glaze

Ruth—Round Rock, TX

Prep: 20 minutes **Bake:** 45 minutes

Method

1. Preheat oven to 350°F. In a large skillet melt margarine over medium heat. Add onion; cook until tender. Stir in bread cubes; cook for 1 minute more.

2. Place crumbled burger into a large bowl. Add onion mixture, cheddar cheese, eggs, garlic powder, and poultry seasoning. Mix thoroughly to combine all ingredients. Spoon into a greased 9×9×2-inch baking dish.

3. For glaze, in a small bowl stir together brown sugar, ketchup, and the water. Pour glaze over the burger loaf. Bake for 45 to 60 minutes or until cooked through.

Makes 8 to 10 servings

Cook's Notes
To speed up the preparation process, I use a food processor to chop the onion (not too fine), then put the bread in separately to make bread crumbs. Preparing the glaze in a 2-cup measure makes it easy to pour over the loaf before baking.

Ingredients

½ cup margarine

1 large onion, chopped

6 slices whole wheat bread, cubed

1 20-ounce package vegetarian burger, crumbled

2 cups shredded cheddar cheese

4 eggs

1 teaspoon garlic powder

1 teaspoon poultry seasoning

½ cup packed dark brown sugar

½ cup ketchup

½ cup water

This vegetarian meat loaf mixes vegetarian burger with corn, black beans, tomatoes, onion, sweet peppers, and carrot and is seasoned with thyme and marjoram.

Western Vegetarian Meat Loaf

Susan—Little Rock, AR

Ingredients

1 cup rolled oats

1 cup vegetable juice

1 20-ounce can vegetarian burger

1 16-ounce can corn, drained

1 15-ounce can black beans, rinsed and drained

1 14.5-ounce can diced tomatoes, undrained

1 medium onion, chopped

1 medium red sweet pepper, chopped

1 medium green sweet pepper, chopped

1 cup shredded carrot

1 tablespoon chopped fresh thyme

1 tablespoon chopped fresh marjoram

½ cup ketchup

Prep: 15 minutes Bake: 40 minutes Stand: 10 minutes

Method

1. Preheat oven to 350°F. In a small bowl combine oats and vegetable juice; set aside. In a large bowl combine vegetarian burger, drained corn, drained black beans, undrained tomatoes, onion, and sweet pepper; add carrot, thyme, and marjoram. Stir in oat mixture.

2. Shape vegetable mixture into a loaf in a 13×9×2-inch baking pan. Bake for 40 to 50 minutes or until hot in center. Top with ketchup; let stand for 10 minutes before serving.

Makes 6 servings

Cook's Notes
The cooking time may vary. You can substitute different seasonings and types of tomatoes.

Prepared with packaged crust mix and lots of veggies, this pizza is colorful, nutritious, and yummy.

Veggie Pizza Supreme

Pamela—Parkersburg, WV

Prep: 20 minutes **Bake:** 25 minutes **Stand:** 10 minutes

Method

1. Preheat oven to 375°F. Prepare pizza dough according to package directions. Coat a baking sheet or baking stone (about 15×12 inches) with nonstick cooking spray. After pizza dough rises, pat out onto prepared baking sheet or stone. Arrange mozzarella cheese strips across the dough, spacing them evenly.

2. Cover cheese strips and dough with pizza sauce.

3. Top the pizza with ingredients in this order: mushrooms, broccoli, red onion, sweet pepper, hot pepper, and shredded cheese.

4. Bake for 25 to 28 minutes or until the crust is brown. Let stand for 10 minutes before slicing.

Makes 8 to 10 servings

Cook's Notes
This pizza is so good and colorful from the vegetables, you don't even miss the meat. Sometimes I prepare a whole wheat crust from scratch to make it even healthier.

Ingredients

1   **6.5-ounce package pizza crust mix**

   Nonstick cooking spray

4   **thin slices low-fat mozzarella cheese, cut into 2-inch strips**

1   **14.5-ounce can pizza sauce**

1   **cup sliced fresh mushrooms**

1   **cup broccoli florets, chopped**

½   **cup chopped red onion**

½   **cup chopped red sweet pepper**

½   **cup chopped green sweet pepper**

1   **cup hot pepper rings**

1½   **cups shredded reduced-fat or nonfat mozzarella cheese**

Meatless

207

Impress your guests with this elegant main dish! It uses purchased piecrust so it's supereasy to make.

Tomato-Spinach Tart

Janet—Bricktown, NJ

208

Ingredients

½ of a 15-ounce package rolled refrigerated piecrust (1 crust), unbaked

1½ cups shredded mozzarella cheese

1 10-ounce package frozen spinach, thawed and well drained

1 cup chopped fresh basil

½ cup mayonnaise

1 egg, beaten

¼ cup grated Parmesan cheese

2 cloves garlic, minced

3 tomatoes, cut into wedges

Prep: 30 minutes Bake: 45 minutes

Method

1. Preheat oven to 325°F. Let piecrust stand according to package directions. Ease piecrust into a 9-inch pie plate; crimp edge. Bake piecrust for 10 minutes. Remove from oven. Increase oven temperature to 350°F.

2. Sprinkle piecrust with ½ cup of the mozzarella cheese. In a large bowl stir together spinach, basil, mayonnaise, egg, Parmesan cheese, garlic, and the remaining 1 cup mozzarella cheese. Arrange tomato wedges on top of melted cheese in piecrust. Spoon spinach mixture over.

3. Bake in the 350° oven for 35 to 40 minutes or until golden brown and bubbly.

Makes 4 main-dish servings

**Knock-Your-Socks-Off
Buffalo Wings**
page 12

Cookie Dough Cheese Ball
page 22

Caesar Chef Salad Sandwiches
page 28

Meatball Subs
page 37

Taco Salad
page 56

Best of Hometown Cooking

Grilled Chicken–Artichoke Salad
page 58

Chicken Parmesan
page 86

**Grilled Chicken with
Sweet Corn Relish**
page 94

Turkey Scallop Skillet
page 118

Mexican Pizza
page 123

Best of Hometown Cooking

Peppercorn Steaks
page 133

**Homemade Meatballs
and Spaghetti**
page 143

Stuffed Pork Loin Roast
page 147

**Pecan-Crusted Salmon
with Glaze**
page 168

Coconut Shrimp
page 179

Family Manicotti
page 199

217

Portobello Caprese
page 226

**Tiny Potato and
Carrot Chowder**
page 263

Festive Fall Chili
page 267

Amazing Twice-Baked Potatoes
page 270

Summer Green Beans
page 281

Chapter 10
Breads & Muffins

220

Best of Hometown Cooking

Chocolate Caramel Candy Cake
page 326

Old-Fashioned Sugar Cookies
page 339

Chapter 12

Pies & Desserts

222

Best of Hometown Cooking

Mixed Berry Cobbler
page 362

**Chocolate-Peanut
Ice Cream Dessert**
page 371

Chapter 13
Holiday

224

Orange-Glazed Ham
page 393

Decadent Caramel Apples
page 397

Serve these tomato tapas as an easy vegetable dish for dinner tonight. Fresh tomatoes and a variety of cheeses make them irresistible.

 # Tomato Tapas

Marjorie–Skaneateles, NY

Ingredients

- ½ cup shredded Italian 6-cheese blend
- ¼ cup crumbled Gorgonzola cheese
- 1 large plum tomato, seeded and chopped
- 2 tablespoons purchased sun-dried tomato pesto
- 2 tablespoons finely chopped sweet onion
- ½ teaspoon dried basil, crushed
- ½ teaspoon finely chopped fresh rosemary
- ⅛ teaspoon garlic powder

  Freshly ground black pepper
- 1 2.1-ounce package baked miniature phyllo dough shells

Prep: 20 minutes Bake: 7 minutes

Method

1. Preheat oven to 350°F. In a small bowl combine cheese blend, Gorgonzola cheese, tomato, pesto, onion, basil, rosemary, garlic powder, and pepper.

2. Place phyllo dough shells on baking sheet or in miniature muffin pans. Spoon cheese mixture into shells, mounding as needed. Bake for 7 to 8 minutes or until cheese melts.

Makes 6 to 8 servings

 Tip

Seeding Tomatoes The simplest way to seed a tomato—whether it's a plum tomato or a regular salad tomato—is to cut it in half horizontally (perpendicular to the stem), then hold it over a bowl and gently squeeze the seeds out. Alternately, you can take the tip of a teaspoon and scoop the seeds out of each seed pocket.

Meaty portobello mushrooms are cooked in the microwave, along with eggplant and tomato and served with sliced fresh mozzarella cheese. See photo on page 217.

Portobello Caprese quick

Tracy—Bloomington, IN

Ingredients

2 **large portobello mushrooms**

Olive oil

Salt

Dried Italian seasoning, crushed

2 **½-inch-thick slices small, firm eggplant**

2 **¼-inch-thick slices firm, ripe tomato**

2 **¼-inch-thick slices (about 1 ounce each) fresh mozzarella cheese**

Start to finish: 25 minutes

Method

1. Remove mushroom stems and discard. Lightly dry mushrooms with paper towels and place gill sides down in a single layer in a microwave-safe, broilerproof dish. Generously drizzle olive oil over mushrooms to cover the entire cap. Lightly salt mushrooms. Flip over and repeat. Sprinkle inside of mushrooms with Italian seasoning. Set aside.

2. Lay eggplant, tomato, and mozzarella slices flat on a plate; lightly drizzle with olive oil, making sure all slices are completely coated. Lightly sprinkle with salt and Italian seasoning. Flip over and repeat.

3. Layer one slice eggplant and one slice tomato onto each mushroom cap. Cover dish; microwave on 100% power (high) about 8 minutes or until eggplant and mushrooms are tender.

4. Meanwhile, preheat broiler. Place one slice of the fresh mozzarella cheese on top of each mushroom stack. Broil for 1 to 2 minutes or just until cheese melts down the sides of the vegetables. Serve immediately.

Makes 2 servings

Cook's Notes
Be sure to use a dish that is both microwave-safe and broilerproof. This recipe is healthy enough for vegetarians and dieters, yet hearty and flavorful enough for non-vegetarians. It is an absolutely delicious entrée that is truly elegant for entertaining but fast enough to throw together after work.

Frozen ravioli are dipped in batter, rolled in an Italian-spiced bread crumb mixture, and deep-fried. Serve them with the spaghetti sauce of your choice.

Provolone Fried Ravioli

Mary—Ada, OK

Prep: 25 minutes **Cook:** 4 minutes per batch **Bake:** 2 minutes

Method

1. Preheat oven to 450°F. In a deep-fat fryer or large heavy saucepan heat oil to 350°F. Meanwhile, for batter, in a large bowl stir together flour, biscuit mix, and seasoned salt; stir in the water. Set batter aside.

2. In a medium bowl stir together bread crumbs, Parmesan cheese, parsley flakes, garlic powder, onion powder, oregano, and pepper; set aside.

3. Dip each ravioli into batter, allowing excess to drip back into bowl. Roll in bread crumb mixture. Fry ravioli, 4 or 5 at a time, for 4 to 6 minutes or until golden brown, turning once. Drain on paper towels.

4. Place fried ravioli 1 inch apart on large baking sheets. Quarter each slice of provolone. Place one piece of provolone on each ravioli. Bake for 2 to 3 minutes or until cheese melts. Serve with warm spaghetti sauce.

Makes 8 servings

Cook's Notes
These wonderful little ravioli are versatile. They're great as an entrée or as an appetizer for a party. Zesty spaghetti sauce makes an easy yet perfect complement. This is a great vegetarian dish.

Ingredients

6 **cups cooking oil for deep-frying**

1¼ **cups all-purpose flour**

1 **cup packaged biscuit mix**

½ **teaspoon seasoned salt**

1⅔ **cups water**

2 **cups seasoned fine dry bread crumbs**

2 **tablespoons grated Parmesan cheese**

1 **teaspoon dried parsley flakes, crushed**

½ **teaspoon garlic powder**

½ **teaspoon onion powder**

¼ **teaspoon dried oregano, crushed**

¼ **teaspoon freshly ground black pepper**

1 **25-ounce package frozen cheese ravioli, thawed**

1 **pound thinly sliced provolone cheese**

1 **26.5-ounce jar spaghetti sauce, warmed**

Purchased ravioli is breaded, browned in olive oil, and served with a savory tomato and red pepper sauce.

Toasted Ravioli with Dipping Sauce ◆quick◆

Toylynn—Amarillo, TX

Ingredients

2 eggs

1 tablespoon milk or half-and-half

⅛ teaspoon salt

⅛ teaspoon ground black pepper

1½ cups seasoned fine dry bread crumbs

½ cup grated Parmigiano-Reggiano cheese

¼ cup chopped fresh flat-leaf parsley

12 large fresh spinach and cheese ravioli (about 12 ounces)

5 tablespoons olive oil

3 cloves garlic, minced

Dash crushed red pepper

2 bottled roasted red sweet peppers, drained

1 14-ounce can crushed tomatoes, undrained

Salt

Ground black pepper

Start to finish: 25 minutes

Method

1. In a shallow dish whisk together eggs, milk, the ⅛ teaspoon salt, and the ⅛ teaspoon black pepper. In another shallow dish combine bread crumbs, cheese, and parsley. Coat ravioli with egg mixture, then with bread crumb mixture. In a large skillet heat 3 tablespoons of the olive oil over medium heat. Add ravioli; cook 6 to 8 minutes or until deep golden brown, turning once. Remove to a serving platter to keep warm.

2. In a small saucepan heat the remaining 2 tablespoons olive oil, the garlic, and crushed red pepper over medium-low heat.

3. Pulse the roasted peppers in a food processor and add to garlic mixture after it has cooked for 2 minutes.

4. Stir undrained tomatoes into roasted red pepper mxiture; season to taste with salt and black pepper. When ready to serve, transfer dipping sauce to a small bowl. Serve sauce with toasted ravioli.

Makes 4 servings

These homemade ravioli are stuffed with a spicy pumpkin and ricotta filling and topped with an herbed cream sauce.

Savory Pumpkin Ravioli

Tora-Lynn—East Greenbush, NY

+ +

Method

1. For filling, in medium bowl combine ricotta cheese, pumpkin, mozzarella cheese, Parmesan cheese, 2 tablespoons of the parsley, 1 tablespoon of the sage, 1 teaspoon of the nutmeg, the salt, ¼ teaspoon of the ground black pepper, and the cloves. Set aside.

2. Cut each egg roll wrapper in half to make two rectangular sheets. For each ravioli, place a heaping teaspoon of the pumpkin mixture onto one half of the rectangle, leaving edges free. Brush edges lightly with water. Fold the rectangle in half and crimp the edges together using the tines of a fork. If desired, dust each ravioli with a little all-purpose flour; set aside.

3. Start boiling a large pot of water while making the sauce. For sauce, cook shallot and garlic in hot butter about 5 minutes or until tender. Add the remaining 1 tablespoon sage, the remaining 1 tablespoon parsley, the rosemary, the remaining ½ teaspoon nutmeg, and the remaining ¼ teaspoon ground black pepper. Add wine; cover and simmer for 5 minutes. Add whipping cream; heat through.

4. When the water comes to a boil, add ravioli carefully. Reduce the water to a simmer and cook the ravioli for 6 to 7 minutes or until they are puffed in the center and soft on the edges. Drain carefully.

5. To serve, arrange ravioli on a large platter. Spoon sauce over ravioli. If desired, garnish with sage leaves and parsley sprigs.

Makes 4 to 6 servings

Cook's Notes
This is an impressive dish to serve to company. It pleases both vegetarian and meat-eating guests!

Ingredients

1 ½	cups ricotta cheese
1 ¼	cups canned pumpkin
½	cup shredded mozzarella cheese
¼	cup shredded Parmesan cheese
3	tablespoons finely chopped fresh parsley
2	tablespoon finely chopped fresh sage
1½	teaspoons freshly grated nutmeg
½	teaspoon salt
½	teaspoon ground black pepper
⅛	teaspoon ground cloves
1	16-ounce package egg roll wrappers
	All-purpose flour
2	shallots, minced
2	cloves garlic, minced
½	cup butter
2	teaspoons finely chopped fresh rosemary
¼	cup dry red wine
½	cup whipping cream

This healthy vegetarian pasta dish is made with broccoli, tofu, and sweet peppers in a creamy low-fat sauce with tangy blue cheese.

Creamy Broccoli-Topped Pasta ◆quick◆

Marjorie—Skaneateles, NY

Ingredients

Nonstick cooking spray

1 cup finely chopped onion

1 cup finely chopped red sweet pepper

1 small clove garlic, minced

8 ounces extra-firm tofu (fresh bean curd), crumbled

1 cup nonfat milk

1 teaspoon vegetable base or vegetable bouillon

8 ounces blue cheese, crumbled

3 tablespoons nonfat cream cheese

4 cups broccoli florets, blanched and chopped

3 cups hot cooked penne pasta

Start to finish: 30 minutes

Method

1. Coat an unheated large skillet with nonstick cooking spray. Preheat over medium heat. Add onion, sweet pepper, and garlic; cook until onion is tender, stirring occasionally.

2. In a blender combine tofu, milk, and vegetable base; cover and blend until smooth. Pour over vegetable mixture in skillet; cook and stir until slightly thickened.

3. Reduce heat to low. Stir in blue cheese and cream cheese; cook and stir until cheese melts. Stir in broccoli; heat through. Serve over hot cooked pasta.

Makes 4 to 6 servings

Here's a quick and easy—and tasty—way to get some vitamin C and A. Combined with half-and-half, pasta, mushrooms, and cheese, broccoli just couldn't taste better!

quick Pasta con Broccoli

Mary Jo—Wentzville, MO

Start to finish: 25 minutes

Method

1. Cook pasta shells according to package directions until nearly tender. Drain pasta; return to hot pan.

2. Add half-and-half, broccoli, butter, tomato sauce, and garlic powder. Bring to boiling; reduce heat. Simmer, uncovered, about 8 minutes or until broccoli and pasta are tender. Stir in drained mushrooms.

3. Remove from heat. Stir in Parmesan cheese.

Makes 4 to 6 servings

Ingredients

1   **pound dried medium pasta shells**

4   **cups (1 quart) half-and-half or light cream**

1   **pound fresh or frozen broccoli florets**

½   **cup butter**

½   **of an 8-ounce can tomato sauce**

1½   **teaspoons garlic powder**

1   **8-ounce can sliced mushrooms, drained**

1½   **to 2 cups grated Parmesan cheese**

This rich and luscious sauce is made with Brie cheese and served with bow tie pasta and tomatoes.

Bow-Tie Pasta with Brie

Dawn—Neptune Beach, FL

Ingredients

1   8-ounce round Brie cheese

1   16-ounce package
     bow tie pasta

1   cup olive oil

3   cloves garlic, finely chopped

2   cups chopped plum tomatoes

1   cup chopped fresh basil

     Freshly grated Parmigiano-
     Reggiano cheese

Start to finish: 30 minutes

Method

1. Put the Brie cheese in the freezer (to makes it easier to remove the rind). Cook pasta according to package directions; drain.

2. For the sauce, in a large skillet heat olive oil over medium heat. Add garlic; cook for 1 minute. Add tomatoes; cook for 10 minutes.

3. Meanwhile, cut rind off the Brie; cut Brie into chunks.

4. Add basil to tomato mixture; cook for 5 minutes. Add Brie; cook and stir just until cheese melts. Add pasta; toss to coat. Serve with freshly grated Parmigiano-Reggiano cheese.

Makes 6 servings

Cook's Notes
We love to make garlic bread and serve it and a salad with this meal.

For this easy vegetarian pasta dish, warm Gorgonzola cheese with olive oil and toss the mixture with penne pasta. Sprinkle chopped pistachios on top.

quick Penne with Gorgonzola and Pistachios

Lauren—Iowa City, IA

Start to finish: 25 minutes

Method

1. Cook penne according to package directions; drain.

2. Meanwhile, in a small skillet heat olive oil over low heat. Add Gorgonzola cheese; heat just enough to melt the cheese and mix it with the oil, stirring constantly so the cheese does not stick to the skillet.

3. When the cheese is melted, remove from heat immediately. Pour melted cheese over penne; toss to coat. Sprinkle with chopped pistachios. Serve immediately.

Makes 2 servings

Cook's Notes
This is a vegetarian dish for two. It can be a starter, a side dish accompaniment, or a main course. I had this dish at Vini Da Gigio, a wonderful Venetian trattoria. I never asked the chef how it was prepared (although I'm sure the restaurant used fresh homemade penne). This is my attempt to reproduce it.

Ingredients

8   ounces dried penne pasta

2   tablespoons olive oil

6   ounces Gorgonzola cheese or other sharp blue cheese, crumbled

½   cup pistachio nuts, lightly toasted and chopped

This yummy vegetarian dish is perfect for a last-minute dinner. It's made with tomatoes, artichokes, rigatoni, and black beans for plenty of protein.

Artichoke-Bean Rigatoni **quick**

Michelle—Costa Mesa, CA

Ingredients

8 ounces dried rigatoni

2 tablespoons olive oil

2 cloves garlic, sliced

8 cherry tomatoes, quartered

1 15-ounce can black beans, rinsed and drained

1 14-ounce can artichoke hearts, drained and quartered

Dash dried basil, crushed

Dash dried thyme, crushed

Salt

Black pepper

Parmesan cheese (optional)

Start to finish: 25 minutes

Method

1. Cook rigatoni according to package directions; drain.

2. Meanwhile, in a medium skillet heat olive oil over medium heat. Add garlic; cook for 1 minute. Stir in tomatoes, drained beans, drained artichoke hearts, basil, and thyme. Cook and stir about 5 minutes or until heated through.

3. Drain pasta; toss with tomato mixture.

4. Season with salt and pepper to taste. If desired, top with Parmesan cheese.

Makes 3 servings

This dish is fast, easy, and healthy. No one will ever miss the meat in a main dish this hearty and satisfying.

quick Black Bean Pasta

Kimberly—Montgomery, AL

Start to finish: 25 minutes

Method

1. In a large skillet heat olive oil over medium heat. Add celery; cook for 2 minutes. Stir in garlic; cook for 3 minutes more, stirring frequently.

2. Stir in undrained beans, undrained tomatoes, and, if desired, crushed red pepper. Add pasta; toss to mix well. Cook about 3 minutes more or until heated through. Serve with Parmesan cheese.

Makes 4 servings

Cook's Notes
I am a very busy mother of four young boys ranging in age from 10 years to 21 months. I created this recipe because it can be made in one skillet, it is superfast and very inexpensive to make, and it's a way to sneak some protein in from the black beans.

Ingredients

- 2 tablespoons olive oil
- 4 stalks celery, chopped
- 2 cloves garlic, minced
- 1 15-ounce can black beans, undrained
- 1 14.5-ounce can diced tomatoes, undrained, or 3 plum tomatoes, chopped
- 1 teaspoon crushed red pepper (optional)
- 8 ounces dried penne or ziti pasta, cooked according to package directions

  Parmesan cheese

Tip

Peeling Garlic Do you often find yourself fumbling with the papery peel on fresh garlic? Here's a superfast way to peel garlic before chopping or mincing it: Lay a clove on a cutting board and place the flat, broad side of a chef's knife on top of it. With your fist, pound the blade of the knife one or two times, crushing the garlic clove. The peel will split and slide off easily.

Spaghetti is cooked with tofu and mushrooms and flavored with five-spice powder, crushed red pepper, and toasted sesame for a new Far East favorite.

Szechwan Spaghetti Skillet ◆quick◆

Roxanne—Albany, CA

236

Ingredients

1 **14.5-ounce can diced tomatoes**

1 **14-ounce can vegetable broth**

½ **cup dry sherry or water**

½ **teaspoon five-spice powder**

¼ **teaspoon crushed red pepper**

8 **ounces dried thin spaghetti, broken in half**

1 **cup extra-firm tofu (fresh bean curd) cut into small cubes**

½ **cup sliced fresh mushrooms**

1 **clove garlic, minced**

½ **cup frozen green peas, thawed**

1 **green onion, finely chopped**

1 **tablespoon rice vinegar**

1 **tablespoon toasted sesame oil**

1 **tablespoon soy sauce**

Fresh cilantro sprigs

Start to finish: 30 minutes

Method

1. In a large nonstick skillet combine undrained tomatoes, vegetable broth, sherry, five-spice powder, and crushed red pepper. Stir in uncooked spaghetti, tofu, mushrooms, and garlic. Bring to boiling; cook for 6 to 8 minutes or until pasta is al dente.

2. Stir in peas, green onion, rice vinegar, toasted sesame oil, and soy sauce; heat through. Top servings with cilantro.

Makes 4 servings

Cook's Notes
This is easy, quick, nutritious, and delicious. Szechwan is a kind of Chinese cuisine that is hot and spicy. These dishes often include cinnamon, cloves, fennel seeds, star anise, and Szechwan peppercorns.

The noodles are tossed in a savory sauce made of soy sauce, peanut butter, and balsamic vinegar and topped with peanuts and chopped green onions.

quick Noodles with Peanut Sauce

Vicki—Dowagiac, MI

Start to finish: 25 minutes

Method

1. Toss warm noodles with sesame oil. Keep warm or chill as desired.

2. For the sauce, in a blender combine peanut butter, the water, soy sauce, balsamic vinegar, sugar, and cayenne pepper; cover and blend until smooth. Toss noodles with sauce. Sprinkle with peanuts and green onion.

Makes 4 to 6 servings

Ingredients

1 pound dried noodles or spaghetti, cooked and drained

1 tablespoon toasted sesame oil

¼ cup peanut butter

2 tablespoons water

1 tablespoon soy sauce

2 teaspoons balsamic vinegar

1 teaspoon sugar

⅛ teaspoon cayenne pepper

2 tablespoons peanuts, chopped

2 tablespoons chopped green onion

This healthy stir-fry is made with a colorful assortment of vegetables and tofu in a sauce made with garlic, soy sauce, and peanuts.

Tofu Stir-Fry quick

Mitali—Los Angeles, CA

Ingredients

1 16-ounce package extra-firm tofu

½ teaspoon cooking oil

1 teaspoon peanuts

¼ teaspoon garlic paste

1 16-ounce package frozen stir-fry vegetables (any combination of vegetables)

2 to 3 tablespoons soy sauce

   Salt

   Cayenne pepper

¼ of a lemon

Start to finish: 20 minutes

Method

1. Cut the tofu into ½-inch cubes; pat dry with paper towels. Set aside.

2. In a large nonstick skillet heat oil over medium-high heat. Add tofu, peanuts, and garlic paste; cook for 2 minutes. Stir in vegetables and soy sauce; cook and stir for 5 to 6 minutes or until vegetables are tender. Season to taste with salt and cayenne pepper. Squeeze the lemon over tofu mixture.

Makes 4 servings

Cook's Notes
This is a dry stir-fry. If a sauce is desired, add some coconut milk to the skillet with the vegetables and soy sauce.

Chapter 8

Soups, Stews & Chili

Wild rice, chicken, and a creamy broth make this soup a favorite choice when the weather forces you to stay inside.

Cream of Chicken and Wild Rice Soup

Celeste—Redding, CA

Ingredients

10	cups chicken broth
1	cup wild rice
¼	cup butter
2	cups sliced fresh mushrooms
4	stalks celery, sliced
4	medium carrots, sliced
1	large white onion, chopped
2	to 3 cloves garlic, minced
½	cup all-purpose flour
2	teaspoons dried savory, sage, or thyme, crushed
3	cups cubed cooked chicken
2	to 3 tablespoons lemon juice
	Salt
	Ground black pepper
	Fresh dillweed, parsley, thyme, or savory (optional)

Prep: 25 minutes Cook: 1 hour 20 minutes

Method

1. In a medium saucepan combine 4 cups of the chicken broth and the wild rice. Bring to boiling; reduce heat. Cover and simmer for 50 to 60 minutes or until rice is tender. (Do not drain.)

2. Meanwhile, in a Dutch oven melt butter over medium heat. Add mushrooms, celery, carrot, onion, and garlic; cook until vegetables are tender. Stir in flour and dried herb, stirring well. Add the remaining 6 cups chicken broth to vegetables; cook until slightly thickened and bubbly. Stir in cooked wild rice and chicken. Simmer on very low heat for 30 minutes.

3. Stir in lemon juice just before serving; season to taste with salt and pepper. If desired, garnish with a fresh herb.

Makes 6 to 8 servings

This soup is made with sliced mushrooms in a lightly thickened butter and milk mixture. Crumbled bacon is sprinkled on top.

quick Cream of Mushroom Soup with Bacon

Sondra—East Liverpool, OH

Start to finish: 25 minutes

Method

1. In a large saucepan melt butter over medium heat. Add mushrooms; cook until tender. Remove from heat. Stir in flour until mushrooms are completely coated. Stir in milk and salt. Add bouillon cube.

2. Bring to boiling over medium heat; cook and stir until slightly thickened and bubbly. Cook and stir for 1 minute more. Sprinkle servings with crumbled bacon.

Makes 4 to 6 servings

Cook's Notes
Perfect when you aren't sure what time dinner will be or when guests will be grazing all afternoon. This soup is quick to make and holds up well left in a slow cooker on a warm setting. Don't forget croutons or bread to go with it.

Ingredients

¼   cup unsalted butter

1   8-ounce container fresh sliced mushrooms

¼   cup all-purpose flour

5   cups milk

1   teaspoon salt

1   chicken bouillon cube

6   slices bacon, crisp-cooked and crumbled

This creamy, delicious soup will convince anyone—even kids—to eat their broccoli and maybe even indulge in a second or third helping!

Creamy Broccoli Soup

Karla—Cedar Rapids, IA

Ingredients

3	tablespoons olive oil
2	tablespoons butter
1	small yellow onion, chopped
3	cloves garlic, minced
1	head broccoli, cut into florets
3	small carrots, cut into small pieces
1	teaspoon dried thyme, crushed
4	cups chicken broth
½	cup dry white wine
2	cups whipping cream
	Salt
	Ground black pepper

Prep: 30 minutes   Cook: 10 minutes

Method

1. In a large saucepan heat olive oil and butter over medium heat. Add onion and garlic; cook about 3 minutes or until tender. Add broccoli, carrot, and thyme; cook for 5 minutes, stirring occasionally.

2. Add chicken broth and white wine. Bring to boiling; reduce heat. Simmer, uncovered, about 10 minutes or until broccoli and carrot are tender. Cool slightly.

3. Ladle broccoli mixture into blender in batches; blend until smooth. Return all of broccoli mixture to saucepan. Stir in whipping cream; cook over low heat until slightly thickened and heated through. Season to taste with salt and pepper.

Makes 8 servings

This thick creamy-rich soup combines cauliflower, whipping cream, and nutmeg for a sophisticated, restaurant-style dish.

quick Creamy Cauliflower Soup

Lynn—San Jose, CA

Prep: 15 minutes   Cook: 10 minutes

Method

1. Break cauliflower into florets; steam about 10 minutes or until very soft. Drain cauliflower. Using an electric hand mixer, beat cauliflower until nearly smooth. (Soup will have some small pieces of cauliflower.)

2. In a medium saucepan stir together cauliflower, whipping cream, kosher salt, white pepper, and nutmeg. Heat through over medium-low heat. Sprinkle individual servings with Parmesan cheese.

Makes 6 to 8 servings

Cook's Notes
This soup is rich and fresh enough to serve in any restaurant, but it is incredibly easy to make.

Ingredients

1   head fresh cauliflower

1   cup whipping cream

1   teaspoon kosher salt (or to taste)

1   teaspoon white pepper (or to taste)

½   teaspoon freshly grated nutmeg

½   cup grated Parmesan cheese

Potatoes, ham, onion, and chicken bouillon are cooked together and enriched with whipping cream for this slightly smoky-flavored soup.

Creamy Potato and Ham Soup

Kristina—Gilbert, AZ

Ingredients

12	**cups diced russet potatoes (about 4 pounds)**
8	**cups water**
6	**chicken bouillon cubes**
¾	**teaspoon garlic powder**
½	**cup chopped onion**
3	**cups cubed smoked ham**
2½	**teaspoons salt (or to taste)**
¾	**teaspoon white pepper**
2	**cups whipping cream**

Prep: 20 minutes   Cook: 20 minutes

Method

1. In a large Dutch oven combine potato, water, bouillon cubes, and garlic powder. Bring to boiling over high heat, stirring occasionally. Reduce heat to medium-low and simmer about 20 minutes or until potato is very mushy, stirring occasionally.

2. When the potato mixture begins to simmer, remove about 2 cups of the liquid and place in a blender with the chopped onion. Cover and blend until onion is pureed and integrated into the broth. Return liquid to Dutch oven.

3. When potatoes are very mushy and broth has thickened, stir in ham, salt, and white pepper. Heat through. Stir in whipping cream. Heat through.

Makes 6 to 8 servings

Cook's Notes
If the soup becomes too thick, stir in more cream to thin the broth.

This rich and earthy soup is made with three delicious varieties of hearty mushrooms— portobello, porcini, and cremini—and flavored with sherry.

Three-Mushroom Soup

Deb—Champaign, IL

Prep: 25 minutes   **Cook:** 10 minutes

Method

1. Pour chicken stock into a large saucepan; set aside. Remove gills and stems from all of the mushrooms. Finely chop or grind the mushrooms. In a large skillet melt butter over medium heat. Add mushrooms and chives; cook and stir for 3 minutes.

2. Stir in whipping cream, salt, and pepper. Bring to a simmer. Stir mushroom mixture into chicken stock. Bring to boiling; reduce heat. Simmer, covered, for 10 minutes. Stir in sherry.

Makes 4 servings

Ingredients

- 4 cups clear homemade chicken stock or chicken broth
- 1 pound fresh portobello mushrooms
- 4 ounces fresh porcini mushrooms
- 4 ounces fresh cremini or chanterelle mushrooms
- ¼ cup butter
- 3 tablespoons chopped fresh chives, shallot, or green onion
- 1 cup whipping cream
- ¼ teaspoon salt
- ⅛ teaspoon ground black pepper
- ½ cup dry sherry

This spring-fresh soup for two contains asparagus and chicken breast in a thickened mixture of milk and chicken broth. Shredded Cheddar cheese tops each serving.

Hearty Chicken and Asparagus Soup ◆quick◆

Deborah—Lilburn, GA

Ingredients

1	tablespoon margarine
⅓	cup finely chopped onion
1	14-ounce can chicken broth
6	fresh asparagus tips (use only the top 3 inches of the stalk)
1½	cups milk
2	tablespoons cornstarch
3	ounces purchased honey-roasted chicken breast, diced
⅓	cup shredded cheddar cheese

Start to finish: 30 minutes

Method

1. In a medium saucepan melt margarine over low heat. Add onion; cook for 4 minutes or until light golden, stirring occasionally. Add chicken broth and asparagus. Bring to boiling over medium heat; cook about 5 minutes or until asparagus is tender.

2. In a small bowl mix ½ cup of the milk with the cornstarch until smooth. Slowly stir into mixture in saucepan. Stir in the remaining 1 cup milk; cook until thickened and bubbly, stirring occasionally. Stir in chicken; cook 2 minutes more. Sprinkle with cheese. Serve immediately.

Makes 2 servings

Cook's Notes
When using fresh asparagus, be sure to rinse the stalks thoroughly to remove all the grit and sand.

Bottled sweet-and-sour sauce provides the flavor while rotisserie chicken makes this soup quick. Rice noodles, straw mushrooms, peanuts, and cilantro add an Asian flair.

Polynesian Chicken Noodle Soup

Beth—Richmond, VA

+ · · + · + · + · + · ++ · + · + + · + + · + · + · + + · ++ · + + · + · + · +

Prep: 25 minutes **Cook:** 10 minutes

Method

1. In a large saucepan combine chicken broth, carrot, and sweet-and-sour sauce. Bring to boiling. Stir in rice noodles. Simmer about 10 minutes or until noodles are softened.

2. Stir in chicken and drained mushrooms; heat through. Sprinkle servings with cilantro and peanuts.

Makes 4 servings

*Note: Rice noodles and straw mushrooms can be found in the Asian section of most grocery stores. Angel hair pasta and canned button mushrooms may be substituted.

Cook's Notes
This is a fun twist on traditional chicken noodle soup. Using rotisserie chicken makes this a quick and easy dinner for our family. My husband and sons love it, and the bonus is that I have more time to spend with them.

Ingredients

7 cups chicken broth

2 large carrots, grated

½ cup bottled sweet-and-sour sauce

½ of a 6-ounce package rice noodles* (also called rice sticks), broken in half

1 whole deli-roasted chicken (about 22 ounces), skinned, boned, and chopped

1 15-ounce can whole straw mushrooms,* drained

½ cup chopped fresh cilantro

½ cup chopped salted peanuts

With white kidney beans, tomatoes, basil, and oregano, this is truly an Italian-flavored soup. Fresh spinach and basil add oodles of color.

Tuscan Beef and Barley Soup

Patricia—Baden, PA

+ · + · + · + · + · + · + · + + · + · + · + · + · + · + + · + · + · + · + · + · + + · + · + · +

Ingredients

1   **tablespoon olive oil**

1½   **pounds beef stew meat, cut into 1-inch cubes**

1   **cup chopped onion**

1   **large clove garlic, minced**

2   **cups torn fresh spinach**

1   **15-ounce can white kidney beans (cannellini beans), undrained**

1   **14.5-ounce can Italian-style diced tomatoes, undrained**

1   **14-ounce can chicken broth**

1   **cup quick-cooking barley**

1   **cup water**

2   **tablespoons chopped fresh basil**

1   **teaspoon dried oregano, crushed**

¼   **teaspoon crushed red pepper (optional)**

    Grated Romano cheese

Prep: 25 minutes   **Cook:** 20 minutes

Method

1. In a Dutch oven heat olive oil over medium heat. Brown stew meat in hot oil. Add onion and garlic; cook until onion is tender. Stir in spinach, undrained white kidney beans, undrained tomatoes, broth, barley, water, basil, oregano, and, if desired, crushed red pepper.

2. Bring to boiling; reduce heat. Cover and simmer for 20 to 25 minutes or until barley is tender. Sprinkle servings with Romano cheese.

Makes 5 to 6 servings

Cook's Notes
Just add crusty Italian bread and a fresh green salad for a complete meal.

This easy stew recipe is great to mix up the night before and refrigerate, so in the morning you can just pop everything in the slow cooker and plug it in.

Slow-Cooker Savory Pot Roast Stew

Allison—Ogden, IL

Prep: 20 minutes **Cook:** 6 hours on low-heat setting or 4 hours on high-heat setting

Method

1. In a medium bowl combine beef broth, cream of mushroom soup, garlic powder, salt, pepper, and bay leaves. Pour mixture into a 5- to 6-quart slow cooker. Place roast in slow cooker. Add potatoes, carrots, and onion.

2. Cover and cook for 6 to 8 hours on low-heat setting or 4 to 6 hours on high-heat setting.

3. Discard bay leaves. Remove roast from slow cooker. Using two forks, shred warm roast; return to cooker and stir.

Makes 10 servings

Cook's Notes
Serve this stew hot with crusty French bread or warm biscuits on a cold evening.

Ingredients

8 cups beef broth

1 10.75-ounce can condensed cream of mushroom soup

1 tablespoon garlic powder

1 tablespoon salt

1 tablespoon black pepper

3 bay leaves

1 3-pound boneless top round roast

5 medium potatoes, cubed

1 16-ounce package peeled baby carrots

1 large yellow sweet onion, chopped

Lentils, two varieties of Italian sausage, celery, onion, and more star in this rich, tomato-based soup.

Classic Italian Sausage and Lentil Soup

Julie—Keller, TX

Ingredients

1 tablespoon olive oil

1 medium onion, diced

2 carrots, diced

2 stalks celery, diced

1 pound spicy Italian sausage (casings removed)

1 pound sweet Italian sausage (casings removed)

6 cloves garlic, crushed

1 6-ounce can tomato paste

1 16-ounce can whole plum tomatoes, undrained

8 cups beef broth

1 8-ounce can tomato sauce

1 tablespoon dried Italian seasoning, crushed

1 cup dried brown lentils, rinsed and picked free of stones

½ cup grated Parmesan cheese

Ground black pepper

Prep: 35 minutes Cook: 1 hour

Method

1. In a large Dutch oven heat olive oil over medium heat. Add onion, carrots, and celery; cook about 10 minutes or until tender.

2. Remove vegetables from pan, reserving drippings in pan. Add sausages; cook until brown, breaking sausages apart with a wooden spoon. For the last 2 minutes of browning sausage, add garlic. Remove sausage and garlic; set aside. Drain off fat. Add tomato paste to pan; quickly cook over low to medium heat for 2 minutes.

3. Deglaze the pan with juice from the undrained plum tomatoes, scraping bottom to get up all of the crusty bits.

4. Gently crush tomatoes with a large spoon. Add tomatoes, sausage mixture, and vegetables back to pan. Stir in beef broth, tomato sauce, and Italian seasoning. Bring to boiling; reduce heat to low. Simmer, stirring occasionally, for 10 to 15 minutes.

5. Stir in lentils; cook for 20 minutes. (If you think you are going to need more liquid, add some water because the lentils will absorb some liquid.) Remove from heat. Sprinkle with Parmesan cheese. Season to taste with black pepper.

Makes 6 to 10 servings

Cook's Notes
Serve this soup with a salad and crusty bread for a complete meal. Leftovers taste even better when reheated the next day.

This creamy soup made of butternut squash will warm up any chilly evening. It would also make an elegant appetizer for a dinner party.

Butternut Squash Soup

Mary—Henderson, NC

* *

Prep: 25 minutes **Bake:** 1 hour **Cook:** 20 minutes

Method

1. Preheat oven to 400°F. Cut squash in half lengthwise. Spread butter over squash; sprinkle with brown sugar. Bake about 1 hour or until tender. Cool.

2. In a medium saucepan heat olive oil over medium-high heat. Add onion and garlic; cook until onion is tender. Carefully add broth. Bring to boiling; reduce heat. Simmer, uncovered, for 20 minutes. Cool slightly.

3. Scoop out squash pulp with a spoon (or an ice cream scoop) and discard all skin and seeds.

4. Transfer squash and broth mixture to food processor or blender. Add milk, salt, and pepper. Cover and process or blend until smooth. Transfer to a medium saucepan; heat until nearly boiling.

Makes 4 servings

Ingredients

1   medium butternut squash

¼   cup butter

¼   cup packed brown sugar

1   teaspoon olive oil

½   of a medium onion, chopped

2   cloves garlic, minced

4   cups chicken broth or water

1   cup milk

¼   teaspoon kosher salt

¼   teaspoon freshly ground black pepper

This supereasy, heart-warming beef and vegetable soup is simmered in a slow cooker to get maximum flavor.

Slow-Cooker Italian Vegetable Soup

Jennifer—Lebanon, OR

Ingredients

1   to 2 pounds ground beef

1   16-ounce can whole kernel corn

1   14.5-ounce can zucchini with tomato sauce, undrained

1   14.5-ounce can diced tomatoes, undrained

2   to 3 potatoes, diced

1   8-ounce can tomato sauce

2   tablespoons dried oregano, crushed

3   bay leaves

Pinch dried basil, crushed

Few dashes garlic salt

Prep: 15 minutes   Cook: 6 hours on low-heat setting

Method

1. In a large skillet cook ground beef until brown. Drain off fat.

2. In a 3½- or 4-quart slow cooker combine ground beef, corn, undrained zucchini, undrained tomatoes, potato, tomato sauce, oregano, bay leaves, basil, and garlic salt. Cover and cook on low-heat setting for 6 to 8 hours. Discard bay leaves before serving.

Makes 4 to 6 servings

Cook's Notes
This recipe doubles nicely. Simmer this hearty beef and vegetable soup in a slow cooker all day for an easy dinner.

This creamy soup would make a great appetizer for your next dinner party.

New England Leek and Cucumber Soup

Donna—Gray, ME

Start to finish: 40 minutes

Method

1. In a large saucepan combine cucumber, chicken broth, potato, leek, parsley, salt, dry mustard, and savory. Bring to boiling; reduce heat. Cover and simmer for 8 to 10 minutes or until potato is tender. Cool slightly.

2. Press through a food mill or sieve, pushing as much of the vegetable mixture through as possible.

3. Return to saucepan. Stir in whipping cream and white pepper. Cook and stir over low heat until heated through.

Makes 6 to 8 servings

Cook's Notes

For an attractive garnish, use dried chives and a pinch of nutmeg. For those of us who live in New England, this soup is the year-end bounty of our own fresh garden vegetables.

Ingredients

4   cups chopped unpeeled cucumbers

4   cups chicken broth

1   cup finely chopped potato

⅔   cup sliced leek

¼   cup chopped fresh parsley

1   teaspoon salt (or more to taste)

¼   teaspoon dry mustard

¼   teaspoon dried savory, crushed

⅔   cup whipping cream

¼   teaspoon white pepper

Tip

Cleaning Leeks Leeks have many circular layers, and lots of soil and grit gets trapped in them as they grow. Cleaning leeks thoroughly before cooking means you won't crunch down on something unpleasant. The best way to clean leeks is to cut them down the center lengthwise and then into half-circle slices. Put the sliced leeks in a salad spinner filled with cool water and swish them around. Let the dirt settle to the bottom, then pull the basket out and repeat. Empty the second round of water out and spin the leeks dry. If you don't have a salad spinner, you can put the leeks in a strainer or colander and then in a bowl of cool water, rinsing and changing the water several times.

This creamy corn soup with shrimp has a tantalizing hint of spice from the addition of green chile paste.

Thai-Style Sweet Corn Soup quick

Chris—Cedar Rapids, IA

Ingredients

½   **teaspoon toasted sesame oil**

2   **green onions, thinly sliced**

1   **clove garlic, minced**

2½ **cups chicken broth**

2   **cups peeled and deveined shrimp**

1   **15-ounce can cream-style corn**

1   **teaspoon green chile paste**

Sea salt

White pepper

Fresh cilantro leaves

Start to finish: 20 minutes

Method

1. In a large saucepan heat sesame oil over low heat. Add green onion and garlic; cook until onion is tender. Stir in chicken broth, shrimp, corn, and chile paste.

2. Bring to boiling; cook for 1 to 2 minutes or until shrimp turn opaque, stirring occasionally. Season to taste with sea salt and white pepper. Sprinkle with cilantro.

Makes 4 servings

Cook's Notes
This soup is quick, healthy, and tasty. To make a complete meal, serve this soup with Thai sticky rice and egg rolls.

This traditional Italian soup is made with white kidney beans, pasta, and rosemary. It makes a warm and savory main dish or starter soup.

quick Pasta Fagioli Soup

Lisa—Far Hills, NJ

Start to finish: 25 minutes

Method

1. In a Dutch oven heat olive oil over medium heat. Add garlic; cook and stir for 30 seconds. Stir in chicken broth. Bring to boiling. Stir in the undrained white kidney beans, rosemary, tomato paste, the ¼ teaspoon salt, and the ¼ teaspoon pepper. Cook over medium-low heat for 8 minutes.

2. Meanwhile, cook pasta according to package directions. Stir cooked pasta into bean mixture. Season to taste with additional salt and pepper. If desired, sprinkle individual servings with Romano cheese.

Makes 6 servings

Cook's Notes
"Fagioli" is the Italian word for beans. Ditalini are tiny tubes of macaroni pasta.

Ingredients

2 teaspoons olive oil

3 cloves garlic, thinly sliced

8 cups chicken broth

3 19-ounce cans white kidney beans (cannellini beans), undrained

¼ cup fresh rosemary, coarsely chopped

1 tablespoon tomato paste

¼ teaspoon salt

¼ teaspoon ground black pepper

1 pound dried ditalini pasta

Salt

Ground black pepper

Grated Romano cheese (optional)

Soups, Stews & Chili

255

This soup combines canned black beans with onion, stewed tomatoes, and chile peppers and is seasoned with cumin, lemon juice, and crushed red pepper.

Jessica's Black Bean Soup `quick`

Jessica—Boynton Beach, FL

Ingredients

1 **large onion, chopped**

2 **cloves garlic, minced**

1 **tablespoon cooking oil**

2 **15-ounce cans black beans, rinsed and drained**

1 **14.5-ounce can stewed tomatoes, undrained**

1 **14-ounce can chicken broth or vegetable broth**

1 **cup water**

1 **4-ounce can chopped green chile peppers, drained**

1 **tablespoon lemon juice**

2 **teaspoons ground cumin**

Dash crushed red pepper

Sour cream

Tortilla chips

Prep: 15 minutes   Cook: 10 minutes

Method

1. In a large saucepan cook onion and garlic in hot oil until tender. Add 1 can of the black beans; mash with a potato masher or fork. Stir in the remaining can black beans, the undrained tomatoes, broth, water, drained chile peppers, lemon juice, cumin, and red pepper flakes. Bring to boiling; reduce heat. Simmer, uncovered, for 10 minutes, stirring occasionally.

2. Serve soup with sour cream and tortilla chips.

Makes 6 servings

Cook's Notes
This is best served with a scoop of sour cream and tortilla chips. By mashing half the black beans in this recipe, the soup gains a thicker texture and richer flavor.

Traditional ham and bean soup is enhanced with fresh vegetables and herbs for a great new twist.

Mediterranean Bean Soup

Margaret—Bellingham, WA

Prep: 40 minutes **Cook:** 2 hours

Method

1. In a Dutch oven cook carrot, celery, and onion in hot olive oil until tender. Add garlic, mint, oregano, thyme, and bay leaf; cook for 1 minute.

2. Using your hands, crush undrained tomatoes in batches and add them to the mixture in the Dutch oven. Cook and stir for 3 minutes.

3. Add the water, drained beans, and ham. Bring to boiling; reduce heat. Cover and simmer about 2 hours or until beans are tender. (If using canned beans, cook for 30 minutes to develop flavors.)

4. Stir in red wine vinegar. Discard bay leaf. Season to taste with salt and pepper.

Makes 6 servings

Ingredients

3 **carrots, chopped**

2 **stalks celery, chopped**

1 **medium onion, diced**

2 **tablespoons olive oil**

2 **cloves garlic, minced**

2 **tablespoons dried mint, crushed**

1 **teaspoon dried oregano, crushed**

1 **teaspoon dried thyme, crushed**

1 **bay leaf**

1 **15-ounce can diced tomatoes, undrained**

7½ **cups water**

2 **cups dried Great Northern beans, sorted and soaked overnight, or two 15-ounce cans Great Northern beans, rinsed and drained**

1 **large meaty ham hock, baked and meat removed and diced**

1 **tablespoon red wine vinegar**

Salt

Black pepper

Tip

Quick-Soaking Beans This recipe gives an option to use canned beans if you didn't soak your dried beans overnight. But you can still use dried beans by using the quick-soak method: Bring the beans and fresh water to a rolling boil. Boil for 2 minutes, then cover the pot and turn off the heat. Let sit for 1 hour and then proceed with the recipe.

This tomato-based Italian soup is loaded with healthy vegetables and hunger-satisfying pasta, cannellini beans, and lentils.

Melissa's Minestrone

Melissa—Springville, UT

Ingredients

1 cup dried lentils

2 tablespoons olive oil

3 medium carrots, sliced

1 cup finely chopped onion

4 cloves garlic, minced

6 cups water

3 chicken bouillon cubes

2 medium zucchini, quartered and sliced

1 19-ounce can white kidney beans (cannellini beans), rinsed and drained

2 14.5-ounce cans Italian-style diced tomatoes, undrained

1 6-ounce can tomato paste

2 teaspoons salt

2 teaspoons dried oregano, crushed

2 teaspoons dried basil, crushed

½ teaspoon ground black pepper

2 cups dried small shell pasta

Prep: 35 minutes Cook: 20 minutes

Method

1. Cook lentils according to package directions; set aside.

2. In a Dutch oven heat olive oil over medium heat. Add carrot, onion, and garlic; cook and stir until carrot is tender. Add the water and bouillon cubes; bring to boiling and boil for 4 minutes. Add zucchini and drained white kidney beans; cook for 3 minutes more.

3. Add undrained diced tomatoes, tomato paste, salt, oregano, basil, and pepper. Return to boiling; reduce heat to low. Simmer, uncovered, for 20 minutes.

4. Meanwhile, prepare pasta according to package directions, cooking for the minimum time recommended on package. Stir pasta and lentils into soup.

Makes 12 servings

Applejack brandy makes this a grown-up soup perfect for any autumn activity. Substitute apple cider to make the soup nonalcoholic.

Autumn Apple Bisque

Julia—Pacific Palisades, CA

+ +

Prep: 45 minutes **Chill:** overnight

Method

1. In a large saucepan combine quartered apples and the water. Bring to boiling; reduce heat. Cover and simmer until apples are tender. Remove from heat. Cool slightly.

2. Transfer apples to a food processor; process until smooth. Stir whipping cream and applejack into apples.

3. To caramelize sugar, in a heavy medium skillet cook sugar over medium-high heat until sugar begins to melt, shaking skillet occasionally. Do not stir. When sugar starts to melt, reduce heat to low and cook until all the sugar is melted, stirring as needed with a wooden spoon. Carefully add the apple cider, stirring until the sugar dissolves.

4. Stir sugar mixture into apple mixture; chill overnight. Serve in soup bowls garnished with thin apple slices.

Makes 12 servings

Ingredients

9   apples, peeled, cored, and quartered

¾   cup water

2   cups whipping cream

1   cup applejack (apple brandy) or apple cider or apple juice

1¼   cups sugar

1   pint (2 cups) apple cider or apple juice

    Thin apple slices

Chunks of lobster are added to a saucy mixture of milk, chicken broth, and tomato puree flavored with sherry, garlic, and jalapeño chile pepper.

Cilantro-Lobster Bisque

Jodie—San Antonio, TX

Ingredients

Butter flavor nonstick cooking spray

1 onion, finely chopped

1 clove garlic, minced

½ teaspoon finely chopped fresh jalapeño chile pepper

1 tablespoon water

2 tablespoons whole wheat flour

3½ cups nonfat chicken broth

½ cup tomato puree

½ cup dry sherry

½ teaspoon salt

1 pound cooked lobster meat, cut into 1-inch pieces

1½ cups nonfat milk

1 tablespoon cornstarch

1 teaspoon paprika

1 plum tomato, chopped

2 tablespoons chopped fresh cilantro

Prep: 35 minutes Cook: 21 minutes

Method

1. Coat an unheated large saucepan generously with nonstick cooking spray. Preheat saucepan over medium heat. Add onion, garlic, and jalapeño chile pepper; cook about 5 minutes or until tender, stirring occasionally. Add the water. Cook for 2 minutes more. Add flour; cook and stir about 3 minutes.

2. Stir in broth, tomato puree, sherry, and salt. Bring to boiling; reduce heat to low. Cover; simmer for 10 minutes. Add lobster. Cover; simmer about 6 minutes.

3. Stir in 1 cup of the milk. Whisk cornstarch and the remaining ½ cup milk until smooth; add it and the paprika to the saucepan. Cook over medium heat for 5 minutes. Stir in the tomato and cilantro.

Makes 4 servings

Cook's Notes
Served warm, this bisque is perfect on a cold winter night. However, the soup can also be chilled and served cold— making it an ideal summer recipe!

 Tip

How Hot? The hottest part of a jalapeño is actually the seeds, not the flesh. So if you like your food spicy, add the seeds with the rest of the chile. If you like a little less tongue-tingling, scrape out the seeds and membrane and use only the green flesh of the jalapeño. Always wash your hands when you're done chopping—and keep your hands away from your eyes. Chile oils are very potent!

Green and red sweet peppers lend a festive look and taste to this smoky-flavored cream-based chowder.

Smoked Turkey Chowder

Devin—Raleigh, NC

· ·

Prep: 40 minutes **Cook:** 15 minutes

Method

1. Cut turkey meat off bones; dice meat. In a Dutch oven heat olive oil over medium heat. Add turkey; cook until brown. Add onion and sweet pepper; cook about 5 minutes or until vegetables are tender.

2. Stir in flour; cook for 3 minutes. Add the water; bring to boiling. Add potato, corn, celery seeds, salt, and black pepper. Return to boiling; reduce heat to medium-low. Cover and cook about 15 minutes or until potato is tender.

3. Stir in half-and-half; heat through. Stir in margarine until melted.

Makes 12 servings

Ingredients

2 **pounds smoked turkey legs**

2 **tablespoons olive oil**

1 **onion, diced**

1 **green sweet pepper, finely chopped**

1 **red sweet pepper, finely chopped**

2 **tablespoons all-purpose flour**

2 **cups water**

6 **small red potatoes, diced**

1 **cup fresh white corn kernels (cut off the cob)**

2 **tablespoons celery seeds**

2 **teaspoons salt**

1 **teaspoon ground black pepper (or to taste)**

1 **cup half-and-half or light cream**

1 **tablespoon margarine**

261

Prepackaged ingredients, such as frozen hash browns, frozen corn, canned green chile peppers, and packaged cheese, make this soup quick and easy to prepare.

Nacho Corn Chowder   *quick*

Tracy—Penfield, NY

Ingredients

1 ½ **cups frozen hash brown potatoes (not shredded)**

1 ½ **cups frozen whole kernel corn, thawed**

1 **14-ounce can reduced-sodium chicken broth**

1 **tablespoon chili powder**

1 ½ **teaspoons ground cumin**

1 **teaspoon salt**

½ **teaspoon paprika**

¼ **teaspoon garlic powder**

¼ **teaspoon onion powder**

3 **cups low-fat milk**

½ **cup all-purpose flour**

1 **4-ounce can green chile peppers, drained**

1 **8-ounce package shredded sharp cheddar cheese**

2 **cups nacho-flavor corn chips, coarsely crushed**

Start to finish: 25 minutes

Method

1. In a medium saucepan combine potatoes, corn, chicken broth, chili powder, cumin, salt, paprika, garlic powder, and onion powder. Cover and bring to boiling over medium heat.

2. While vegetable mixture is heating, in a screw-top jar combine 1 cup of the milk and the flour. Shake vigorously until no lumps of flour remain. When the vegetable mixture comes to a boil, stir in the flour mixture, the remaining 2 cups milk, and the drained chile peppers. Bring to boiling, stirring frequently.

3. Reduce heat to medium-low. Simmer until mixture is slightly thickened and the potato is tender, stirring frequently. Remove from heat. Add the cheddar cheese; stir until melted. Serve hot. Sprinkle corn chips over servings.

Makes 4 to 6 servings

Cook's Notes
This soup is so easy to put together and is ready in about 25 minutes. I enjoy serving it for casual winter gatherings such as football parties.

New potatoes are combined with carrots, green chile peppers, onion, cumin, vegetable broth, milk, and cheddar cheese. See photo on page 218.

Tiny Potato and Carrot Chowder

Gretchen—Seattle, WA

Prep: 35 minutes **Cook:** 25 minutes

Method

1. In a large saucepan heat olive oil over medium heat. Add carrot, onion, undrained chile peppers, cumin seeds, and garlic; cook about 10 minutes or until vegetables are tender. Add broth, potato, and salt. Bring to boiling; reduce heat. Cover and simmer about 25 minutes or until potato is tender.

2. In a medium bowl whisk together milk and flour. Stir milk mixture into potato mixture. Cook and stir over medium heat until thickened and bubbly; cook and stir for 1 minute more. Remove from heat. Add cheese, stirring until melted.

Makes 4 servings

Cook's Notes
This is flavorful yet kid-friendly fare that is simple to make and sure to please the whole family. It's one of our most successful one-dish meals!

Ingredients

2	tablespoons olive oil
2	cups chopped carrots
1½	cups finely chopped onion
1	4-ounce can diced green chile peppers, undrained
½	teaspoon cumin seeds, crushed
5	cloves garlic, minced
4	cups vegetable broth
4	cups halved or quartered tiny new potatoes or regular potatoes, cubed
½	teaspoon salt
2½	cups milk
⅓	cup all-purpose flour
1½	cups shredded cheddar cheese

This sensational beef stew slow cooks all day in a rich red wine and tomato sauce. It's well worth the wait.

Beef Stew

Debi—Milwaukee, WI

Ingredients

1   **pound lean beef stew meat**

1   **pound baby carrots**

4   **medium red potatoes, finely chopped**

4   **stalks celery, finely chopped**

1   **onion, diced**

1   **10.75-ounce can reduced-fat and reduced-sodium condensed tomato soup**

1   **cup dry red wine or cooking wine**

4   **cloves garlic, minced**

1   **bay leaf**

4   **whole cloves**

¼   **teaspoon salt**

⅛   **teaspoon ground black pepper**

1   **10-ounce package frozen peas**

Prep: 20 minutes   Cook: 8 hours on low-heat setting

Method

1. In a 3½- or 4-quart slow cooker combine all ingredients, except peas. Cover and cook on low-heat setting for 8 to 10 hours. Stir in peas. Discard bay leaf and cloves before serving.

Makes 6 to 8 servings

Lamb and potatoes form the base of this hearty Irish stew. Simmer it slowly for about an hour to unlock the flavors of all the ingredients and allow them to mingle.

Irish Stew

Marjorie—Skaneateles, NY

Prep: 20 minutes Cook: 1 hour

Method

1. In a Dutch oven cook onion in hot margarine until tender. Stir in lamb, potato, beef broth, thyme, bay leaf, a few dashes salt, and a few dashes pepper.

2. Bring to boiling; reduce heat. Simmer, uncovered, about 1 hour. Discard bay leaf before serving.

Makes 4 servings

Ingredients

¾ cup chopped onion

1 tablespoon margarine

2 pounds lamb, cubed

2 cups peeled cubed potato

2 cups beef broth

2 teaspoons dried thyme, crushed

1 bay leaf

Salt

Ground black pepper

This thick, hearty stew is the perfect way to reenergize after a long day. It combines cooked ground turkey, smoked sausage, and four kinds of canned beans.

Tired and Tuckered Stew

Pat—Lee's Summit, MO

Ingredients

- 1 **pound kielbasa, cut into bite-size pieces**
- 1 **pound uncooked ground turkey, cooked and drained**
- 1 **28-ounce can baked beans**
- 1 **15-ounce can light red kidney beans, rinsed and drained**
- 1 **15-ounce can dark red kidney beans, rinsed and drained**
- 1 **15-ounce can lima beans, drained**
- 1 **14.5-ounce can white whole kernel corn, drained**
- 1 **cup bottled chili sauce**
- 1 **cup packed dark brown sugar**
- 1 **cup finely chopped onion**
- 1 **tablespoon bottled hot pepper sauce**

Prep: 20 minutes Cook: 4 hours on low-heat setting or 2 hours on high-heat setting

Method

1. In a 5- to 6-quart slow cooker combine kielbasa pieces, cooked ground turkey, baked beans, kidney beans, lima beans, corn, chili sauce, brown sugar, onion, and hot pepper sauce.

2. Cover and cook for 4 to 6 hours on low-heat setting or 2 to 3 hours on high-heat setting.

Makes 8 servings

Cook's Notes
This is a great, hearty protein-packed stew. It is fabulous with biscuits and cheese.

This fall chili is like Thanksgiving with a kick: pumpkin and turkey plus red beans and red wine. See photo on page 218.

Festive Fall Chili

Roxanne—Albany, CA

Prep: 25 minutes **Cook:** 18 minutes

Method

1. In a large saucepan heat oil over medium heat. Add onion, celery, and garlic; cook and stir for 3 minutes. Stir in undrained tomatoes, drained red beans, pumpkin, tomato sauce, wine, chili powder, and poultry seasoning. Bring to boiling; reduce heat. Cover and simmer about 15 minutes or until pumpkin is tender.

2. Stir in turkey and baby spinach; cook about 3 minutes or until chili is heated through and spinach is wilted. Top servings with croutons.

Makes 4 servings

Cook's Notes
Leftovers from Thanksgiving dinner inspired this recipe.

Ingredients

1   tablespoon cooking oil

1   onion, chopped

1   stalk celery, sliced

1   large clove garlic, minced

2   14.5-ounce cans diced tomatoes, undrained

1   15-ounce can small red beans, rinsed and drained

1   cup finely chopped peeled pumpkin or butternut squash

1   8-ounce can tomato sauce

½   cup dry red wine or water

1   tablespoon chili powder

½   teaspoon poultry seasoning

2   cups finely chopped cooked turkey

2   cups fresh baby spinach

    Croutons

If you're tired of the same beef-and-tomato-based chili, this chicken-and-bean variety is a fresh alternative.

White Bean-Chicken Chili

Jaime—Ozark, MO

Ingredients

2 to 3 tablespoons olive oil

3 skinless, boneless chicken breast halves, cubed

½ of a white onion, finely chopped

1 tablespoon minced garlic

Chili powder

1 lime wedge

2 15-ounce cans Great Northern beans, undrained

1 14.5-ounce can white whole kernel corn, undrained

1 4-ounce can green chile peppers, undrained

1½ teaspoons ground cumin

⅛ teaspoon cayenne pepper

4 to 5 fresh cilantro leaves

2 green onions, chopped

Shredded Monterey Jack cheese with jalapeño chile peppers

Prep: 25 minutes Cook: 15 minutes

Method

1. In a large skillet heat olive oil over medium heat. Add chicken, onion, and garlic; cook until chicken is tender and no longer pink. Sprinkle with chili powder; squeeze lime wedge over. Transfer to a large saucepan.

2. Stir in undrained beans, undrained corn, undrained chile peppers, cumin, and cayenne pepper. If desired, stir in additional chili powder. Stir in cilantro leaves. Cover and cook over medium heat for 10 minutes. Reduce heat to medium-low; simmer, uncovered, for 5 minutes more. Sprinkle servings with green onion and Monterey Jack cheese with jalapeño chile peppers.

Makes 3 to 4 servings

Cook's Notes
The amount of chicken and corn should be adjusted according to the number of people served. I hope you enjoy!

Chapter 9
Sides

What makes these potatoes so good is the twice-baked filling of sour cream, cheddar cheese, and green onion. See photo on page 219.

Amazing Twice-Baked Potatoes

Allison—Ogden, IL

Ingredients

- 6 **baking potatoes**
- 1 **pound bacon**
- 1 **8-ounce carton light sour cream**
- ½ **cup margarine (reduced fat, if desired), melted**
- 1 **bunch green onions, thinly sliced**
- 1 **4-ounce package shredded sharp cheddar cheese**
- 1 **teaspoon salt**
- 1 **teaspoon ground black pepper**

Prep: 25 minutes   Bake: 1 hour 10 minutes

Method

1. Preheat oven to 375°F. Wrap each potato in foil. Bake for 1 hour. Meanwhile, in a large skillet cook bacon, in batches, until crisp. Drain on paper towels and crumble. Set aside.

2. In small bowl combine sour cream, melted margarine, and green onion. Set aside.

3. Remove foil from potatoes. Cut potatoes in half lengthwise. Scoop pulp out of potatoes leaving a ¼-inch-thick shell.

4. In a large bowl combine pulp and sour cream mixture. Beat with an electric mixer on low to medium speed until well mixed. Stir in half of the cheese, the salt, and pepper.

5. Scoop mixture back into potato shells. Top with remaining cheese. Place potatoes on a foil-lined baking pan. Bake for 10 to 15 minutes more or until cheese is melted.

Makes 12 servings

Tip

One Potato, Two Baking potatoes—also called Idaho or russet potatoes—are prized for baking, mashing, and oven roasting because of their low moisture/high starch content. Their mealy texture makes for light and tender baked potatoes, fluffy mashed potatoes, and oven fries with a crisp exterior and an airy interior. If you want to make potato salad, look for waxy white potatoes, which hold their shape much better than baking potatoes when boiled.

This make-ahead recipe combines mashed potatoes with cream cheese and sour cream. The mixture is refrigerated and baked as needed.

Icebox Mashed Potatoes

Valerie—Wichita, KS

Prep: 20 minutes **Cook:** 20 minutes **Bake:** 30 minutes

Method

1. In a covered large Dutch oven cook potatoes in enough boiling salted water to cover for 20 to 25 minutes or until fork-tender; drain. Mash potatoes. Stir in cream cheese, sour cream, salt, and white pepper. Cover and store in the refrigerator for up to 48 hours.

2. To reheat, preheat oven to 350°F. Put as much of the potato mixture as you want into a buttered casserole. Dot with butter. Bake until hot and just starting to brown around the edges (30 to 60 minutes, depending on how much you are heating). The full recipe makes about 12 cups of potato mixture.

Makes 12 servings

Cook's Notes
These potatoes store extremely well in the refrigerator for a few days. They taste best after being refrigerated at least 36 to 48 hours. Double or triple the recipe as needed.

Ingredients

5 pounds white potatoes, peeled and quartered

1 8-ounce package cream cheese

1 ⅓ cups sour cream

1 tablespoon salt

¼ teaspoon ground white pepper

Butter

sides

271

These better-for-you mashed potatoes are enriched with light cream cheese and Parmesan cheese, then moistened with nonfat milk and garnished with chives.

Cheesy Low-Fat Mashed Potatoes

Heather—League City, TX

272

Ingredients

5   medium russet potatoes (1 ¾ to 2 pounds total), peeled and quartered

3   tablespoons light cream cheese with chive and onion

½   cup nonfat milk

2   tablespoons grated Parmesan cheese

    Salt

    Ground black pepper

3   tablespoons chopped fresh chives (optional)

Prep: 15 minutes   Cook: 20 minutes

Method

1. In a covered Dutch oven cook potatoes in enough boiling water to cover for 20 to 25 minutes or until fork-tender; drain.

2. While potatoes are still hot, add cream cheese; mash until combined. Add milk and Parmesan cheese to potatoes; stir to combine. (Add a little more milk, if needed for desired consistency.) Season to taste with salt and pepper. If desired, garnish with chives. Serve hot.

Makes 4 servings

Cook's Notes
Use up to ¾ cup of nonfat milk to achieve desired consistency. These are so rich and creamy you won't miss the butter or whole milk!

Frozen hash brown potatoes are covered with a mixture of sour cream, cream of chicken soup, and cheddar cheese, then topped with buttery cornflake crumbs.

Hash Brown Casserole

Courtney—Houma, LA

Prep: 20 minutes   Bake: 40 minutes

Method

1. Preheat oven to 375°F. Place hash browns in a 13×9×2-inch baking dish.

2. In a medium saucepan cook onion in ½ cup of the butter. Stir in cream of chicken soup, sour cream, and cheese. Cook and stir until smooth. Pour mixture over hash browns.

3. Sprinkle cornflakes over mixture in baking dish. In a small saucepan melt remaining ½ cup butter; pour evenly over cornflakes. Bake for 40 to 45 minutes or until heated through.

Makes 8 to 10 servings

Cook's Notes
Try this easy casserole for brunch or the next time you get a craving for breakfast food at dinnertime.

Ingredients

1   **2-pound package Southern-style frozen hash browns, thawed**

1   **onion, chopped**

1   **cup butter**

1   **10.75-ounce can condensed cream of chicken soup**

1   **8-ounce carton sour cream**

1   **8-ounce package shredded cheddar cheese**

2   **cups crushed cornflakes**

Sides

273

These potato wedges are flavored with thyme, rosemary, and paprika and baked—not fried—to use less fat.

Oven-Roasted Potato Fries

Lisa—Austin, TX

274

Ingredients

6 **baking potatoes, cut lengthwise into eighths**

3 **tablespoons cooking oil**

¼ **teaspoon salt**

¼ **teaspoon dried thyme, crushed**

¼ **teaspoon dried rosemary, crushed**

¼ **teaspoon paprika**

⅛ **teaspoon ground black pepper**

Prep: 15 minutes Bake: 65 minutes

Method

1. Preheat oven to 425°F. Divide potatoes between two large greased baking pans; spread potatoes into single layers. Sprinkle potatoes with oil, salt, thyme, rosemary, paprika, and pepper. Toss well to coat.

2. Cover pans with foil. Bake for 45 minutes. Remove foil; turn potatoes over. Bake about 20 minutes more or until potatoes are golden.

Makes 8 servings

Mashed canned sweet potatoes are combined with butter, eggs, and brown sugar, formed into mounds, and topped with a sweetened apple mixture.

Apple-Filled Sweet Potatoes

Jan—Scottsdale, AZ

Prep: 20 minutes **Cook:** 10 minutes **Bake:** 25 minutes **Stand:** 1 minute

Method

1. Preheat oven to 400°F. In a large bowl combine drained sweet potatoes, eggs, melted butter, brown sugar, vanilla, and nutmeg. Beat with an electric mixer on low speed until combined; increase speed to medium and beat until light and fluffy. Using a large ice cream scoop, scoop mounds of the sweet potato mixture onto a greased baking sheet. Using the back of a spoon, make a depression in the center of each mound.

2. In a medium saucepan combine chopped apple and the water; bring to boiling over medium heat. Reduce heat to low. Cover and simmer about 10 minutes or until apple is tender. Stir in granulated sugar. Using a slotted spoon, divide apple mixture among depressions in the sweet potato mounds. Sprinkle with cinnamon.

3. Bake for 25 to 30 minutes or until golden brown. Let stand on baking sheet for 1 minute; using a wide metal spatula, carefully remove mounds from baking sheet.

Makes 8 servings

Cook's Notes
Whether you serve these sweet potato and apple delights as a side dish or a nontraditional dessert, they look very pretty on a plate.

Ingredients

2 **16-ounce cans sweet potatoes, drained**

2 **eggs**

¼ **cup butter, melted**

2 **tablespoons packed brown sugar**

1 **teaspoon vanilla**

½ **teaspoon ground nutmeg**

6 **medium apples, peeled, cored and chopped**

½ **cup water**

1 **cup granulated sugar**

Ground cinnamon

This side dish starts with quick-cooking long grain and wild rice mix, then adds celery, onion, dates, and cashews for superb flavor and crunch!

Sweet and Savory Pilaf `quick`

Andrea—Freeport, IL

Best of Hometown Cooking

Ingredients

1	teaspoon olive oil
4	stalks celery, finely chopped
½	of a medium onion, chopped
1	6.25-ounce package quick-cooking long grain and wild rice mix
2	cups water
¾	cup chopped dates
½	cup cashew halves

Prep: 15 minutes   **Cook:** 8 minutes   **Stand:** 5 minutes

Method

1. In a large skillet heat olive oil over medium-high heat. Add celery and onion; cook and stir for 2 to 3 minutes or until crisp-tender. Add rice mix, seasoning packet from rice mix, and the water. Bring to boiling; reduce heat. Cover tightly and simmer for 8 to 10 minutes or until most of the liquid is absorbed.

2. Remove from heat. Stir dates into rice mixture. Cover and let stand for 5 minutes to allow dates to soften. Sprinkle with cashew halves.

Makes 6 servings

Cook's Notes
This dish is quick and easy yet looks quite elegant next to anything from filet mignon to meat loaf! The use of a boxed quick-cooking long grain and wild rice mix saves valuable time without sacrificing flavor.

A variety of exotic flavors—apricots, cinnamon, cumin, orange zest, and crushed red pepper—combine in this sensational couscous side dish.

quick Casablanca Carrot Couscous

Roxanne—Albany, CA

Prep: 15 minutes Stand: 10 minutes

Method

1. In a large saucepan combine broth and apricot nectar. Bring to boiling; remove from heat. Stir in uncooked couscous, carrot, dates, dried apricots, green onion, olive oil, lemon juice, cinnamon, cumin, orange zest, and crushed red pepper. Cover and let stand for 10 minutes. Fluff with a fork. If desired, garnish with mint and cashews.

Makes 6 to 8 servings

Cook's Notes
This is a quick, easy, nutritious, and delicious side dish. It's great with chicken or pork loin.

Ingredients

1 **14-ounce can vegetable broth**

1 **11.5-ounce can apricot nectar**

2 **cups quick-cooking couscous**

1 **cup shredded carrot**

⅓ **cup pitted date pieces**

⅓ **cup slivered dried apricots**

⅓ **cup finely chopped green onion**

2 **tablespoons olive oil**

2 **tablespoons lemon juice**

½ **teaspoon ground cinnamon**

½ **teaspoon ground cumin**

½ **teaspoon grated orange zest**

¼ **teaspoon crushed red pepper**

Chopped fresh mint (optional)

Cashews (optional)

Broccoli florets are cooked with penne pasta, drained, then tossed with garlic and oil and sprinkled with lemon juice and Parmesan cheese.

Penne con Broccoli `quick`

Leona–Redlands, CA

278

Ingredients

1 **pound dried penne pasta**

2 **cups chopped broccoli florets**

3 **tablespoons olive oil**

4 **cloves garlic, sliced**

2 **lemon wedges**

⅓ **cup grated Parmesan cheese (optional)**

Start to finish: 20 minutes

Method

1. In a Dutch oven cook penne pasta and broccoli in a large amount of boiling salted water according to pasta package directions until pasta is almost tender.

2. Meanwhile, in a large skillet heat olive oil over medium heat. Add garlic; cook for 1 minute. Remove from heat.

3. Drain pasta mixture. Add pasta mixture to oil mixture; toss to coat. Cook for 2 minutes. Squeeze lemon wedges over; toss well. If desired, sprinkle with Parmesan cheese.

Makes 8 servings

Cook's Notes
This two-in-one dish allows you to cook the pasta and vegetable at the same time and in the same pot.

This yummy broccoli casserole features a cheesy sauce that's crowned with a crunchy stuffing-mix topper. Serve it alongside grilled chicken or pork chops.

Broccoli Supreme

Cindy—Bradenton, FL

Prep: 20 minutes **Bake:** 30 minutes

Method

1. Preheat oven to 350°F. Place steamed broccoli spears in an 11×7×1½-inch baking dish.

2. In a medium bowl lightly beat eggs; stir in cream of mushroom soup, mayonnaise, and onion. Pour over broccoli. Sprinkle with cheese. In a small bowl combine stuffing mix and melted butter; sprinkle over casserole. Bake for 30 minutes.

Makes 5 servings

Ingredients

1   bunch fresh broccoli, trimmed, cut into spears, and steamed

2   eggs

1   10.75-ounce can condensed cream of mushroom soup

½   cup mayonnaise

1   small onion, chopped

1   8-ounce package shredded cheddar cheese

1   cup stuffing mix

¼   cup butter, melted

Sides

279

Ground beef, bacon, and a trio of beans—baked, kidney, and garbanzo—make this more of a meal than a side dish.

Best-Ever Baked Beans

Wayne—Surrey, BC

Ingredients

- 8 ounces bacon
- 1 pound ground beef
- 2 onions, sliced and separated into rings
- 2 16-ounce cans baked beans in tomato sauce, undrained
- 1 15.5-ounce can red kidney beans, rinsed and drained
- 1 15-ounce can garbanzo beans (chickpeas), rinsed and drained
- 2 cups ketchup
- ¼ cup granulated sugar
- ¼ cup packed brown sugar
- 3 tablespoons white vinegar
- 1 tablespoon Dijon-style mustard

Prep: 25 minutes Cook: 7 hours on low-heat setting or 3½ hours on high-heat setting

Method

1. In a large nonstick skillet partially cook bacon; drain. Coarsely chop; set aside. Add ground beef and onions to skillet; cook until beef is brown and onion is tender, stirring to break up meat. Using a slotted spoon, transfer meat mixture to a 3½- or 4-quart slow cooker.

2. Add bacon, undrained baked beans, drained kidney beans, drained garbanzo beans, ketchup, granulated sugar, brown sugar, vinegar, and mustard to meat mixture in cooker, stirring to combine.

3. Cover and cook on low-heat setting for 7 to 9 hours or high-heat setting for 3½ to 4½ hours.

Makes 6 servings

Walnuts add extra crunch to fresh green beans while lemon peel adds zesty flavor. See photo on page 219.

quick Summer Green Beans

Megan—Ruston, LA

Start to finish: 30 minutes

Method

1. In a covered large saucepan cook green beans in a large amount of boiling salted water for 10 to 15 minutes or until crisp-tender. Drain. Rinse with cold water; drain well.

2. In a large nonstick skillet heat olive oil over medium heat. Add mushrooms, garlic, and lemon peel; cook for 8 to 10 minutes or until mushrooms are tender and liquid has evaporated.

3. Stir in green beans; heat through. Season to taste with salt and pepper. Sprinkle with walnuts and Parmesan cheese.

Makes 6 servings

Cook's Notes
Try this with grilled chicken or fresh seafood that you buy—or, better yet, catch!

Ingredients

1 **pound fresh green beans, trimmed**

1 **tablespoon olive oil**

8 **ounces fresh mushrooms, sliced**

2 **cloves garlic, minced**

1 **teaspoon finely grated lemon peel**

  Salt

  Freshly ground black pepper

¼ **cup chopped walnuts, toasted if desired**

¼ **cup freshly grated Parmesan cheese**

Here's a new twist on old-fashioned green bean casserole: Jack cheese with peppers and ground cumin add a Southwestern flavor.

Pepper-Jack Green Bean Casserole

Judy—Arlington, TX

Ingredients

1   10.75-ounce can condensed cream of celery soup

½   cup milk

⅛   teaspoon ground black pepper

1   cup shredded Monterey Jack cheese with jalapeño chile peppers

1   cup diced red sweet pepper

1   teaspoon ground cumin

2   10-ounce packages frozen cut green beans, thawed

1⅓   cups canned french-fried onions

Prep: 15 minutes   Bake: 35 minutes

Method

1. Preheat oven to 350°F. In a large bowl stir together cream of celery soup, milk, and black pepper. Stir in cheese, sweet pepper, and cumin. Fold in green beans and half of the onions. Spoon into a 1½-quart rectangular baking dish.

2. Bake for 30 minutes. Carefully stir green bean mixture. Sprinkle with remaining onions. Bake about 5 minutes more or until onions are golden.

Makes 8 servings

This is the perfect way to enjoy fresh summer corn without the mess of eating it on the cob. A bit of honey and fresh basil add dimension to the traditional flavors!

quick Corn "Off" the Cob

Melissa—Studio City, CA

+ · · + · · + + · · + + · · + + · · + · + · + · + · + · + · + · + · + · + + · · + + · · + · · +

Start to finish: 20 minutes

Method

1. Using a sharp knife, cut corn from cobs. In a large skillet heat butter and olive oil over medium heat until butter is melted. Add corn, salt, and pepper. Cook for 8 to 10 minutes or until corn is tender and butter starts to brown. Add honey; stir to coat corn. Remove from heat. Toss with basil.

Makes 4 servings

Ingredients

6	large ears corn
2½	tablespoons butter
1½	tablespoons olive oil
1	teaspoon salt
½	teaspoon black pepper
2	tablespoons honey
2	tablespoons fresh basil, cut into thin strips

This simple recipe uses frozen corn and combines it with the richness of cream cheese and butter. Use the slow cooker or the oven to create this creamy dish.

South Dakota Creamed Corn

Sue—Ranchester, WY

Ingredients

1   16-ounce package frozen corn (thawed)

4   ounces cream cheese, cut up

¼   cup butter, cut up

2   tablespoons sugar

Prep: 5 minutes   Cook: 2 hours on low-heat setting

Method

1. In a 1½-quart slow cooker combine corn, cream cheese, butter, and sugar. Cover and cook on low-heat setting for 2 hours. (Or preheat oven to 350°F. In a 1½-quart casserole combine corn, cream cheese, butter, and sugar. Bake for 40 minutes.)

Makes 6 servings

Cook's Notes
This is awesome! You can multiply the recipe as needed. I've even used a can of corn with less of the other ingredients for just my hubby and me and heated it in the microwave.

This colorful side dish goes together in a hurry and makes a great accompaniment for your Easter ham.

Southwest Creamy Corn Casserole

Mary—Ada, OK

Prep: 20 minutes Bake: 50 minutes

Method

1. Preheat oven to 350°F. Coat a 2-quart baking dish with nonstick cooking spray; set aside.

2. In a large bowl combine cream-style corn, drained whole kernel corn, corn bread mix, sour cream, cheese, onion, eggs, sweet pepper, roasted pepper, butter, sugar, and salt. Transfer to prepared baking dish.

3. Bake for 50 to 60 minutes or until top is golden and center is set.

Makes 8 servings

Cook's Notes
The versatility of corn allows for endless creativity in the kitchen so I am always trying it in new ways. This delicious and easy recipe I created is now a family favorite. It has a very short preparation time.

Ingredients

Nonstick cooking spray

1   **15.5-ounce can cream-style corn**

1   **15.5-ounce can whole kernel corn, drained**

1   **8.5-ounce package corn bread mix**

1   **cup sour cream**

1   **cup shredded cheddar cheese**

¾   **cup finely chopped onion**

2   **eggs, lightly beaten**

¼   **cup finely chopped green sweet pepper**

¼   **cup bottled roasted red sweet pepper, drained and chopped**

3   **tablespoons butter, melted**

2   **tablespoons sugar**

½   **teaspoon seasoned salt**

These Brussels sprouts, cooked with bacon, will have even your most reluctant little diners asking for seconds.

Bacon Brussels Sprouts

Chris—Cedar Rapids, IA

+ · +

Ingredients

2	tablespoons olive oil
6	ounces bacon, diced
8	ounces Brussels sprouts, trimmed and halved
¾	teaspoon sea salt
¾	teaspoon freshly ground white pepper
¾	cup chicken broth
	Sea salt
	Freshly ground white pepper

Start to finish: 35 minutes

Method

1. In a large skillet heat olive oil over medium heat. Add bacon; cook for 5 to 10 minutes or until bacon is golden brown and crisp, stirring frequently. Drain bacon on paper towels, reserving oil and drippings in skillet.

2. Add Brussels sprouts, the ¾ teaspoon sea salt, and the ¾ teaspoon white pepper to oil and drippings in skillet. Cook over medium heat about 5 minutes or until golden. Carefully add the chicken broth. Reduce heat. Cook, uncovered, about 15 minutes or until Brussels sprouts are tender, stirring occasionally. (If necessary, add additional chicken broth during cooking.)

3. Stir bacon into Brussels sprouts mixture. Season to taste with additional sea salt and white pepper.

Makes 4 servings

Cook's Notes
This is a carnivore's veggie side dish.

Sliced cucumber and onion are combined to create a vegetable salad side dish in a creamy dressing of mayonnaise, milk, vinegar, sugar, and hot pepper sauce.

Creamed Cucumbers

Lindacay—Lewiston, ID

Prep: 15 minutes Chill: several hours

Method

1. In a large bowl combine cucumber and green onion. In a small bowl stir together mayonnaise, milk, vinegar, sugar, salt, parsley flakes, garlic salt, onion salt, and hot pepper sauce. Pour mayonnaise mixture over cucumber mixture, tossing to coat. Chill for several hours before serving, stirring occasionally.

Makes 6 to 7 servings

Cook's Notes
This recipe was given to me by my mother-in-law, Ruby.

Ingredients

5	cucumbers, thinly sliced
1	bunch green onions, chopped
1	cup mayonnaise
¼	cup evaporated milk
¼	cup vinegar
¼	cup sugar
1	teaspoon salt
1	teaspoon dried parsley flakes, crushed
¼	teaspoon garlic salt
¼	teaspoon onion salt
12	drops bottled hot pepper sauce

Fresh asparagus is coated lightly with olive oil and butter, then roasted at a high temperature with shallot, garlic, and poppy seeds. The finishing touch is lime juice.

Roasted Asparagus with Poppy Seeds ◀quick▶

Tom—Somerset, NJ

Ingredients

2 pounds fresh asparagus, trimmed

1 tablespoon olive oil

1 tablespoon butter, melted

2 tablespoons minced shallot

2 tablespoons poppy seeds

1 tablespoon minced garlic

2 tablespoons lime juice

   Salt

Prep: 15 minutes   Bake: 6 minutes

Method

1. Preheat oven to 500°F. In a large shallow baking pan toss the asparagus with the olive oil and butter until well coated. Add shallot, poppy seeds, and garlic. Bake for 6 to 8 minutes or until crisp-tender. Sprinkle with lime juice; season to taste with salt.

Makes 4 servings

Cook's Notes
This is excellent as a side dish for chicken or fish. If the asparagus stems are tough, you can use a vegetable peeler to remove the outer layer.

Frozen whole baby carrots are cooked in orange juice, honey, margarine, and nutmeg until tender and glazed with the sauce.

quick Honey-Orange Carrots

Janelle—Mount Holly, NJ

Start to finish: 15 minutes

Method

1. In a medium saucepan combine carrots, orange juice, honey, margarine, and nutmeg; cook over medium-high heat until mixture begins to boil. Reduce heat; cover and simmer for 5 minutes. Uncover; continue cooking for 5 to 10 minutes more or until carrots are tender and glazed with honey mixture. Stir in parsley.

Makes 4 servings

Ingredients

1   14-ounce package frozen whole baby carrots, thawed

3   tablespoons orange juice

2   tablespoons honey

1   tablespoon margarine

⅛   teaspoon ground nutmeg

2   tablespoons chopped fresh parsley

Mango chutney and curry add a touch of India to these pecan-topped carrots.

Candied Chutney Carrots quick

Elaine—Dallas, TX

Ingredients

6 large carrots

2 teaspoons packed brown sugar

½ teaspoon salt

3 tablespoons unsalted butter

1 teaspoon curry powder

½ teaspoon ground cinnamon

½ teaspoon ground allspice

½ cup prepared mango chutney

¼ cup pecans, toasted and chopped

3 tablespoons coconut, toasted

2 tablespoons chopped fresh parsley

Start to finish: 25 minutes

Method

1. Peel and slice carrot. Place carrot in a large saucepan; cover with water and add brown sugar and salt to saucepan. Bring mixture to boiling; reduce heat to medium-low. Cover and simmer for 7 to 9 minutes or until carrot is crisp-tender. Drain; return to pan. Toss with butter, curry powder, cinnamon, and allspice. Spread the mango chutney over the carrot mixture; cook over medium-low heat for 5 minutes.

2. Transfer carrot mixture to a serving bowl; sprinkle with pecans and coconut. Sprinkle with parsley. Serve immediately.

Makes 6 servings

Cook's Notes
These spicy-sweet carrots have a crunchy topping.

Tip

What's Chutney? Chutney is a condiment from India made from fruit (most commonly mango), vinegar, sugar, spices, and sometimes, chiles. It can be chunky or smooth, sweet and mild or fiery. For this recipe, you can make it sweet or hot, depending on your taste. The sweetness of candied carrots is delicious piqued with a little heat!

An herbed butter mixture flavors these halved tomatoes. Try serving them warm or refrigerate them and serve later.

quick Broiled Herb Tomatoes

Susan—Spring Hill, FL

✦ ✦ · ✦ · · ✦ · · ✦ ✦ ✦ · ✦ · · ✦ ✦ · ✦ · ✦ · ✦ · ✦ · ✦ · ✦ · · ✦ ✦ · ✦ · ✦ · ✦ · ✦ · ✦ · ✦ ✦ · ✦ · ✦ · ✦ ✦ · ✦ · ✦ · ✦

Prep: 10 minutes **Broil:** 3 minutes

Method

1. Preheat broiler.

2. Using a sharp knife, make deep scores into the cut surface of each tomato half.

3. In a small bowl combine margarine, parsley, salt, pepper, and thyme. Sprinkle over scored surface of tomatoes. Broil for 3 to 4 minutes or just until tomatoes are heated through.

Makes 8 servings

Cook's Notes
This is a terrific side dish my family loves, and yours will too. It goes with any kind of main dish—meats, chicken, etc. And my sister wraps the tomatoes in foil and packs them in her kids' lunches. The kids always enjoy them, and they actually ask for more!

Ingredients

4 **medium tomatoes, halved crosswise**

2 **tablespoons margarine, melted**

2 **teaspoons chopped fresh parsley**

¼ **teaspoon salt**

¼ **teaspoon ground black pepper**

⅛ **teaspoon ground thyme**

Green tomatoes are coated and fried in this side-dish recipe—but you can easily adapt it if only red tomatoes are available.

Fried Green Tomatoes quick

Linda—Timberlake, NC

Ingredients

¾ cup all-purpose flour

1 teaspoon sugar

½ teaspoon salt

¼ teaspoon ground
   black pepper

4 medium green tomatoes,*
   sliced ½ inch thick

2 tablespoons butter
   or margarine

Start to finish: 20 minutes

Method

1. Mix flour, sugar, salt, and pepper on piece of waxed paper. Coat tomato slices with flour mixture.

2. In a large skillet melt 1 tablespoon of the butter over medium heat. Add half of the tomato slices in single layer.

3. Cook for 6 to 8 minutes or until light brown and just tender, turning once. Remove to a serving platter. Repeat with remaining butter and tomato slices.

*Note: If only red ripe tomatoes are available, decrease sugar by half and cooking time by half.

Makes 4 servings

Thickly sliced half circles of onion are threaded onto skewers, brushed with olive oil and balsamic vinegar, sprinkled with thyme, and grilled to perfection.

Gorgeous Grilled Onions and Thyme

Marianne—Chicago, IL

Prep: 15 minutes Grill: 10 minutes Stand: 10 minutes

Method

1. Thread the onion slices onto flat metal skewers. In a small bowl combine olive oil and balsamic vinegar; brush over all sides of onions. Sprinkle with thyme leaves. Let stand for 15 to 20 minutes.

2. Place skewers on rack of an uncovered grill directly over medium coals. Grill about 10 minutes or until brown on both sides and tender in the center, turning once. Season with salt and pepper.

Makes 6 servings

Cook's Notes
This recipe is great as an accompaniment to grilled beef steaks or chicken. Prepare these onion slices while your meat or poultry is grilling, then let the onions grill while you ready the meat for serving.

Ingredients

3   **large onions, cut into ½-inch slices and halved crosswise**

¼   **cup olive oil**

1   **tablespoon balsamic vinegar**

2   **teaspoons fresh thyme leaves**

    Salt

    Ground black pepper

These tangy beets can be made ahead and chilled until dinnertime, then reheated when you're ready to serve them.

Roasted Beets with Tangerine Sauce

Tom–Somerset, NJ

294

Ingredients

4 **large beets, trimmed**

1 **cup tangerine juice**

2 **tablespoons sugar**

2 **tablespoons butter**

1 **tablespoon minced fresh ginger**

2 **teaspoons rice wine vinegar**

1 **teaspoon crushed red pepper**

Salt

Ground black pepper

Prep: 15 minutes   Bake: 1¼ hours   Cook: 8 minutes

Method

1. Preheat oven to 400°F. Wrap 2 beets together in foil. Repeat with remaining beets. Place on baking sheet. Bake about 1¼ hours or until tender; cool. Peel beets. Cut each into 8 wedges.

2. In a medium non-aluminum saucepan combine beet wedges, tangerine juice, sugar, butter, ginger, rice wine vinegar, and red pepper flakes. Bring to boiling; reduce heat to medium. Simmer, uncovered, about 8 minutes or until sauce is syrupy, stirring frequently. Season to taste with salt and black pepper.

Makes 4 servings

Cook's Notes
This can be made a day ahead and chilled. Reheat over low heat, stirring often. Serve hot.

Slices of eggplant are sprinkled with chili powder, baked, then topped with slices of red onion, tomato, avocado, and pepper-Jack cheese and broiled to melt the cheese.

Tex-Mex Eggplant Melts

Roxanne—Albany, CA

Prep: 15 minutes Bake: 30 minutes Broil: 1 minute

Method

1. Preheat oven to 350°F. Brush both sides of each eggplant slice with the olive oil. Place on a baking sheet. Sprinkle the top side of each slice with chili powder. Bake about 30 minutes or until tender.

2. Remove the baking sheet from the oven; turn oven to broil. Top each eggplant slice with red onion, tomato, avocado, and Monterey Jack cheese.

3. Broil for 1 to 2 minutes or until the cheese melts and is bubbly. Garnish with sour cream and cilantro.

Makes 4 servings

Cook's Notes
This is a great side dish with a Southwestern-style dinner.

Ingredients

1 **large eggplant, cut into ½-inch slices**

2 **tablespoons olive oil**

½ **teaspoon chili powder**

4 **slices red onion**

4 **slices tomato**

1 **avocado, halved, pitted, peeled and cut into 8 wedges**

4 **slices Monterey Jack cheese with jalapeño chile peppers**

Sour cream

Chopped fresh cilantro

Sides

295

This so-easy (and superfun!) vegetable dish is made with spaghetti squash prepared in your microwave oven.

Tropical Spaghetti Squash

Sarah—Narberth, PA

Ingredients

1	spaghetti squash
¼	cup water
2	mangoes, finely chopped
1	red sweet pepper, finely chopped
1	orange sweet pepper, finely chopped
½	of a small red onion, finely chopped
½	cup orange juice
	Juice of 2 limes
¼	cup chopped fresh cilantro
	Salt

Prep: 25 minutes **Cook:** 17 minutes **Stand:** 5 minutes

Method

1. Halve squash lengthwise; remove and discard seeds. Place squash halves, cut sides down, in a microwave-safe baking dish large enough for squash to lay flat. Pour water into baking dish. Prick squash skin all over with a fork. Cover with vented plastic wrap. Microwave on 100% power (high) for 17 to 20 minutes or until squash is tender. Let stand for 5 minutes. Using a fork, rake the stringy pulp from the squash shell, separating the pulp into spaghetti-like strands.

2. In a large bowl combine squash, mango, sweet pepper, red onion, orange juice, lime juice, and cilantro. Season to taste with salt.

Makes 6 servings

Tip

Prepping Spaghetti Squash Spaghetti squash is an amazing thing. Once cooked, it really does shred into toothsome strands that resemble spaghetti. Even kids love it! Using a pot holder, hold a cooked squash half in your hand and drag a fork from top to bottom. The strands will come right out. Spaghetti squash is also delicious with a simple tomato sauce and Parmesan cheese as a low-carb, healthy alternative to real spaghetti.

Zucchini and spinach are cooked with garlic, ginger, green onion, and red pepper flakes and topped with toasted almonds.

quick Spinach and Zucchini

Megan—Ruston, LA

Start to finish: 20 minutes

Method

1. In a large nonstick skillet heat olive oil over high heat. Add garlic, ginger, salt, and pepper flakes; cook and stir a few seconds until fragrant. Add zucchini; cook for about 5 minutes, stirring occasionally.

2. Add spinach and green onion; cook and stir just a few seconds or until wilted. Top with toasted almonds.

Makes 3 to 4 servings

Cook's Notes
Try this light and refreshing veggie dish with grilled salmon.

Ingredients

1	tablespoon olive oil
2	cloves garlic, minced
1	teaspoon minced fresh ginger
½	teaspoon kosher salt
¼	teaspoon crushed red pepper
1	zucchini, thinly bias-sliced
1	10-ounce package fresh baby spinach
1	green onion, thinly sliced
¼	cup sliced almonds, toasted

Red cabbage, carrot, and raisins are simmered with sugar, vinegar, and water. Chopped walnuts are added before serving.

Sweet Red Cabbage

Gwen—Orem, UT

Ingredients

1   medium red cabbage, chopped

1   large carrot, shredded

1   cup sugar

½   cup water

½   cup raisins

¼   cup vinegar

     Pinch of salt

½   cup chopped walnuts

Prep: 15 minutes   Cook: 1 hour 10 minutes

Method

1. In a Dutch oven combine cabbage, carrot, sugar, water, raisins, vinegar, and salt. Bring to boiling; reduce heat. Simmer, uncovered, for 10 minutes. Cover and cook for 1 hour. Just before serving, stir in walnuts.

Makes 10 to 12 servings

Cook's Notes
This is easy to make and tastes sweet. It's a great side dish.

Chapter 10
Breads & Muffins

You will need a large-capacity bread machine to make this loaf, which blends the flavors of ranch salad dressing mix and crumbled bacon.

Savory Bacon-Ranch Bread

Patricia—Jefferson, WI

Ingredients

- 1¼ cups water
- 1 tablespoon butter or margarine, softened
- 3¾ cups bread flour
- 6 slices bacon, crisp-cooked and crumbled
- 2 tablespoons sugar
- 2 tablespoons dry ranch salad dressing mix (from a 1-ounce packet)
- ½ teaspoon salt
- 1¼ teaspoons active dry yeast

Prep: 5 minutes Bake: per bread machine directions

Method

1. Using a 1½- to 2-pound capacity bread machine, place all ingredients into pan according to manufacturer's directions. Select the basic white bread cycle and, if available, light crust color. (Check dough during kneading stages; if dough sticks to sides of bread pan, sprinkle with a little additional flour, 1 tablespoon at a time, until dough no longer sticks.)

2. Remove hot bread from machine as soon as it is done. Cool on wire rack.

Makes 12 servings

Cook's Notes
Combine the remaining dry ranch salad dressing mix (about 1½ tablespoons) with softened butter or a package of cream cheese to make a tasty spread for the bread.

You can prepare the batter for these buttermilk pancakes the night before so everything is ready to go in the morning.

Old-Fashioned Oatmeal-Pecan Pancakes

Linda—Chagrin Falls, OH

Prep: 30 minutes **Chill:** several hours

Method

1. In a large bowl combine rolled oats, pecans, all-purpose flour, whole wheat flour, brown sugar, baking soda, baking powder, cinnamon, and salt. In a medium bowl whisk together buttermilk, eggs, egg white, the 5 tablespoons melted butter, and the vanilla until well mixed. Add the buttermilk mixture to the flour mixture; stir just until combined. Cover and refrigerate for several hours or overnight. (The batter will thicken as it stands.)

2. Heat a large skillet over medium heat. Brush skillet with additional melted butter. For each pancake, pour about ¼ cup batter onto skillet. (Use a ¼-cup measure to transfer batter.) (Do not stir batter excessively.) Spread batter out to form a pancake about 4 inches in diameter. Repeat, making about four pancakes at a time or as many as can fit in the pan. Cook over medium-low heat until bubbles form on the pancake surface; flip. Cook 3 to 4 minutes or until the second sides are golden.

3. Transfer to a plate and keep warm until ready to serve (the pancakes may be kept warm in a low oven). To serve, stack three pancakes on each plate. Sprinkle with powdered sugar and chopped pecans. If desired, serve with butter and warmed maple syrup.

Makes 6 servings (3 pancakes per serving)

Tip

Perfect Pancakes Pancakes are easy to make and easy to burn if you aren't careful about moderating the heat as you cook them. Be sure to use medium or medium-low heat so you don't end up with pancakes that are black and crusty on the outside and doughy on the inside. When there are bubbles all over the top surface of the pancake, flip it.

Ingredients

2¼ cups quick-cooking rolled oats

½ cup finely chopped pecans

⅓ cup all-purpose flour

⅓ cup whole wheat flour

¼ cup packed brown sugar

1 teaspoon baking soda

1 teaspoon baking powder

1 teaspoon ground cinnamon

½ teaspoon salt

2½ cups buttermilk

2 eggs

1 egg white

5 tablespoons unsalted butter, melted, plus additional for skillet

1 teaspoon vanilla

Powdered sugar

Coarsely chopped pecans

Butter (optional)

Warmed maple syrup (optional)

Make these quick-rising rolls for breakfast. There's a spiral of butter, sugar, and cinnamon inside and a topping of brown-sugar icing. See photo on page 220.

Big Fluffy Cinnamon Rolls

Kim—Idaho Falls, ID

Ingredients

7½	cups all-purpose flour
⅔	cup granulated sugar
2	packages quick-rising yeast
2	teaspoons salt
1	cup nonfat milk
½	cup water
¼	cup butter, cut up
2	eggs (at room temperature)
¼	cup butter, melted
1	cup granulated sugar mixed with 2 teaspoons ground cinnamon
1	cup powdered sugar
⅓	cup packed brown sugar
3	tablespoons butter, melted
½	teaspoon vanilla
4	to 5 teaspoons fat-free milk

Prep: 35 minutes **Stand:** 15 minutes **Rise:** 1 hour **Bake:** 20 minutes

Method

1. In a large bowl combine 6½ cups of the flour, the ⅔ cup granulated sugar, the yeast, and salt. In a microwave-safe bowl combine the 1 cup milk, the water, and the ¼ cup cut-up butter. Microwave on 100% power (high) just until mixture reaches 120°F to 130°F; mix into flour mixture. Stir in eggs and enough of the remaining 1 cup flour to make a moderately soft dough. Knead on a floured surface for 5 to 10 minutes or until smooth and elastic. Cover and let stand 15 minutes.

2. On a lightly floured surface, roll out dough to form a 20×14-inch rectangle. For filling, brush with the ¼ cup melted butter; sprinkle with sugar-cinnamon mixture. Roll up from the long side. Moisten and pinch the seam closed.

3. Using a sharp knife, cut into sixteen 1¼-inch slices. Arrange on a greased cookie sheet with sides or a jelly-roll pan in five rows of three, placing cut sides of rolls up. Cover and let rise in a warm draft-free place until doubled in size (about 1 hour).

4. Preheat oven to 375°F. Bake rolls for 20 to 25 minutes or until light brown. Meanwhile, for icing, combine powdered sugar, brown sugar, the 3 tablespoons melted butter, and the vanilla. Stir in enough of the 4 to 5 teaspoons milk to make icing of spreading consistency. Spread over warm rolls.

Makes 16 servings

Cook's Notes
When I discovered baking several years ago, I developed this recipe to make as a special treat for my little girls and husband. The brown sugar icing adds a nice touch and is lighter than the heavy white frosting that most recipes call for.

Frozen cinnamon roll dough shortcuts this recipe. The mixture of butter, pecans, and ice cream that's baked with them makes them gooey-rich.

Ice Cream-Caramel Pecan Rolls

Julie—Port Orchard, WA

Prep: 15 minutes **Chill:** overnight **Bake:** 30 minutes

Method

1. In a medium saucepan combine brown sugar, ice cream, butter, and granulated sugar. Cook and stir over medium heat until all ingredients have melted and blended. Place pecans in the bottom of a 13×9×2-inch baking pan. Place frozen cinnamon rolls on top of the pecans. Pour warm brown sugar mixture over the top of the rolls. Cover pan with foil. Chill in refrigerator overnight to rise.

2. In the morning, remove rolls from refrigerator; remove foil and let rolls stand while preheating oven to 350°F. Bake rolls about 30 minutes or until golden brown. Flip hot rolls onto a baking sheet as soon as you take them out of the oven. Serve warm.

Makes 6 servings

Cook's Notes
This recipe doubles and triples very well!

Ingredients

1 ½	cups packed brown sugar
1 ½	cups vanilla ice cream
¾	cup butter
¾	cup granulated sugar
1 ½	cups chopped pecans
6	jumbo frozen cinnamon rolls

These little sticks are made from sheets of puff pastry flavored with a mix of powdered sugar and cinnamon and sprinkled with pecans.

Breakfast Cinnamon Sticks `quick`

Deborah—Lilburn, GA

Ingredients

1 **sheet puff pastry (from a 17.3-ounce box), thawed about 40 minutes at room temperature**

⅓ **cup butter or margarine, melted**

¾ **cup powdered sugar**

1½ **teaspoons ground cinnamon**

1 **cup chopped pecans**

Prep: 15 minutes   Bake: 10 minutes

Method

1. Preheat oven to 400°F. On a lightly floured surface, use a rolling pin to roll the pastry sheet into a 12×10-inch sheet. Brush with melted butter. Combine the powdered sugar and cinnamon and sift evenly across the dough. Sprinkle with the pecans.

2. Cut into five 2×12-inch strips. Roll each strip into a 12-inch long "pencil" shape. Cut each of the "pencils" into three pieces. Place on a lightly greased baking sheet.

3. Bake for 10 to 15 minutes or until golden. Serve warm.

Makes 4 to 5 servings

Cook's Notes
This is a special breakfast treat that doesn't take that long to fix.

These "muffins" are made with a batter of packaged biscuit mix, eggs, and cream or milk that's poured over cooked sausage in muffin cups.

Breakfast Casserole Muffins

Vicki—Dowagiac, MI

Prep: 20 minutes **Bake:** 25 minutes

Method

1. Preheat oven to 350°F. Coat 24 muffin cups with nonstick cooking spray. Divide drained sausage evenly among the muffin cups.

2. In a medium bowl stir together eggs, half-and-half, biscuit mix, salt, and pepper. Pour evenly over the sausage. Top with cheddar cheese. Bake about 25 minutes or until toothpick inserted in centers comes out clean.

Makes 24 servings

Cook's Notes
While browning the sausage, you can add chopped onion, chopped green sweet pepper, and sliced mushrooms. Bacon or ham can be substituted for the sausage.

Ingredients

Nonstick cooking spray

1 pound bulk pork sausage, browned and drained

6 eggs, beaten

2 cups half-and-half or milk

1 cup packaged biscuit mix

¼ teaspoon salt

¼ teaspoon ground black pepper

2 cups finely shredded cheddar cheese

These muffins will fill your home with the scent of oranges and spices. They're made with powdered biscuit mix for a fast and simple recipe.

Orange Blossom Special Muffins

Randy—Carrollton, TX

Ingredients

- 1 egg, lightly beaten
- 1 cup orange juice
- ½ cup sugar
- 4 tablespoons butter, melted
- 2 cups packaged biscuit mix
- ¼ cup orange marmalade
- ¼ cup chopped pecans
- 1½ tablespoons all-purpose flour
- ¼ teaspoon ground cinnamon
- ¼ teaspoon ground nutmeg

Prep: 20 minutes   Bake: 20 minutes

Method

1. Preheat oven to 400°F. In a large bowl combine egg, orange juice, ¼ cup of the sugar, and 2 tablespoons of the melted butter. Add biscuit mix; mix for 30 seconds. Stir in marmalade and pecans.

2. Grease 12 muffin cups or line with paper baking cups. Fill muffin cups two-thirds full of batter. In a small bowl combine the remaining ¼ cup sugar, the flour, cinnamon, and nutmeg; stir in the remaining 2 tablespoons melted butter. Sprinkle over batter. Bake for 20 to 25 minutes or until toothpick inserted in centers comes out clean.

Makes 12 servings

Kids are guaranteed to love these decadent morning treats—chocolate pancakes with chocolate chips!

quick Chocolate Pancakes

Davontae—Cleveland Heights, OH

+ · +

Start to finish: 25 minutes

Method

1. Preheat oven to 200°F. In a medium bowl sift together flour, sugar, cocoa powder, baking powder, and salt. Stir in chocolate pieces. In small saucepan combine milk and butter; heat over low heat, stirring often just until butter is melted (the milk should be warm but must not be hot). Remove from heat. In a small bowl beat egg with a fork; gradually beat in milk-butter mixture. Add liquid mixture all at once to flour mixture. Stir just until combined.

2. Heat griddle (preferably nonstick) over medium heat until a few drops of water scattered on it move around rapidly before evaporating. Drop pancake batter onto heated griddle by rounded tablespoons (not measuring tablespoons), spreading batter slightly. Leave room between pancakes, as they will expand somewhat during cooking. Cook only two pancakes in first batch. These two will give you some indication of timing and whether your heat is too high or too low.

3. Watch pancakes carefully. As the first side cooks, the pancakes will puff up and become full of bubbles. When done, the edges will appear set and bubbles that break on surface will no longer fill in with batter. This should take anywhere from 1½ to 2½ minutes on the first side. Flip pancakes over; cook until lightly browned on second side (about 45 seconds). Do not burn. Transfer pancakes that are done to heatproof plate; keep warm in oven.

Makes 12 servings

Cook's Notes
Serve the hot pancakes with butter or with slightly softened vanilla ice cream, warm hot fudge topping, and strawberries.

Ingredients

½ **cup all-purpose flour**

⅓ **cup sugar**

3 **tablespoons unsweetened cocoa powder (not Dutch-processed)**

½ **teaspoon baking powder**

Dash salt

¼ **cup miniature semisweet chocolate pieces**

⅓ **cup plus 1 tablespoon milk**

2 **tablespoon unsalted butter, cut into small pieces**

1 **egg**

Breads & Muffins

307

These low-fat waffles contain no oil. The batter combines plenty of pumpkin, brown sugar, egg, milk, and flour with spices to make them rich and delicious.

Pumpkin Pie Waffles quick

Carole—Cleveland, OH

Ingredients

1	cup all-purpose flour
2	teaspoons baking powder
¾	teaspoon ground cinnamon
⅛	teaspoon salt
⅛	teaspoon ground ginger
⅛	teaspoon ground cloves
1	egg, lightly beaten
1	cup milk
½	cup canned pumpkin (not prepared pumpkin pie mix)
¼	cup packed dark brown sugar
	Butter (optional)
	Maple syrup (optional)

Prep: 15 minutes Bake: 5 minutes

Method

1. In a medium bowl combine flour, baking powder, cinnamon, salt, ginger, and cloves. In a small bowl whisk together egg, milk, pumpkin, and brown sugar. Pour the pumpkin mixture over the flour mixture; stir just until combined.

2. Preheat waffle iron according to manufacturer's directions. Put ¼ cup of the batter (or as directed) in the center of the grid. Close iron and cook for 5 to 7 minutes or until the steam starts to subside. Open iron and remove waffle. Repeat with remaining batter. Cooked waffles can be kept warm, covered with foil, in a 300°F oven.

3. If desired, serve with butter and maple syrup.

Makes 8 servings

Cook's Notes
This is a very easy recipe for that special day. For a great combination, serve with hot apple cider.

These waffles are based on flavors from a banana bread recipe. Butterscotch pieces are folded into the batter for extra sweetness.

Butterscotch Banana-Bread Waffles

Charmie—Fontana, CA

Prep: 20 minutes   **Bake:** per waffle baker directions

Method

1. In a large bowl sift together flour, brown sugar, cinnamon, baking powder, baking soda, salt, and nutmeg.

2. In a medium bowl beat egg yolks. Add buttermilk and mashed bananas. Stir banana mixture into flour mixture until well mixed.

3. In a clean medium bowl beat egg whites with an electric mixer on medium speed until stiff peaks form. Fold into batter. Gently stir in butterscotch pieces.

4. Heat waffle iron and brush with oil. Pour batter into iron. Close lid quickly; do not open until done. Bake according to manufacturer's directions. If desired, serve with maple syrup.

Makes 6 to 8 servings

Cook's Notes
I created these by combining my favorite banana bread and waffle recipes! They're so delicious with syrup, powdered sugar, or sliced bananas. NOTE: I wipe off any melted butterscotch from the iron between batches so it doesn't burn.

Ingredients

2¼ cups all-purpose flour

¼ cup packed brown sugar

1 teaspoon ground cinnamon

½ teaspoon baking powder

½ teaspoon baking soda

½ teaspoon salt

½ teaspoon ground nutmeg

3 eggs, separated

2 cups buttermilk or sour milk

2 ripe bananas, well mashed

1 cup butterscotch pieces

Cooking oil

Maple syrup or butter (optional)

Tip

Making Sour Milk If you don't have buttermilk on hand, you can easily substitute homemade sour milk in your recipe. Just add 1 tablespoon of white or cider vinegar or lemon juice to a measuring cup, then add enough milk (it can be whole, 2 percent, 1 percent, or skim) to the cup to make 1 cup. Let the mixture sit 5 minutes until it begins to curdle, then use it in your recipe.

French bread "sandwiches" filled with cream cheese, marshmallow creme, bananas, nuts, and raisins are dipped in a mixture of milk and eggs, then cooked.

Ultimate Skillet Stuffed French Toast

Allison—Ogden, IL

Ingredients

1   large loaf French bread

1   8-ounce package cream cheese

1   7-ounce jar marshmallow creme

2   medium bananas

1   cup chopped walnuts

½   cup raisins

4   eggs

2   cups milk

1   tablespoon vanilla

2   cups packed brown sugar

2   tablespoons butter

    Maple syrup (optional)

Prep: 20 minutes   Cook: 4 minutes per sandwich

Method

1. Cut French bread into 1-inch slices. In a medium bowl stir together cream cheese and marshmallow creme. Slice bananas; stir into cream cheese mixture. Stir in walnuts and raisins.

2. Spread cream cheese mixture on half of the French bread slices; top with remaining French bread slices. In a medium bowl whisk together eggs, milk, and vanilla. Place brown sugar in a shallow bowl.

3. Dip both sides of each "sandwich" in egg mixture, then dip in brown sugar. In a large nonstick skillet or on a griddle melt 1 tablespoon of the butter over medium heat; add half of the "sandwiches" and cook for 2 to 3 minutes on each side or until golden brown. Repeat with remaining butter and "sandwiches." Serve warm. If desired, serve with maple syrup.

Makes 6 servings

Cook's Notes
This will impress your hardest-to-please guests—and keep the kids asking for more at the table! It's filling and heartwarming for a special family breakfast. And it's great for the holidays!

This make-ahead breakfast strata has a brown sugar–butter syrup in the bottom of the baking dish with French bread and an egg-milk mixture poured over.

Baked French Toast with Fresh Berries

P.J.–Cary, NC

· · · · · ✦ · · · · · · ✦✦ · · · · · ✦✦ · · · · ✦ · · · · · · ✦ · · · · · ✦ · · · · · · ✦ · · · ✦ · · · ✦

Prep: 20 minutes **Chill:** overnight **Bake:** 40 minutes

Method

1. In a medium saucepan combine brown sugar, butter, and corn syrup. Cook and stir over medium heat until butter melts and mixture boils. Pour syrup in a 13×9×2-inch baking dish. Place bread slices in syrup. In a medium bowl whisk together eggs, milk, vanilla, and salt; pour over bread slices. Sprinkle with cinnamon. Cover with foil. Refrigerate overnight.

2. Preheat oven to 350°F. Uncover. Bake about 40 minutes or until golden brown and bubbly. Serve topped with fresh berries.

Makes 6 to 8 servings

Cook's Notes
There's just enough time while this bakes for you to take a walk—when you return you'll open the door to an incredibly inviting aroma!

Ingredients

2 cups packed brown sugar

1 cup butter

¼ cup light-color corn syrup

8 to 10 slices French bread

6 eggs, beaten

1½ cups milk

1 teaspoon vanilla

Dash salt

Ground cinnamon

Fresh berries

These healthy breakfast or brunch treats contain brown sugar substitute, buttermilk, and a small amount of butter along with dried tart cherries and toasted almonds.

Cherry-Almond Scones

Alma—Sarasota, FL

Ingredients

Nonstick cooking spray

2 cups all-purpose flour

3 tablespoons brown sugar substitute

2 teaspoons baking powder

½ teaspoon salt

2 tablespoons cold unsalted butter

½ cup dried tart cherries, chopped

¼ cup almonds, toasted and chopped

1 cup buttermilk

1 tablespoon water

1 to 2 drops almond extract

Prep: 20 minutes   Bake: 15 minutes

Method

1. Preheat oven to 425°F. Coat a baking sheet with nonstick cooking spray. In a large bowl stir together flour, 2 tablespoons of the brown sugar substitute, the baking powder, and salt. Using a pastry blender, cut in butter until coarse crumbs form. Stir in cherries and almonds. Make a well in center of flour mixture. Add buttermilk all at once to flour mixture. Using a fork, stir just until moistened.

2. Turn dough out onto a lightly floured surface. Knead dough by folding and gently pressing it for 10 to 12 strokes or until dough is nearly smooth. Divide dough in half. Pat or lightly roll each half into an 8-inch circle. Cut each circle into 8 wedges.

3. Place wedges 2 inches apart on prepared baking sheet. In a small bowl mix water with almond extract; brush on scones. Sprinkle on the remaining 1 tablespoon brown sugar substitute. Bake for 15 to 18 minutes or until golden. Remove scones from baking sheet; serve warm.

Makes 16 servings

This easy-to-make corn bread has an extra twist—creamed corn and maple syrup are added to a packaged mix for extra flavor.

quick Sweet Corn Bread

Sheena—Atlanta, GA

Prep: 10 minutes Bake: 20 minutes

Method

1. Preheat oven to 375°F. Grease an 8×4×2-inch loaf pan.

2. In a medium bowl combine corn, corn bread mix, butter, milk, maple syrup, egg, and sugar. Beat with an electric mixer on medium speed until combined. Spoon into prepared pan. Bake about 20 minutes or until toothpick inserted in center comes out clean.

Makes 6 servings

Cook's Notes
You may add butter to the top.

Ingredients

1	15-ounce can creamed corn
1	7-ounce box corn bread mix
½	cup butter, softened
½	cup milk
⅓	cup maple syrup
1	egg
2	tablespoons sugar

This traditional Easter bread with raisins is braided and topped with a sugar glaze.

Glazed Raisin Braid

Diane—Louisville, KY

Ingredients

1   **package active dry yeast**

¼   **cup warm water (105°F to 115°F)**

1   **cup milk, scalded**

½   **cup sugar**

½   **cup softened butter or shortening**

2   **teaspoons salt**

4½   **to 5 cups sifted all-purpose flour**

2   **eggs**

1   **cup dark or golden raisins**

2   **teaspoons grated lemon zest**

¼   **teaspoon ground mace (optional)**

1   **recipe Sugar Glaze**

Prep: 30 minutes **Rise:** 3 hours **Stand:** 10 minutes **Bake:** 25 minutes

Method

1. In a small bowl combine yeast and warm water; let stand for 5 minutes to soften. In a large bowl combine scalded milk, sugar, butter, and salt; cool to lukewarm. Stir in about 2 cups of the flour; add the eggs and mix well. Stir in softened yeast. Stir in raisins, lemon zest, and, if desired, mace. Stir in enough of the remaining flour to make a soft dough.

2. On a lightly floured surface, knead dough until smooth and elastic. Place in a lightly greased bowl, turning once. Cover; let rise in a warm place until double in size (about 1½ hours).

3. Punch dough down. Let rise until almost doubled in size (about 1 hour). Divide dough in half; shape each half into a ball. Cover and let rest for 10 minutes.

4. For each loaf, divide one of the balls into quarters. Shape three of the quarters into 12-inch-long ropes, tapering the ends. Line up ropes 1 inch apart on a lightly greased baking sheet. Braid loosely without stretching the dough, beginning at the middle and working toward either end. Seal ends well. Divide remaining quarter into 3 pieces; shape each into an 8- to 9-inch-long rope, tapering ends. Braid loosely and place on top of large braid, tucking ends of small braid into large one. Repeat process with remaining dough. Cover and let rise until doubled in size (30 to 45 minutes).

5. Preheat oven to 350°F. Bake loaves for 25 to 30 minutes or until bread is golden and sounds hollow when lightly tapped. While warm, spread with Sugar Glaze.

Sugar Glaze: Combine 2 cups powdered sugar, ¼ cup hot water, and 1 teaspoon butter; stir until well mixed. If necessary, thin with more water to reach drizzling consistency.

Makes 2 loaves

This traditional Italian yeast bread is braided, then topped with sesame or poppy seeds, which makes a very attractive loaf.

Italian Bread

Jacquelyn—Lucerne Mines, PA

Prep: 40 minutes   **Rise:** 2¾ hours   **Bake:** 40 minutes

Method

1. In a large bowl stir together the water, salt, yeast, and sugar; stir in 6 cups of the flour. Stir in enough of the remaining flour to make a dough that is stiff but not too dry. Turn out onto floured surface; knead about 8 minutes or until dough is smooth and elastic, working in ½ cup to 1 cup additional flour as necessary.

2. Pour oil into a large bowl; swirl to coat the bowl's interior. Put dough in bowl, turning to coat thoroughly with oil. Cover with plastic wrap; let rise in warm place for 2 to 3 hours (it won't rise a great deal).

3. Punch down dough; divide in half. Divide each half into three parts; braid each set of three on a greased cookie sheet, ending up with two large braids.

4. Let rise in a warm place for 45 minutes. Brush braids with milk; sprinkle with sesame seeds.

5. Preheat oven to 350°F. Bake braids for 25 minutes. Remove braids from pans; lay braids directly on oven rack. Bake 15 to 25 minutes more or until bread is very pale tan and instant-read thermometer inserted in center registers 160°F. Cool on wire rack.

Makes 10 to 12 servings

Ingredients

3 **cups warm water**

1 **tablespoon salt**

1 **teaspoon fast-rising active dry yeast**

1 **teaspoon sugar**

7 **to 8 cups all-purpose flour**

2 **tablespoons cooking oil**

2 **tablespoons milk**

2 **tablespoons sesame seeds or poppy seeds**

Garlic, provolone cheese, dried tomatoes, and green onions are all added to the batter to flavor this delicious quick bread.

Italian Provolone Dried Tomato Bread

Barbara—Park Hills, MO

Ingredients

1 ¼ cups buttermilk

2 eggs, beaten

¼ cup olive oil

2 tablespoons sugar

2 teaspoons minced garlic

2⅔ cups bread flour

2 teaspoons baking powder

1 ½ teaspoons salt

½ teaspoon baking soda

4 ounces provolone cheese, shredded (1 cup)

3 ounces dried tomatoes, (oil-packed) drained and chopped

⅓ cup finely chopped green onion (including some tops)

¼ cup chopped fresh parsley

1 teaspoon freshly ground black pepper

Prep: 20 minutes Bake: 50 minutes Cool: 10 minutes

Method

1. Preheat oven to 350°F. Grease bottom and sides of a 9×5x3-inch loaf pan. Set aside.

2. In a large bowl combine buttermilk, eggs, olive oil, sugar, and garlic; stir until smooth. In another large bowl combine flour, baking powder, salt, and baking soda. Stir provolone cheese, dried tomato, green onion, parsley, and pepper into flour mixture.

3. Add the buttermilk mixture to the flour mixture; stir just until combined. Pour the batter into prepared loaf pan. Smooth top with the back of a wet spoon. Bake about 50 minutes or until golden. Cool in pan on wire rack for 10 minutes; remove from pan.

Makes 1 loaf

The dough is mixed in the bread machine, then topped with kalamata olives, garlic, goat cheese, Parmesan-Asiago cheese, and rosemary. See photo on page 220.

Rosemary Olive Focaccia

Anne—Des Moines, IA

Prep: 30 minutes Rise: 30 minutes Bake: 20 minutes

Method

1. Make the bread dough in your bread machine or mixer as directed on the package; set machine on the dough cycle. Remove dough from bread machine.

2. On a lightly floured surface, press dough into two loose circles. Drizzle and brush with some of the 3 to 4 tablespoons olive oil. Cover with plastic wrap. Let rise in a warm place until doubled in size (30 to 40 minutes).

3. Preheat oven to 400°F. Press olives into top of dough circles; drizzle with a little more olive oil and dot with garlic. Bake for 7 minutes. Remove from oven; drizzle a little more olive oil and dot with crumbled goat cheese. Bake for 10 to 12 minutes more. Remove from oven; sprinkle with Parmesan and Asiago cheese blend, rosemary, and more olive oil if needed. Bake for 3 to 4 minutes more or until light brown.

4. For dipping oil, in small bowl combine the 3 tablespoons olive oil, the Parmesan cheese, and pepper. Serve with the focaccia.

Makes 16 servings

Cook's Notes
If you like, you can make your own dough or substitute frozen bread dough for the bread machine mix and top with remaining ingredients as directed.

Ingredients

1 1½-pound package bread machine bread mix

3 to 4 tablespoons olive oil

½ cup pitted and sliced kalamata olives

6 cloves garlic, crushed

½ cup goat cheese, crumbled

½ cup grated Parmesan and Asiago cheese blend

3 tablespoons chopped fresh rosemary

3 tablespoons olive oil

1 tablespoon freshly grated Parmesan cheese

   Freshly ground black pepper

This supereasy yeast bread is made in the bread machine. In addition to the usual ingredients, it contains onion soup mix for flavor.

Sunday Dinner Onion Bread

Marla—St. Paul, MN

Ingredients

¾	cup water
4	teaspoons olive oil
4	teaspoons dry onion soup mix
4	teaspoons sugar
2¼	cups bread flour
1	teaspoon bread machine yeast

Prep: 5 minutes   Bake: per bread machine directions

Method

1. Place all ingredients into bread machine pan according to manufacturer's directions. Select the basic white bread cycle and, if available, medium crust color. Remove hot bread from machine as soon as it is done. Serve warm.

Makes 10 servings

Cook's Notes
One of the best-flavored white loaves I've ever made. Everyone loves it, especially for dinner with a roast and vegetables.

This yeast bread is made with extras such as beer, oil and honey, and rolled oats. For a treat, serve the baked bread with cinnamon-flavored butter.

Honey-Wheat Beer Bread

Jodie—San Antonio, TX

Prep: 30 minutes   Rise: 1¾ hours   Bake: 30 minutes

Method

1. In a small saucepan combine beer, canola oil, and honey; heat and stir until mixture is 110°F to 120°F. In a large bowl stir together bread flour and whole wheat flour.

2. In another large bowl combine 2 cups of the flour mixture, the yeast, and salt. Add the warm beer mixture to yeast mixture; beat with electric mixer on medium speed for 2 minutes. Knead in the remaining flour mixture until dough is smooth. Let rise in a warm place for 1 hour. Split dough in half; shape dough into two loaves. Place loaves in two greased 8×4×2-inch loaf pans. Let rise in a warm place until doubled in size (about 45 minutes).

3. Preheat oven to 350°F. Bake loaves for 15 minutes. Remove from oven; quickly brush tops with egg mixture and sprinkle lightly with oats. Bake for 15 to 20 minutes more or until loaves are brown on top.

4. For cinnamon butter, in a small bowl stir together butter and cinnamon; chill. Serve with bread.

Makes 6 servings

Ingredients

1   12-ounce bottle honey-wheat beer (at room temperature)

½   cup canola oil

⅓   cup honey

3   cups bread flour

2   cups whole wheat flour

4   teaspoons active dry yeast

1½   teaspoons salt

1   egg yolk beaten with 1 tablespoon water

½   cup old-fashioned rolled oats

½   cup butter, softened

½   teaspoon ground cinnamon

Pineapple and pecans add interesting flavor dimensions to this lusciously moist zucchini bread.

Extreme Zucchini Bread

Christine—Windsor, CA

Ingredients

1	cup granulated sugar
¾	cup packed brown sugar
1	cup cooking oil
3	eggs
1	teaspoon vanilla
2¾	cups all-purpose flour
½	cup rolled oats
1	teaspoon baking soda
1	teaspoon ground cinnamon
½	teaspoon baking powder
½	teaspoon salt
2½	cups shredded zucchini
1	8-ounce can crushed pineapple, drained
1	cup chopped pecans

Prep: 25 minutes Bake: 50 minutes Cool: 10 minutes

Method

1. Preheat oven to 350°F. Grease and flour two loaf pans. In a large bowl combine granulated sugar, brown sugar, oil, eggs, and vanilla. Beat with an electric mixer on medium speed until smooth.

2. In a medium bowl combine flour, oats, baking soda, cinnamon, baking powder, and salt; add to the sugar mixture, beating until smooth. Stir in the zucchini, drained pineapple, and pecans. Pour batter into prepared loaf pans.

3. Bake for 50 to 55 minutes or until toothpick inserted in centers comes out clean. Let cool in pans on wire rack for 10 minutes. Remove from pans.

Makes 2 loaves

These savory cornmeal-buttermilk drop biscuits are flavored with green onion, chives, and cheddar cheese.

◆quick◆ Cheddar-Onion Biscuits

Pat—Lee's Summit, MO

Prep: 15 minutes   Bake: 12 minutes

Method

1. Preheat oven to 400°F. In a large bowl combine flour, cornmeal, baking powder, baking soda, and salt. Using a pastry blender or fork, cut in shortening until coarse crumbs form. Add cheddar cheese, green onion, and chives; mix well. Make a well in the center of the flour mixture. Add buttermilk. Stir just until flour mixture is moistened.

2. Drop by full tablespoons onto a parchment-lined baking sheet. Bake for 12 to 15 minutes or until delicate golden.

Makes about 16 biscuits

Cook's Notes
These are great with honey!

Ingredients

1 ½	cups all-purpose flour
½	cup cornmeal
2	teaspoons baking powder
½	teaspoon baking soda
¼	teaspoon salt
¼	cup shortening
½	cup grated sharp cheddar cheese
½	cup chopped green onion
2	tablespoons chopped fresh chives
1	cup buttermilk

These tender cheese-filled biscuits are spiced up with a little chili powder. They would go great with a thick, meaty chili.

Chili Cheese Pinwheels

Donna—Gray, ME

Ingredients

2 cups sifted all-purpose flour

1 tablespoon baking powder

½ teaspoon salt

½ cup shortening

1 cup grated sharp cheddar cheese

⅔ cup milk

2 tablespoons butter, melted

¼ to ½ teaspoon chili powder

Prep: 20 minutes Bake: 12 minutes

Method

1. Preheat oven to 450°F. In a large bowl sift together flour, baking powder, and salt. Using a pastry blender, cut in shortening and ½ cup of the cheddar cheese until mixture resembles coarse meal. Gradually stir in enough milk to form a soft dough.

2. On a lightly floured surface, roll dough to ½-inch thickness. Brush melted butter over dough. In a small bowl combine the remaining ½ cup cheddar cheese and the chili powder; sprinkle over dough. Roll up starting at the long side. Cut into ½-inch slices. Place on well-greased baking sheet. Bake for 12 to 15 minutes or until golden.

Makes 16 biscuits

Cook's Notes
These are great with supper or the next day in your lunch box.

Spinach, fresh basil, and lots of garlic give these quick-and-easy dinner rolls a distinctive flavor.

Herbed-Spinach Dinner Rolls

Kim–Kingwood, TX

Prep: 30 minutes **Rise:** 45 minutes **Bake:** 20 minutes

Method

1. Place frozen spinach in a microwave-safe dish; microwave on 100% power (high) about 5 minutes or until fully defrosted. Set aside to cool. (To speed this process, return the spinach to the freezer or the refrigerator while preparing the bread dough.)

2. In a large bowl sprinkle yeast into warm water. Let stand for 3 minutes. Add sugar and the ¼ cup olive oil; stir gently. Using a garlic press, crush garlic cloves directly into the yeast mixture. Stir in whole wheat flour and salt. Squeeze water from defrosted spinach one handful at a time. Stir spinach and basil into dough. Add all-purpose flour, 1 cup at a time, using hands to knead in the last cup of flour thoroughly.

3. Coat a 13×9×2-inch baking dish with nonstick cooking spray. Form rolls by breaking off 2-inch balls of bread dough. Line up rolls in prepared baking dish. Cover with a damp towel. Let rise in a warm place for 45 minutes.

4. Preheat oven to 350°F. Bake rolls for 15 minutes. Brush tops of rolls with the 2 tablespoons olive oil. Bake about 5 minutes more or until tops are light brown.

Makes 15 servings

Ingredients

- 1 **10-ounce package frozen spinach**
- 1 **package active dry yeast**
- 1 **cup warm water**
- ¼ **cup sugar**
- ¼ **cup olive oil**
- 1 **bulb garlic (about 14 cloves)**
- 1 **cup whole wheat flour**
- 1 **teaspoon salt**
- ¼ **cup fresh basil, chopped**
- 2 **cups all-purpose flour**
  Nonstick cooking spray
- 2 **tablespoons olive oil**

Cook's Notes
This yeast bread recipe takes half the time of a traditional bread because the dough rises only once. The result is delicious, savory dinner rolls.

These soft rolls with cottage cheese, onions, and dillweed are baked en masse in a lasagna pan for great pull-apart bites.

Dilly Rolls

Tina—Edmore, MI

Ingredients

2	cups cottage cheese
2	tablespoons butter
2	packages active dry yeast
½	cup warm water
2	eggs
¼	cup sugar
2	tablespoons minced dried onion
2	tablespoons chopped fresh dillweed
1	tablespoon salt
½	teaspoon baking soda
4½	to 5 cups all-purpose flour

Prep: 25 minutes   **Rise:** 1¾ hours   **Bake:** 20 minutes

Method

1. In a small saucepan combine cottage cheese and butter; heat and stir until butter is melted. Cool to 110°F to 115°F. In a large bowl dissolve yeast in warm water. Add cottage cheese mixture, eggs, sugar, minced dried onion, dillweed, salt, and baking soda.

2. Add 3 cups of the flour and beat until smooth. Add enough of the remaining flour to make a soft dough. Knead until smooth and elastic (just a little kneading will do).

3. Place in greased bowl. Cover. Let rise in a warm place until dough doubles in size (about 1 hour). Punch down dough. Divide into 24 balls. Put in greased lasagna pan or other 13×9×2-inch baking pan. Let rise until double (about 45 minutes).

4. Preheat oven to 350°F. Bake rolls for 20 to 25 minutes or until light brown.

Makes 2 dozen rolls

Chapter 11
Cakes, Cookies & Candies

This chocolate cake is topped with caramel ice cream topping and whipped topping.
See photo on page 221.

Chocolate Caramel Candy Cake

Liz—Hillsborough, NJ

Ingredients

3 **cups all-purpose flour**

2 **cups sugar**

6 **tablespoons unsweetened cocoa powder**

2 **teaspoons baking soda**

1 **teaspoon salt**

2 **cups water**

⅔ **cup cooking oil**

2 **tablespoons vinegar**

2 **teaspoons vanilla**

1 **6-ounce jar caramel or butterscotch ice cream topping**

1 **8-ounce container frozen whipped dessert topping, thawed**

1 **2.1-ounce bar chocolate-covered crisp peanut butter candy, crushed**

Prep: 25 minutes **Bake:** 35 minutes

Method

1. Preheat oven to 350°F. In a large mixing bowl combine flour, sugar, cocoa powder, baking soda, and salt. Add water, oil, vinegar, and vanilla; beat with an electric mixer on low to medium speed until well mixed.

2. Spoon batter into a greased and floured 13×9×2-inch baking pan. Bake for 35 to 40 minutes or until a toothpick inserted in center comes out clean. Cool in pan on a wire rack.

3. Using a long fork, poke holes all over top of cake. Pour ice cream topping over cake. Spread cake with whipped dessert topping. Sprinkle with crushed candy bar. Store in the refrigerator.

Makes 12 to 16 servings

326

What could make this rich chocolate cake recipe even better? Serve it topped with spoonfuls of whipped cream.

Cocoa Cola Cake

Linda–San Antonio, TX

Prep: 20 minutes **Bake:** 30 minutes

Method

1. Preheat oven to 350°F. In a large bowl stir together flour, sugar, and baking soda; set aside. In a medium saucepan combine cola, butter, and cocoa powder; bring to boiling over medium heat. Add the hot mixture to the flour mixture; stir just until combined. Add eggs, buttermilk, and vanilla; stir until combined. Gently stir in marshmallows (they will float to the top).

2. Pour the cake batter into a greased and floured 13×9×2-inch baking pan. Bake about 30 minutes or until a toothpick inserted near the center of the cake comes out clean. Transfer cake in pan to a wire rack. Immediately spread Cocoa Topping over cake. Cool completely on wire rack.

Cocoa Topping: In a medium saucepan combine ½ cup butter, ¼ cup unsweetened cocoa powder, and ¼ cup cola; bring to boiling. Add 2½ cups sifted powdered sugar and 1 teaspoon vanilla. Mix with a wire whisk until combined. Stir in 1 cup chopped nuts.

Makes 16 servings

Ingredients

2⅓ cups all-purpose flour

2 cups sugar

1 teaspoon baking soda

1 cup cola

⅔ cup butter

2 tablespoons unsweetened cocoa powder

2 eggs

½ cup buttermilk

2 teaspoons vanilla

1½ cups tiny marshmallows

1 recipe Cocoa Topping

Tip

Confused About Cocoa Powder? There are two types of cocoa powder available—Dutch process, or alkalized, and natural, or nonalkalized. Dutch-process cocoa is reddish and has a mellower, softer flavor. Natural cocoa powder is dark brown and has a sharper, more intense flavor. Unless otherwise specified, either type can be used interchangeably.

Dress up a yellow cake mix by adding pineapple and coconut to the batter and finishing it off with a tropical-tasting whipped topping.

Piña Colada Cake

Gina—Fort Lauderdale, FL

Ingredients

1 2-layer-size package yellow cake mix

¾ cup pineapple juice

½ cup butter, melted

2 eggs

⅓ cup olive oil

1 20-ounce can crushed pineapple (juice pack), undrained

7 ounces flaked coconut

½ of 15-ounce can cream of coconut

1 4-serving-size package instant vanilla pudding mix

1 8-ounce container frozen whipped dessert topping, thawed

Prep: 25 minutes   Bake: 35 minutes   Cool: 30 minutes

Method

1. Preheat oven to 350°F. In a large mixing bowl combine cake mix, pineapple juice, melted butter, eggs, and olive oil; beat with an electric mixer on medium speed about 1 minute or until smooth.

2. Add ½ cup of the undrained pineapple and half of the coconut, stirring until combined. Pour batter into a 13×9×2-inch baking dish (or a dish a bit larger).

3. Bake about 35 minutes or until toothpick inserted near the center comes out clean. Cool in pan on a wire rack for 30 minutes. Prick top all over with a large fork, wiggling it a little to enlarge holes.

4. Drizzle half of the cream of coconut over the top. Refrigerate cake while making topping.

5. For topping, in large bowl mix the remaining undrained pineapple, the pudding mix, and the remaining cream of coconut. Fold in whipped topping and half of the remaining coconut. Spread topping on cake. Sprinkle remaining coconut on top.

6. Store in refrigerator, but serve at room temperature for the best flavor.

Makes 15 to 20 servings

Cook's Notes
A smaller can of cream of coconut can be used for a less sweet and less moist cake.

Clever cuts, tinted coconut, and fresh strawberries can make a plain angel food cake look like a blooming flower.

quick Spring Flower Cake

Tiffani–Biloxi, MS

Start to finish: 20 minutes

Method

1. Toss coconut with food coloring until evenly tinted; set aside. Place cake on a large serving plate. Frost top and sides with whipped topping; sprinkle with coconut.

2. Cut cake into eight slices, leaving all slices in place. Carefully pull out cake slices and separate slightly to resemble the petals of an open flower.

3. Spoon halved strawberries into center of "flower." Store in refrigerator.

Makes 8 servings

Ingredients

1   cup flaked coconut

2   drops food coloring (any color)

1   10-ounce purchased round angel food cake

1   cup frozen whipped dessert topping, thawed

3   cups halved fresh strawberries

329

German chocolate cake mix batter is layered with a topping of melted caramel, pecans, and chocolate chips.

Turtle Cake

Connie—Charlestown, IN

+ · +

Ingredients

1   **2-layer-size package German chocolate cake mix**

20   **ounces caramels (unwrapped)**

1   **14-ounce can sweetened condensed milk (not evaporated milk)**

½   **cup butter**

8   **ounces pecans**

12   **ounces semisweet chocolate pieces**

    Powdered sugar or purchased coconut-pecan frosting

Prep: 25 minutes   **Bake:** per package directions

Method

1. Preheat oven as directed on cake package. Prepare cake batter according to package directions. Pour half of the batter into a greased 13×9×2-inch baking pan. Bake for 15 minutes.

2. Meanwhile, in a medium saucepan combine caramels, sweetened condensed milk, and butter; cook and stir over medium-low heat until melted. Pour caramel mixture over baked cake; sprinkle with pecans, then chocolate pieces. Pour remaining cake batter on top of this and bake the remaining time according to package directions or until toothpick inserted in top layer of cake comes out clean.

3. Cool in pan on wire rack. When cool, dust with powdered sugar or frost with purchased coconut-pecan frosting.

Makes 12 servings

Peanut butter makes this pound cake special. A peanut topping adds an extra dose of nutty goodness.

Peanut Butter Pound Cake

Josie-lynn—Woodbine, GA

Prep: 20 minutes Bake: 1 hour Cool: 10 minutes

Method

1. Preheat oven to 325°F. Grease a 9×5×3-inch loaf pan.

2. In a large bowl combine the 1 cup sugar, butter, and peanut butter; beat with an electric mixer on medium speed until smooth and creamy. Beat in milk and vanilla. Add eggs, one at a time, beating well after each addition.

3. In a medium bowl combine flour, ½ teaspoon of the cinnamon, and the baking powder; add to egg mixture, beating well. Pour batter into prepared loaf pan.

4. For topping, pour peanuts into a resealable bag. Seal bag; roll with a rolling pin to crush peanuts. Add the 1 tablespoon sugar and the remaining 1 teaspoon cinnamon; shake well. Sprinkle over top of cake and press gently into the top of the batter.

5. Bake about 1 hour or until a toothpick inserted in center comes out clean. Cool in pan on wire rack for 10 minutes.

Makes 10 to 12 servings

Ingredients

1 cup sugar

½ cup butter, softened

½ cup creamy peanut butter

1 tablespoon milk

1 teaspoon vanilla

4 eggs

2 cups all-purpose flour

1½ teaspoons ground cinnamon

¼ teaspoon baking powder

¼ cup lightly salted dry roasted peanuts

1 tablespoon sugar

331

This makes a large 10-inch tube pound cake from a batter rich with plenty of butter, eggs, and sour cream.

Nita's Sour Cream Pound Cake

Juanita—Moultrie, GA

Ingredients

2 cups sugar

1 cup butter, softened

1 teaspoon vanilla

6 eggs

3 cups all-purpose flour

½ teaspoon baking powder

1 cup sour cream

Prep: 25 minutes **Bake:** 80 minutes **Cool:** 10 minutes

Method

1. Preheat oven to 300°F. In a large mixing bowl combine sugar, butter, and vanilla; beat with an electric mixer on low to medium speed until well mixed. Add eggs, one at a time, beating well after each.

2. In a small bowl sift together flour and baking powder. Alternately add flour mixture and sour cream to butter mixture, beating on low speed after each addition just until combined. Spread batter into a greased and floured 10-inch tube pan.

3. Bake about 80 minutes or until toothpick inserted in center comes out clean. Cool in pan for 10 minutes; remove from pan and cool on wire rack.

Makes 12 to 14 servings

Pudding and coconut flakes form the filling as well as the topping for this tasty angel food cake.

Coconut Angel Cake

Traci—Port Jervis, NY

Prep: 25 minutes **Chill:** 1¼ hours **Bake:** per package directions **Cool:** 10 minutes

Method

1. Prepare cake mix according to package directions; stir in ⅔ cup of the coconut. Pour batter evenly into two 9×1½-inch round cake pans. Bake according to package directions. Cool cake layers in pans on wire racks for 10 minutes. Loosen cakes from pans; invert onto wire racks and remove pans. Cool completely.

2. Pour milk into a medium bowl. Add dry pudding mix and powdered sugar. Beat with a wire whisk about 2 minutes or until well mixed (mixture will be thick). Gently stir in whipped topping. Refrigerate for 15 minutes.

3. Place one of the cake layers on a serving plate; spread top with 1 cup of the pudding mixture. Sprinkle with ¾ cup of the remaining coconut; cover with second cake layer. Spread top and sides with remaining pudding mixture. Press remaining coconut into pudding mixture. Refrigerate for at least 1 hour.

Makes 8 servings

Ingredients

1 **2-layer-size package yellow cake mix**

1 **7-ounce package flaked coconut**

1 **cup cold milk**

1 **4-serving-size package vanilla-flavor instant pudding and pie filling**

¼ **cup powdered sugar**

1 **8-ounce container frozen whipped dessert topping, thawed**

These cupcakes are made with lemon cake mix. There's strawberry gelatin inside and also in the frosting. They're sure to be a favorite!

Strawberry-Lemonade Cupcakes

Kim—New Whiteland, IN

Ingredients

1 **2-layer-size package lemon cake mix**

1 **6-ounce package strawberry gelatin**

¾ **cup sugar**

2 **egg whites**

⅓ **cup water**

2 **teaspoons light-color corn syrup**

¼ **teaspoon salt**

¼ **teaspoon cream of tartar**

Sliced strawberries (optional)

Lemon twists (optional)

Prep: 40 minutes **Bake:** per package directions **Cook:** 7 minutes

Method

1. Line 24 muffin cups with paper cupcake liners; set aside. Prepare cake mix according to package directions. Spoon batter into prepared muffin cups, filling each half full.

2. Spoon ⅛ teaspoon of the dry gelatin into the center of the batter in each muffin cup; spoon remaining batter over. If desired, sprinkle a little additional dry gelatin on tops; gently swirl into batter. Bake according to package directions.

3. For frosting, in top of a double boiler combine remaining dry gelatin, sugar, egg whites, water, corn syrup, salt, and cream of tartar. Place over rapidly boiling water (do not let water touch the bottom of the pan). Beat with an electric mixer on high speed about 7 minutes or until stiff peaks form. Do not overcook. Remove from heat. Continue to beat about 2 minutes or until frosting holds a deep swirl. Cool frosting in the refrigerator. Spread cooled frosting on cooled cupcakes. If desired, garnish with sliced strawberries and lemon twists.

Makes 24 cupcakes

These brownies topped with walnuts and marshmallows will be a hit with the kids. The melted chocolate drizzle makes them extra yummy.

Rocky Road Brownies

Eve—Olympia, WA

Prep: 25 minutes **Bake:** 28 minutes **Cool:** 10 minutes

Method

1. Preheat oven to 350°F. Coat an 8×8×2-inch baking pan with nonstick cooking spray. Set aside. In a medium bowl combine cocoa powder, flour, baking powder, and salt. In a large bowl whisk together oil, sugars, egg whites, and vanilla until well mixed. Stir cocoa powder mixture into oil mixture. Pour into prepared pan.

2. Bake about 25 minutes or until toothpick inserted in the center comes out clean. Place pan on wire rack; cool for 10 minutes.

3. For topping, in a small saucepan combine chocolate pieces and milk; heat over low heat until chocolate is melted. Sprinkle marshmallows and walnuts over brownies. Drizzle chocolate mixture over top. Return pan to oven for 3 minutes. Cool in pan on wire rack. Cut into squares.

Makes 16 brownies

Ingredients

Nonstick cooking spray

⅔ **cup unsweetened cocoa powder**

½ **cup all-purpose flour**

½ **teaspoon baking powder**

¼ **teaspoon salt**

½ **cup cooking oil**

½ **cup packed light brown sugar**

½ **cup granulated sugar**

4 **egg whites**

1 **teaspoon vanilla**

½ **cup semisweet chocolate pieces**

1 **tablespoon low-fat milk**

1½ **cups tiny marshmallows**

3 **tablespoons chopped walnuts**

What a treat! Make these cakelike brownies with the classic gingerbread ingredients of molasses, ground ginger, and cloves.

Gingerbread Brownies

Linda—San Antonio, TX

Ingredients

1 ½ cups all-purpose flour

1 cup sugar

¼ cup unsweetened cocoa powder

1 teaspoon ground ginger

1 teaspoon ground cinnamon

½ teaspoon baking soda

½ teaspoon ground cloves

¼ cup unsalted butter, melted

⅓ cup molasses

2 eggs

Powdered sugar

Prep: 15 minutes Bake: 20 minutes

Method

1. Preheat oven to 350°F. In a large bowl combine flour, sugar, cocoa powder, ginger, cinnamon, baking soda, and cloves. In a small bowl combine melted butter, molasses, and eggs; add to flour mixture, stirring until combined. Do not beat (the batter will be thick).

2. Spread batter in a greased 13×9×2-inch baking pan. Bake for 20 minutes. Do not overbake. Cool in pan on a wire rack. Dust with powdered sugar sprinkled through a paper doily. Cut into squares.

Makes 24 brownies

Calling all coffee lovers! Here's a bar that will appeal to you—and anybody! Espresso powder is combined with chocolate and beaten into cream cheese for the filling.

Chocolate Espresso Cheesecake Bars

Steffany—Alhambra, CA

Prep: 25 minutes   **Bake:** 55 minutes

Method

1. Preheat oven to 350°F. For crust, in a medium bowl combine chocolate wafer crumbs and butter. Press mixture onto bottom of a 13×9×2-inch baking pan. Bake for 10 minutes. Transfer to wire rack and cool completely.

2. For filling, in a heavy medium saucepan combine whipping cream, chocolate pieces, and espresso powder; cook over low heat until chocolate is melted, stirring frequently. Remove from heat; cool.

3. In a mixing bowl combine cream cheese, sugar, sour cream, and vanilla; beat with an electric mixer on medium speed until smooth. Beat in eggs, one at a time. Stir in cooled chocolate mixture. Pour cream cheese mixture over prepared crust.

4. Bake for 45 minutes. Cool in pan on a wire rack. Cover and chill. Cut into bars.

Makes 24 bars

Ingredients

- 2 cups chocolate wafer crumbs
- 6 tablespoons unsalted butter, melted
- ½ cup whipping cream
- 6 ounces semisweet chocolate pieces
- 2 tablespoons instant espresso coffee powder
- 4 8-ounce packages cream cheese, softened
- 1¼ cups sugar
- ⅓ cup dairy sour cream
- 1 tablespoon vanilla
- 3 eggs

Cook's Notes
For an elegant dessert, serve these bars on dessert plates with chocolate sauce, topped with a rosette of whipped cream and a chocolate-covered espresso bean!

Making Wafer Crumbs There are two ways to make the crumbs for a crumb crust, whether it's out of chocolate or vanilla wafers or graham crackers. You can break them up and quickly pulse them in a food processor. Or you can do it the old-fashioned way: Put the wafers or crackers in a resealable plastic bag, press out all of the air, seal the bag, then crush and roll them with a rolling pin. It works well and is almost mess-free!

Brownie batter—with chopped candy bars folded into it—is drizzled with a cream cheese mixture before baking.

Candy Bar Cookies

Anna—Mebane, NC

Ingredients

1 **18-ounce package brownie mix**

3 **2.05-ounce bars chocolate-covered caramel and nougat, chopped**

1 **8-ounce package cream cheese**

½ **cup sugar**

1 **egg, beaten**

2 **tablespoons milk**

Prep: 20 minutes Bake: 35 minutes

Method

1. Preheat oven to 350°F. Prepare brownie mix according to package directions; stir in chopped candy bars. Pour into a greased 13×9×2-inch baking pan.

2. In a small mixing bowl combine cream cheese and sugar; beat with an electric mixer on low speed until smooth. Add egg and milk to the cream cheese mixture; beat well. Drizzle cream cheese mixture over brownie batter to give a swirled look.

3. Bake for 35 to 40 minutes or until toothpick inserted in center comes out clean. Cool in pan on a wire rack. When cooled, cut into bars with a wet knife.

Makes 20 to 24 cookies

This delectable recipe makes a bunch of cookies, so if you like, freeze them in heavy-duty resealable bags for up to 3 months. See photo on page 221.

Old-Fashioned Sugar Cookies

Susan—Lucerne Valley, CA

Prep: 30 minutes **Chill:** 1 hour **Bake:** 10 minutes per batch **Cool:** 10 minutes **Stand:** 2 minutes

Method

1. In a large bowl combine melted butter, powdered sugar, and 1 cup of the granulated sugar; let cool to room temperature. Beat in eggs, one at a time. Stir in lemon zest, baking soda, cream of tartar, salt, and vanilla. Stir in flour. Chill dough for at least 1 hour or overnight.

2. Preheat oven to 325°F and place rack in middle of oven. Roll pieces of dough into walnut-size balls; roll in the remaining ½ cup granulated sugar. Place balls on greased cookie sheet; flatten balls with the greased bottom of a glass.

3. Bake for 10 to 15 minutes or until brown. Cool on cookie sheet for 2 minutes. Transfer to wire rack to cool completely.

Makes 6 to 7 dozen cookies

Ingredients

2	cups butter, melted
2	cups powdered sugar
1 ½	cups granulated sugar
2	eggs
2	teaspoon grated lemon zest
1	teaspoon baking soda
1	teaspoon cream of tartar
1	teaspoon salt
1	teaspoon vanilla
4 ½	cups all-purpose flour

Tip

Zesting Citrus Any citrus—whether it's lemon, lime, or orange—is easy to zest with a handy tool called a Microplane grater. Just run the citrus peel across the surface and you get very fine citrus zest in no time. It also works great for fresh ginger, garlic cloves; and hard cheeses, such as well-aged Parmesan.

These red-and-white swirled cookies are flavored with almond extract and sprinkled with green sugar crystals before baking.

Almond Swirl Cookies

Kathleen—Wildwood, MO

340

Ingredients

1	cup powdered sugar
½	cup butter, softened
½	cup shortening
½	cup chopped almonds
1	egg
2	teaspoons almond extract
2½	cups all-purpose flour
½	teaspoon salt
½	to 1 teaspoon red food coloring
	Green sugar crystals

Prep: 30 minutes **Bake:** 7 minutes per batch **Stand:** 2 minutes

Method

1. Preheat oven to 375°F. In a large bowl combine powdered sugar, butter, shortening, chopped almonds, egg, and almond extract. Stir in flour and salt.

2. Divide dough in half. Tint half of the dough with red food coloring, ½ teaspoon at a time, to desired darkness. Leave the other half of the dough plain.

3. For each cookie, mold together 1 teaspoonful of the plain cookie dough and 1 teaspoonful of the red cookie dough to give a swirled effect.

4. Place on ungreased cookie sheet and flatten each cookie. Sprinkle with green sugar crystals. If dough gets sticky and hard to handle, refrigerate about 15 minutes.

5. Bake for 7 to 9 minutes or until light brown. Let stand on cookie sheet for 2 minutes. Transfer to wire rack to let cool.

Makes about 3 dozen cookies

These drop cookies feature finely shredded carrots, cinnamon, and walnuts.

Carrot-Spice Cookies

Malinda—Jackson, MS

Prep: 30 minutes **Chill:** 1 hour **Bake:** 8 minutes per batch

Method

1. In a large mixing bowl combine shortening and butter; beat with an electric mixer on medium speed until combined. Beat in brown sugar and granulated sugar. Beat in eggs, one at a time, scraping sides of bowl. Stir in carrots, walnuts, coconut (if desired), and vanilla. In a medium bowl sift together flour, cinnamon, baking powder, baking soda, and salt.

2. Gradually stir flour mixture into carrot mixture, stirring until well mixed. Chill for 1 hour.

3. Preheat oven to 350°F. Drop dough by tablespoons about 2 inches apart onto ungreased cookie sheet. Bake for 8 to 10 minutes or until golden brown around edges. Cool on wire racks.

Makes about 4 dozen cookies

Cook's Notes
For a variation on this cookie, raisins can be stirred into the cookie dough and the cooled baked cookies spread with a cream cheese frosting. To make frosting, beat together 4 ounces cream cheese, 2 cups powdered sugar, 2 tablespoons melted butter, and ½ teaspoon vanilla.

Ingredients

- ½ **cup shortening**
- ½ **cup butter, softened**
- 1 **cup packed brown sugar**
- 1 **cup granulated sugar**
- 2 **eggs**
- 1 **cup finely shredded carrots**
- 1 **cup chopped walnuts**
- ½ **cup coconut (optional)**
- 1 **teaspoon vanilla**
- 2½ **cups all-purpose flour**
- 1 **tablespoon ground cinnamon**
- 1 **teaspoon baking powder**
- 1 **teaspoon baking soda**
- 1 **teaspoon salt**

These cinnamon-honey cookies will literally melt in your mouth.

Cinnamon Melt-Away Cookies

Maggie—Ravenna, OH

Ingredients

¼	cup granulated sugar
1	cup packed brown sugar
¼	cup butter
1	egg
1	tablespoon honey
1½	teaspoons vanilla
2⅓	cups all-purpose flour
2	teaspoons ground cinnamon
1	teaspoon baking soda
1	teaspoon baking powder
1	cup cinnamon chips

Prep: 20 minutes   **Bake:** 8 minutes per batch

Method

1. Preheat oven to 375°F. In a large mixing bowl combine granulated sugar, brown sugar, butter, egg, honey, and vanilla; beat with an electric mixer on medium speed until well mixed. In a medium bowl combine flour, cinnamon, baking soda, and baking powder. Gradually add flour mixture to egg mixture, beating until combined. Stir in cinnamon chips.

2. Line cookie sheet with parchment paper or lightly grease cookie sheet. Drop dough by rounded tablespoonfuls onto prepared cookie sheet. Bake for 8 to 10 minutes or until light brown.

Makes 24 cookies

This light and delicate cookie makes a great holiday treat. If you prefer, leave out the peppermint and just flavor these cookies with chocolate and pecans.

Best Meringue Cookies

Jill—North Canton, OH

Prep: 20 minutes **Bake:** 40 minutes

Method

1. Preheat oven to 250°F. In a small mixing bowl beat egg whites with an electric mixer on high speed until foamy. Add salt and cream of tartar; beat until egg whites form soft peaks, gradually adding sugar while beating. When egg white mixture is stiff, fold in chocolate pieces, pecans, crushed candy (if desired), and vanilla.

2. Drop in small teaspoonfuls onto lightly greased cookie sheets. Bake for 40 minutes. Transfer to wire racks; let cool.

Makes 4 to 5 dozen cookies

Cook's Notes
Sometimes I make two batches (one peppermint, one not) and tint the peppermint batch pink.

Ingredients

- 2 **egg whites (at room temperature)**
- ⅛ **teaspoon salt**
- ⅛ **teaspoon cream of tartar**
- ¾ **cup sugar**
- 1 **cup miniature semisweet chocolate pieces**
- 1 **cup finely chopped pecans**
- 3 **tablespoons crushed peppermint candy canes (optional)**
- ½ **teaspoon vanilla**

All About Meringue Cookies, shells, pie toppings, and frostings can be made from the glossy meringue mixture. Here are some hints to keep meringue at its very best:

- To get great volume, allow the egg whites to stand at room temperature for 30 minutes before beating.

- Always wash bowls and utensils with hot, soapy water. Any amount of oil residue will deflate meringues in an instant.

- If meringue cookies are chewy when removed from the oven, it means they haven't dried out enough. Allow them to stand in the warm, turned-off oven for a while longer.

These tasty truffles—made with rum and dipped in white chocolate—are perfect for tea parties or baby or bridal showers.

Rum Balls for Tea

Edith—Scottsdale, AZ

Ingredients

6 ounces white chocolate, broken up

¼ cup dark rum

3 tablespoons light-color corn syrup

1¼ cups crushed vanilla wafers (about 36)

1 cup finely chopped blanched almonds

½ cup vanilla sugar

White chocolate shavings or melted white dipping chocolate

Prep: 45 minutes   Chill: 3 hours to overnight

Method

1. In top of double boiler melt white chocolate over barely simmering water. When melted, remove from heat. Stir in rum and corn syrup until smooth. Stir in crushed wafers, chopped almonds, and vanilla sugar until well mixed.

2. When cool enough to handle, roll into little balls about the size of filbert nuts. Roll firmly in white chocolate shavings until coated. (Or skewer on a hat pin and dip into melted white dipping chocolate.) Place on waxed paper-lined baking sheet with sides or jelly roll pan.

3. Wrap pan with plastic wrap. Chill in refrigerator for at least 3 hours or overnight. If desired, wrap balls in candy wrappers when cold.

Makes 10 servings

Cook's Notes
My grandma made these for formal teas and very special grown-up occasions.

These tender coconut balls are dipped in melted chocolate for a beautiful (and delicious) candy coating.

Toasted Coconut Balls

Janet—Bricktown, NJ

Prep: 30 minutes **Chill:** 1 hour **Stand:** 1 hour

Method

1. In a large bowl combine powdered sugar and toasted coconut. Mix well.

2. In a small bowl stir together sweetened condensed milk, melted butter, and coconut extract; stir into coconut mixture. Form into 70 balls, each about 1 inch in diameter.

3. Place balls on two waxed paper-lined baking sheets; refrigerate for 1 to 2 hours or until firm.

4. In a medium microwave-safe bowl combine chocolate pieces and oil. Microwave on 100% power (high) for 4 to 4½ minutes or until chocolate is melted and smooth.

5. Dip chilled balls into melted chocolate mixture. Let excess drip off and place on waxed paper-lined baking sheets. Let stand at room temperature about 1 hour or until set. (Balls can be stored in an airtight container in refrigerator for up to 4 weeks.)

Makes 70 balls

Ingredients

- 1 **pound powdered sugar**
- 4 **cups coconut, toasted**
- ⅔ **cup sweetened condensed milk (not evaporated milk)**
- ½ **cup butter, melted**
- 1 **teaspoon coconut extract**
- 3 **cups semisweet chocolate pieces**
- 1½ **tablespoons cooking oil**

Cook's Notes
This is one of my holiday favorites—make them in advance and store for all your holiday get-togethers.

Tip

Toasting Coconut Toasting coconut to a light golden brown brings out its flavor and makes it pretty to look at, too. Because of coconut's high sugar content, it's easy to burn. To toast coconut, spread it out in a single layer in a pan with shallow sides and bake it for about 10 minutes at 325°F, stirring it occasionally.

This fudge recipe can be customized to your tastes with chopped nuts. A foil lining makes it easy to remove the candy from the pan.

Foolproof Fudge

Marie—Goodhue, MN

Ingredients

3 cups semisweet chocolate pieces

1 14-ounce can sweetened condensed milk (not evaporated milk)

Dash salt

½ to 1 cup chopped nuts (optional)

1½ teaspoons vanilla

Prep: 20 minutes Chill: 2 hours

Method

1. Line 8- or 9-inch square pan with foil. Butter foil; set aside.

2. In a heavy medium saucepan combine chocolate pieces, sweetened condensed milk, and salt; heat and stir until chocolate is melted. Remove from heat. Stir in nuts (if desired) and vanilla. Spread evenly in the prepared pan.

3. Chill about 2 hours or until firm. Turn out fudge onto cutting board; peel off foil and cut into squares. Store covered in the refrigerator.

Makes 2 pounds

Sweetened condensed milk is combined with peppermint flavoring, green food coloring, and powdered sugar, then formed into patties and coated with chocolate.

quick Chocolate Peppermint Patties

Diane—Louisville, KY

Start to finish: 30 minutes

Method

1. In a large bowl stir together sweetened condensed milk, peppermint extract, and food coloring. Stir in enough powdered sugar for mixture to form a firm, non-sticky ball. Shape into even-size balls. Flatten to make patties.

2. In a small saucepan heat chocolate and the wax. Skewer the patties with toothpicks, then dip into melted chocolate. Set on a baking sheet and allow chocolate to harden.

Makes 64 patties

Ingredients

2   cups sweetened condensed milk (not evaporated milk)

2   teaspoons peppermint extract

10 drops green food coloring

    About 2 pounds powdered sugar

4   ounces semisweet chocolate

1   ounce edible food wax

This peanut brittle is crunchy, sweet, and salty—just like Mom used to make.

Perfect Peanut Brittle

Charles—Ocoee, FL

Ingredients

2	**cups sugar**
1	**cup light-color corn syrup**
½	**cup water**
¼	**teaspoon salt**
3	**cups raw shelled Spanish peanuts (skins on)**
2	**tablespoons unsalted butter**
1	**teaspoon vanilla**
2	**teaspoons baking soda**

Start to finish: 1 hour

Method

1. In a heavy large saucepan (3 quarts or larger) combine sugar, corn syrup, water, and salt; bring to a rolling boil. Stir in peanuts. Reduce heat to medium. Cook to hard crack stage (300°F to 310°F), stirring constantly.

2. Stir in butter and vanilla. Add baking soda and stir rapidly. (The baking soda will cause contents to quickly increase in size.) Pour onto a very lightly greased baking sheet. Spread to approximately ¼-inch thickness. When cool, break into pieces. Store in an airtight container.

Makes 12 servings

Cook's Notes
To make nice small surprises, place several pieces of peanut brittle on a large square of plastic wrap. Gather and tie at the top with a small piece of festive ribbon.
WARNING: If you make this peanut brittle and share it with others, they will bug you until you do it again.

Chapter 12
Pies & Desserts

Lime juice adds zip to this fruity pudding dessert. Serve it in elegant glasses for an attractive presentation.

Cherry Crunch Cream Parfaits

Patrice—Bemidji, MN

Ingredients

1   20-ounce can crushed pineapple (juice pack), undrained

½   cup nonfat milk

1   teaspoon grated lime zest

1   tablespoon lime juice

1   4-serving-size package sugar-free vanilla instant pudding mix

1½ cups frozen light whipped dessert topping, thawed

1   12-ounce package frozen dark sweet cherries, thawed

⅔   cup chopped pecans, toasted

Prep: 15 minutes Chill: 2 hours

Method

1. Drain pineapple juice into a large bowl. Add milk, lime zest, and lime juice. Sprinkle with dry pudding mix; whisk to mix well. Fold in whipped topping.

2. Add pineapple, cherries, and ½ cup of the pecans; fold all together. Cover and chill for at least 2 hours.

3. To serve, spoon mixture into 8 dessert glasses; sprinkle with remaining toasted pecans.

Makes 8 servings

Cook's Notes
This recipe is so flavorful and satisfying that no one ever guesses that it's light in calories! The different creamy and crunchy ingredients give it an interesting texture.

Choose your favorite flavor of gelatin, mix it with cream cheese and sour cream, and swirl in whipped cream to make this stunning dessert.

Marbled Gelatin Dessert

Zan—Jasper, AL

Prep: 1 hour Chill: 2 hours

Method

1. Prepare gelatin according to package directions. Chill until almost set. Beat with an electric mixer until thick and creamy. Beat in cream cheese and sour cream.

2. In a medium mixing bowl combine whipping cream and sugar substitute; beat with clean beaters of an electric mixer until soft peaks form. Fold into gelatin mixture, creating a marbled effect. Spoon into 8 dessert dishes. Chill for 2 hours.

Makes 8 servings

Cook's Notes
This is a light and refreshing dessert.

Ingredients

- 1 4-serving-size package sugar-free gelatin (any flavor)
- 1 8-ounce tub soft cream cheese
- ½ cup sour cream
- 1 cup whipping cream
- 2 teaspoons sugar substitute

351

This spiced apple pie boasts a sweet, thick glaze and crumbles of streusel over the top.
See photo on page 222.

Apple Crumb Pie

Veronica—Holts Summit, MO

352

Ingredients

1 **recipe Homemade Pastry Shell* or 1 purchased deep-dish 9-inch unbaked pastry shell**

3 **tablespoons all-purpose flour**

1 **teaspoon ground cinnamon**

¼ **teaspoon ground nutmeg**

¼ **teaspoon ground ginger**

⅛ **teaspoon ground allspice**

4 **tablespoons butter, cut into pieces**

5 **cups cored and thinly sliced red and/or green cooking apples**

¼ **cup granulated sugar**

¼ **cup packed dark brown sugar**

¼ **cup all-purpose flour**

¼ **cup packed dark brown sugar**

2 **tablespoons butter, softened**

¼ **teaspoon ground cinnamon**

⅛ **teaspoon ground nutmeg**

⅛ **teaspoon ground ginger**

Dash ground allspice

Prep: 40 minutes Bake: 1 hour

Method

1. Preheat oven to 375°F. Prepare Homemade Pastry Shell. In a small bowl stir together the 3 tablespoons flour, 1 teaspoon cinnamon, ¼ teaspoon nutmeg, ¼ teaspoon ginger, and ⅛ teaspoon allspice. Using a pastry blender, cut in 2 tablespoons of the cut-up butter until coarse crumbs form. In a large bowl stir together apples, granulated sugar, and the ¼ cup brown sugar; stir in flour mixture. Spoon apple mixture into pastry shell; top with the remaining 2 tablespoons cut-up butter.

2. For topping, in a medium bowl stir together the ¼ cup flour, the ¼ cup brown sugar, the 2 tablespoons softened butter, ¼ teaspoon cinnamon, ⅛ teaspoon nutmeg, ⅛ teaspoon ginger, and a dash of allspice. Spoon topping evenly over apple mixture in pastry shell.

3. Cover edge of pie with foil. Bake for 40 minutes. Remove foil; bake for 20 minutes more or until the fruit is tender and filling is bubbly. Cool pie on a wire rack.

*Homemade Pastry Shell: In a medium bowl stir together 1½ cups all-purpose flour and ¼ teaspoon salt. Using a pastry blender, cut in 6 tablespoons shortening until pieces are pea-size. Sprinkle 1 tablespoon cold water over part of flour mixture; gently toss with a fork. Toss moistened pastry to the side of the bowl. Repeat, using 1 tablespoon water at a time, until all the flour mixture is moistened and forms a ball (about 5 to 6 tablespoons water). On a lightly floured surface, slightly flatten pastry. Roll pastry from center to edges into a 12-inch circle. Line a 9-inch deep-dish pie plate with pastry circle. Trim and crimp as desired.

Makes 6 to 8 servings

Fresh pears, blackberries, and raspberries baked in a pie shell make a colorful and delicious dessert.

Pear-Berry Pie

Lisa—Topeka, KS

Prep: 20 minutes **Bake:** 1 hour

Method

1. Preheat oven to 425°F. Let piecrusts stand as directed on package. In a large bowl combine sliced pears, berries, granulated sugar, brown sugar, flour, and cinnamon. Stir in lemon juice and vanilla.

2. Line a 9-inch deep-dish pie plate with one of the unbaked piecrusts, being careful not to stretch piecrust. Spoon pear mixture into crust-lined pie plate. Dab with squares of butter. Cut slits in the remaining piecrust; place on filling. Seal and crimp piecrust edge.

3. Bake for 15 minutes. Reduce oven temperature to 375°F; bake for 45 minutes more.

Makes 6 to 8 servings

Ingredients

1 15-ounce package rolled refrigerated unbaked piecrust (2 crusts)

4 large pears, peeled and sliced

1 pint fresh blackberries

1 pint fresh raspberries

¾ cup granulated sugar

½ cup packed brown sugar

1 tablespoon all-purpose flour

1 teaspoon ground cinnamon

1 tablespoon lemon juice

1 teaspoon vanilla

Butter

Pies & Desserts

353

Serve this ultra-rich pie while still slightly warm or chill it several hours until cold.

Macadamia Fudge Pie

Jeanne—Oxnard, CA

Ingredients

2	eggs
1	16-ounce jar thick hot fudge ice cream topping
⅔	cup sugar
¼	cup butter, melted
1	teaspoon vanilla
1½	cups chopped macadamia nuts, toasted
1	purchased deep-dish 9-inch unbaked pastry shell or 1 recipe Homemade Pastry Shell (page 352)
	Whipped cream (optional)

Prep: 15 minutes   Bake: 40 minutes

Method

1. Preheat oven to 350°F. In a large bowl combine eggs, hot fudge topping, sugar, butter, and vanilla until smooth. Stir in macadamia nuts. Pour into unbaked pastry shell.

2. Bake for 40 to 50 minutes or just until filling is set but center is still slightly jiggly. Cool on wire rack.

3. Serve slightly warm or chilled. If desired, serve with whipped cream.

Makes 8 servings

Cook's Notes
This very rich pie is for people who truly love chocolate and nuts. It is quick and easy to put together.

Everybody's favorite holiday drink makes a stunning appearance in this irresistible pie. A whipped cream topping makes for an attractive presentation.

Eggnog Custard Pie

Kari–Akron, OH

+ +

Prep: 20 minutes **Bake:** 55 minutes

Method

1. Preheat oven to 350°F. In a large bowl beat eggs with a whisk. Add eggnog, granulated sugar, the 2 tablespoons brandy, the vanilla, the ⅛ to ¼ teaspoon nutmeg, and the salt; whisk until well mixed. Pour into pastry shell.

2. Cover with foil and bake for 25 minutes. Remove foil; bake 30 to 40 minutes more or until a knife inserted in center comes out clean. Cool completely.

3. In a small bowl beat whipping cream until soft peaks form. Add powdered sugar and the 1 to 2 teaspoons brandy; beat until stiff peaks form. Spoon whipped cream mixture onto cooled pie; sprinkle with additional nutmeg. Store in refrigerator.

Makes 8 to 12 servings

Ingredients

3   eggs

2   cups dairy eggnog

⅓   cup granulated sugar

2   tablespoons brandy or rum

1   teaspoon vanilla

⅛   to ¼ teaspoon
     ground nutmeg

⅛   teaspoon salt

1   purchased deep-dish 9-inch
     unbaked pastry shell or
     1 recipe Homemade Pastry
     Shell (page 352)

1   cup whipping cream

3   tablespoons
     powdered sugar

1   to 2 teaspoons brandy
     or rum

     Ground nutmeg

Fold pineapple, cherries, strawberries, and bananas into this creamy-sweet mixture, then pile it into graham cracker shells to make a refreshing frozen dessert.

Banana Split Pie

Charlie—Ironton, OH

Ingredients

1 **14-ounce can sweetened condensed milk (not evaporated milk)**

1 **12-ounce container frozen whipped topping, thawed**

1 **15-ounce can crushed pineapple, well drained**

1 **10-ounce jar maraschino cherries, drained**

4 **bananas, sliced and dipped in lemon-lime soda (to deter browning)**

6 **to 8 fresh strawberries, sliced**

2 **graham cracker crumb pie shells**

Chopped nuts (optional)

Prep: 20 minutes Freeze: 1½ hours

Method

1. In a large bowl fold sweetened condensed milk into whipped topping until smooth and creamy. Fold in pineapple, maraschino cherries, bananas, and strawberries.

2. Divide fruit mixture between pie shells, spreading evenly. Cover and freeze about 1½ hours or until firm. If desired, garnish with chopped nuts.

Makes 12 to 14 servings

Cook's Notes
This originally was served in our family as a fruit salad, but we discovered that it made a wonderful "ice cream" pie and it is now a favorite. This can also be made into individual tarts.

This dessert uses packaged brownie bars for its crust and an ice cream filling flavored with raspberry preserves, amaretto, and walnuts. See photo on page 222.

Raspberry Ice Cream Brownie Pie

Bev—Brunswick, MO

+ +

Prep: 20 minutes **Freeze:** 3¼ hours **Stand:** 5 minutes

Method

1. Arrange chopped brownie snack bars in the bottom of a 9- or 10-inch springform pan, pressing into a single layer; freeze for at least 15 minutes. In a small bowl stir together preserves and amaretto; cover and chill ½ cup of the mixture for topping. Stir the remaining preserves mixture and the walnuts into the ice cream. Spread over brownie crust. Cover and freeze for at least 3 hours.

2. To serve, drizzle with reserved preserves mixture; sprinkle with grated chocolate. Let stand for 5 minutes before cutting into wedges. Garnish with fresh raspberries.

Makes 10 servings

Cook's Notes
This recipe calls for all prepared ingredients to make a spectacular dessert.

Ingredients

1 13-ounce package fudge brownie snack bars, chopped

1 12-ounce jar seedless raspberry preserves

⅓ cup amaretto liqueur

½ cup finely chopped walnuts

1½ quarts vanilla ice cream, softened

½ cup grated dark chocolate

   Fresh raspberries

Candy, whipped topping, and ice cream are crowned with hot fudge and caramel in this decadent dessert.

Ice Cream Pie

Dee—North Huntingdon, PA

Ingredients

2   8-ounce containers frozen whipped dessert topping, thawed

9   ice cream sandwiches

1   1½-ounce bar milk chocolate, chopped

4   chocolate-covered peanut butter cups, chopped

½   cup candy-coated chocolate-covered peanuts, chopped

3   tablespoons hot fudge ice cream topping

3   tablespoons caramel ice cream topping

Prep: 20 minutes   Freeze: 2 hours

Method

1. Spoon one container of the whipped topping into the bottom of a 13×9×2-inch baking dish, spreading evenly. Top with ice cream sandwiches, arranging in a single layer. Spoon the remaining container of whipped topping over ice cream sandwiches; sprinkle with chopped chocolate, peanut butter cups, and candy-coated chocolate-covered peanuts.

2. Spoon hot fudge topping and caramel topping into separate small microwave-safe bowls. Microwave each on 100% power (high) about 20 seconds or just until they reach drizzling consistency. Drizzle toppings over dessert; use a fork to swirl slightly. Cover and freeze for at least 2 hours.

Makes 12 servings

Cook's Notes
This simple ice cream cake has a great taste and can be stored in the freezer for weeks.

Blueberries and lemon curd top an almond paste mixture that's flavored with almond extract and vanilla and baked in a piecrust.

Blueberry–Lemon Curd Tart

Jennifer—Pine Beach, NJ

Prep: 20 minutes Bake: 25 minutes Chill: 2 hours

Method

1. Preheat oven to 350°F and place oven rack in middle position. In a small bowl beat almond paste with an electric mixer on low speed until smooth. Beat in butter. Add egg white, vanilla, and almond extract; beat about 4 minutes or until light and fluffy. Spread mixture into the pastry shell.

2. Bake about 25 minutes or until golden brown. Cool in pan on wire rack.

3. Spoon lemon curd on top and spread evenly. Arrange blueberries on top. Chill for at least 2 hours before serving.

Makes 8 servings

Cook's Notes
If you like, serve with vanilla ice cream.

Ingredients

⅓ cup almond paste

3 tablespoons unsalted butter

1 egg white, beaten

½ teaspoon vanilla

½ teaspoon almond extract

1 purchased deep-dish 9-inch unbaked pastry shell or 1 recipe Homemade Pastry Shell (page 352)

1 cup purchased lemon curd

1 pint fresh blueberries, rinsed and drained

These tasty little treats are made with lime juice, lemon peel, and cream cheese and are tinted with a little green food coloring.

Lime Mini Tarts

Pamela—Parkersburg, WV

360

Ingredients

1	**3-ounce package cream cheese**
½	**cup butter**
1	**cup all-purpose flour**
4	**ounces cream cheese**
¼	**cup sugar**
1	**egg**
1	**teaspoon finely shredded lime or lemon peel**
1½	**teaspoons lime juice**
1	**drop green food coloring**
	Whipped cream
	Finely shredded lemon or lime zest

Prep: 25 minutes   **Chill:** 1 hour   **Bake:** 13 minutes

Method

1. In a small mixing bowl combine the 3 ounces cream cheese and the butter; beat with an electric mixer on medium speed until creamy. Add flour; beat until combined. Form dough into a ball; wrap in plastic wrap. Chill for 1 hour.

2. Preheat oven to 350°F. Using a teaspoonful of dough for each, roll dough into small balls. Place each ball of dough into a 1¾-inch muffin cup; using a wooden tart maker or your thumb dipped in flour, press dough into muffin cups to form tart shells.

3. For filling, in a medium bowl combine the 4 ounces cream cheese and the sugar. Add egg; beat until smooth. Stir in lime zest and lime juice; tint with food coloring. Spoon filling into tart shells, using about 1 teaspoon filling for each. Bake for 13 to 15 minutes or until filling is set. Carefully remove tarts from pan; cool on wire rack. Store in refrigerator.

4. Garnish tarts with whipped cream and additional zest.

Makes 16 to 18 mini tarts

Cook's Notes
These are so cute and tasty. They're good to serve at a summer luncheon or tea.

This yummy dessert pizza with chocolate chips and marshmallows is reminiscent of s'mores, the much-loved fireside snack.

quick S'more Cookie Pizza

Kathy – Basking Ridge, NJ

Prep: 15 minutes **Bake:** 14 minutes

Method

1. Preheat oven to 375°F. Press cookie dough into two ungreased 12-inch pizza pans. Bake about 10 minutes or until golden. Remove from oven.

2. In a medium saucepan combine semisweet chocolate pieces and sweetened condensed milk; cook and stir over low heat until chocolate is melted. Spread over crusts. Sprinkle with candy-coated chocolate pieces and marshmallows. Bake about 4 minutes or until marshmallows are lightly toasted; cool. Cut into wedges.

Makes 24 servings

Ingredients

- **1** 18-ounce roll refrigerated sugar-cookie dough
- **2** cups semisweet chocolate pieces
- **1** 14-ounce can sweetened condensed milk (not evaporated milk)
- **2** cups candy-coated milk chocolate pieces
- **2** cups tiny marshmallows

Mixed berries baked over a buttery batter make a sure-to-please dessert—perfect for summer, winter, or any season! See photo on page 223.

Mixed Berry Cobbler

Janet—Keller, TX

Ingredients

2	cups fresh or frozen sliced strawberries
1	cup fresh or frozen raspberries
1	cup fresh or frozen blueberries
1½	cups sugar
1	cup all-purpose flour
½	teaspoon baking powder
½	teaspoon salt
1	cup milk
¼	cup butter

Prep: 20 minutes   Bake: 30 minutes

Method

1. Preheat oven to 375°F. In a medium mixing bowl combine strawberries, raspberries, and blueberries. Add ½ cup of the sugar; mix gently. Set aside.

2. In another medium mixing bowl combine remaining 1 cup sugar, the flour, baking powder, and salt. Add milk; beat with an electric mixer on medium speed about 2 minutes or until smooth.

3. Place butter in a 2-quart casserole. Place casserole in oven to melt butter; remove from oven. Spoon batter evenly over melted butter.

4. Spoon berries over batter; do not stir. Bake 30 to 35 minutes or until golden. Serve cobbler warm or cooled to room temperature.

Makes 6 servings

Here's comfort food at its best—baked peaches with a brown sugar, toffee, and pecan crumb topping.

Toffee Pecan Peach Cobbler

Kanthy—Athens, GA

Prep: 20 minutes   Bake: 40 minutes

Method

1. Preheat oven to 400°F. Place peaches in a large bowl. Sprinkle with the 1 tablespoon granulated sugar; toss. Transfer peaches to two 13×9×2-inch baking dishes.

2. In a large bowl combine flour, pecans, toffee pieces, the ½ cup granulated sugar, and the brown sugar. Add chopped butter; using a pastry blender or fork, cut in butter until small crumbs form (you can add more flour if it is needed). Sprinkle crumb mixture evenly over peaches in both dishes.

3. Bake for 40 minutes. If desired, serve with ice cream and caramel sauce.

Makes 12 servings

Cook's Notes
I like to make this cobbler when I am having a get-together for friends and family because it serves so many. You can also make individual cobblers by evenly distributing the peaches and topping into small soufflé dishes. Just place the individual cobblers onto baking sheets and bake at 400°F for 40 minutes.

Ingredients

5   **pounds frozen unsweetened peach slices, thawed**

1   **tablespoon granulated sugar**

1   **cup all-purpose flour**

1   **cup chopped pecans**

¾   **cup chopped toffee pieces**

½   **cup granulated sugar**

¼   **cup packed brown sugar**

1   **cup butter, chopped into small squares**

Vanilla ice cream (optional)

Purchased caramel sauce (optional)

This dessert features fresh apples, pears, plums, and grapes with a sweet and crunchy topping made with oatmeal and nuts.

Autumn Fruit Crisp

Mona—Livonia, MI

Ingredients

2   cups peeled, cored, and sliced apples (3 to 4 medium apples)

1   cup peeled, cored, and sliced pears (2 medium pears)

1   cup pitted and sliced plums (3 to 4 plums)

1   cup seedless red or green grapes

¾   cup all-purpose flour

⅓   cup granulated sugar

1   teaspoon ground cinnamon

¼   teaspoon ground nutmeg

1   cup quick-cooking rolled oats

⅓   cup packed light brown sugar

2   tablespoons chopped walnuts or pecans

¼   cup unsalted butter, melted

    Vanilla ice cream or whipped cream (optional)

Prep: 35 minutes   **Bake:** 25 minutes

Method

1. Preheat oven to 350°F. In a medium bowl combine fruit; set aside.

2. In a small bowl stir together ¼ cup of the flour, the granulated sugar, ½ teaspoon of the cinnamon, and the nutmeg. Add mixture to the fruit; toss until well mixed. Spoon into an 8×8×2-inch baking dish

3. For topping, in another small bowl stir together rolled oats, the remaining ½ cup flour, the brown sugar, walnuts, and the remaining ½ teaspoon cinnamon. Stir in melted butter. Sprinkle oat topping over fruit mixture.

4. Bake for 25 to 30 minutes or until filling is bubbly and top is golden brown. Serve warm. If desired, serve with vanilla ice cream.

Makes 6 servings

Cook's Notes
This recipe can easily be doubled and baked in a 13×9×2-inch baking dish.

Ginger flavors the dumplings as well as the sauce in this dessert. Pineapple, mandarin oranges, and raisins give the sauce a tropical twist.

Gingered Fruit and Dumplings

Roxanne—Albany, CA

Prep: 30 minutes **Cook:** 20 minutes

Method

1. For dumpling batter, in a medium bowl combine flour, brown sugar, baking powder, and ground ginger. Using a pastry blender, cut in butter until the mixture is crumbly. Add the egg and ⅓ cup of the orange juice; stir until evenly moistened. Set aside.

2. In a blender combine mandarin orange segments, marmalade, and the remaining orange juice. Cover and blend until smooth. Pour into a 12-inch skillet. Stir in undrained pineapple, raisins, and lemon juice. Bring to boiling. Drop the dumpling batter by tablespoons into the bubbling sauce, making 8 dumplings in all. Cover; reduce heat to low. Cook about 20 minutes or until toothpick inserted in dumplings comes out clean (do not lift cover during cooking).

3. To serve, spoon dumplings into dessert dishes. Stir crystallized ginger and almonds into the sauce and spoon sauce over and around the dumplings.

Makes 8 servings

Cook's Notes
This is a quick and easy dessert, yet it's impressive enough for company. If desired, serve it with frozen yogurt or ice cream.

Ingredients

1	cup all-purpose flour
2	tablespoons packed brown sugar
1 ½	teaspoons baking powder
½	teaspoon ground ginger
3	tablespoons butter
1	egg
½	cup orange juice
2	15-ounce cans mandarin orange segments, drained
½	cup orange marmalade
1	8-ounce can crushed pineapple (juice pack), undrained
½	cup raisins
1	tablespoon lemon juice
¼	cup finely chopped crystallized ginger
¼	cup sliced almonds

What's Crystallized Ginger? Crystallized ginger is fresh ginger that has been candied—cooked in a sugar syrup and then coated in coarse sugar. It has an intense, sweet, slightly fiery ginger taste and crunchy texture. Look for it in the baking or gourmet section of your grocery store. It is usually sold in small chunks; it is easily minced in a food processor, mini chopper, or electric coffee mill.

This comfort food is made with bread cubes, milk, eggs, butter, and nutmeg and served with a divine vanilla sauce.

Old-Fashioned Bread Pudding

Emily—Forked River, NJ

Ingredients

4	cups cubed white bread
½	cup raisins
2	cups milk
¾	cup butter
1	cup granulated sugar
2	eggs, lightly beaten
2	teaspoons vanilla
½	teaspoon ground nutmeg
½	cup packed brown sugar
½	cup whipping cream

Prep: 20 minutes Stand: 10 minutes Bake: 40 minutes

Method

1. Preheat oven to 350°F. For pudding, in a large bowl combine bread and raisins. In 1-quart saucepan combine milk and ¼ cup of the butter; cook and stir until butter has melted. Pour milk mixture over bread; let stand for 10 minutes. Stir in ½ cup of the granulated sugar, eggs, 1 teaspoon of the vanilla, and the nutmeg. Pour into greased 1½-quart casserole. Bake for 40 to 50 minutes or until set in center.

2. Meanwhile, for vanilla sauce, in a small saucepan combine the remaining ½ cup granulated sugar, the brown sugar, whipping cream, and the remaining ½ cup butter. Cook over medium heat for 5 to 8 minutes or until mixture thickens and comes to a full boil, stirring occasionally. Stir in the remaining 1 teaspoon vanilla. Serve sauce over warm pudding.

Makes 6 servings

Heavenly treat indeed! Sweetened with sugar and marshmallows, with pineapple and maraschino cherries stirred in, this is sure to make it onto your "favorites" list.

Heavenly Rice

Tim—Lake, MI

Prep: 45 minutes Chill: 1 hour

Method

1. Cook rice according to package directions. Stir marshmallows and sugar into hot rice; cool.

2. Stir pineapple and maraschino cherries into cooled rice. Fold in dessert topping. Tint pink with red food coloring. Chill for 1 hour before serving.

Makes 10 to 12 servings

Cook's Notes
I usually double this recipe because my six children always want me to make it for holidays and big get-togethers.

Ingredients

1	**cup long grain rice**
8	**ounces tiny marshmallows**
½	**cup sugar**
1	**8-ounce can crushed pineapple, drained**
1	**8-ounce jar maraschino cherries, drained and chopped**
1	**8-ounce container frozen whipped dessert topping, thawed**
	Red food coloring

This luscious fudge pudding cake is spiced with cinnamon. Top warm pieces of cake with scoops of vanilla ice cream for a taste sensation second to none.

Hot Fudge Pudding

Donna—Chesapeake, VA

Ingredients

- 1 cup all-purpose flour
- ⅔ cup granulated sugar
- ½ cup unsweetened cocoa powder
- 2 teaspoons baking powder
- 1 teaspoon ground cinnamon
- ½ teaspoon salt
- ½ cup milk
- 2 tablespoons butter or margarine, melted
- 1 teaspoon vanilla
- 1 cup packed brown sugar
- 1½ cups boiling water
- Vanilla ice cream (optional)

Prep: 15 minutes Bake: 30 minutes Cool: 10 minutes

Method

1. Preheat oven to 350°F. Grease an 8×8×2-inch baking dish or shallow 2-quart casserole

2. In a medium bowl combine flour, granulated sugar, ¼ cup of the cocoa powder, baking powder, cinnamon, and salt. Whisk in milk, melted butter, and vanilla just until smooth. Spread batter into prepared baking dish.

3. In a small bowl combine brown sugar and the remaining ¼ cup cocoa powder; sprinkle evenly over batter. Carefully pour the boiling water over cocoa mixture in baking dish. Do not stir.

4. Bake for 30 minutes (batter will separate into cake and pudding layers). Cool in pan on wire rack for 10 minutes. Serve warm in dessert bowls. If desired, serve with ice cream.

Makes 6 servings

A rich egg custard made with whipping cream and a vanilla bean is poured over semisweet chocolate in small dessert cups.

Chocolate Chip Crème Brûlée

Linda–San Antonio, TX

Prep: 25 minutes **Bake:** 25 minutes **Chill:** 3 hours

Method

1. Preheat oven to 350°F. Divide the ½ cup chocolate pieces among six 4-ounce ramekins or ovenproof dessert cups. In a small saucepan, heat whipping cream and vanilla bean until nearly boiling, stirring or whisking frequently. Do not boil.

2. In a medium bowl whisk together eggs, egg yolks, and granulated sugar until frothy. While whisking, pour heated cream into sugar mixture. Remove vanilla bean. Strain mixture back into the saucepan. Cook over low heat, stirring constantly, until thick enough to coat the back of a spoon. Stir in vanilla. Pour egg mixture into ramekins.

3. Set ramekins in a baking dish and fill dish with hot water that reaches halfway up the sides of the ramekins. Bake for 25 to 30 minutes or until knife inserted in centers comes out clean. Let ramekins cool, then cover and chill for 3 hours.

4. Just before serving, preheat broiler. Press the brown sugar through a sieve onto surface of custards. Broil 3 to 4 minutes or until brown sugar starts to caramelize. Garnish with mint leaves and additional chocolate pieces.

Makes 6 servings

Ingredients

- ½ cup miniature semisweet chocolate chips pieces
- 3 cups whipping cream
- 1 vanilla bean, split lengthwise
- 2 eggs
- 4 egg yolks
- ¼ cup granulated sugar
- 1 teaspoon vanilla
- ¼ cup packed light brown sugar
- 8 fresh mint leaves

  Miniature semisweet chocolate pieces

Tip

Using Vanilla Beans Nothing compares to the wonderfully intense vanilla flavor that comes from using real vanilla beans. To split the bean, lay it flat side down on a hard surface and cut it lengthwise with the tip of a paring knife. For extra vanilla flavor, scrape out the tiny seeds into the cream before adding the split bean. You'll still need to remove the bean when it's done steeping in the cream, but the tiny seeds will add taste and eye appeal to the finished dessert.

This frozen mixture is topped with a pomegranate syrup and coconut. Cream cheese gives the mousse a rich, smooth texture.

Frozen Tropical Mousse

Laurie—Lynden, WA

Ingredients

1 **cup whipping cream**

⅓ **cup powdered sugar**

4 **ounces cream cheese, softened**

2 **tablespoons sour cream**

1 **10- to 12-ounce jar pineapple curd or lemon curd**

1 **cup pomegranate juice**

⅓ **cup granulated sugar**

¼ **cup coconut, toasted**

Prep: 20 minutes Freeze: 4 hours

Method

1. In a large bowl beat whipping cream until soft peaks form. Add powdered sugar, cream cheese, and sour cream. Whip until stiff peaks form. Fold in pineapple curd. Pour mixture into an 8×8×2-inch baking pan. Freeze for 4 hours.

2. In a small saucepan combine pomegranate juice and granulated sugar. Bring to boiling; boil until reduced to ½ cup. Set aside.

3. To serve, scoop frozen mixture into 6 sundae bowls. Pour pomegranate juice mixture over. Sprinkle with toasted coconut.

Makes 6 servings

Chocolate sandwich cookies layered with ice cream, chocolate sauce, and peanuts makes an ooey-gooey frozen treat. Kids will love it! See photo on page 223.

Chocolate-Peanut Ice Cream Dessert

Vicki—Dowagiac, MI

Prep: 30 minutes   **Freeze:** 2 hours

Method

1. In a small saucepan combine powdered sugar, evaporated milk, chocolate pieces, and the ⅓ cup butter. Bring to boiling; cook and stir for 8 minutes. Stir in vanilla; cool.

2. Soften ice cream. Crush cookies and mix with the ½ cup melted butter.

3. In a 13×9×2-inch baking pan layer in order: cookie mixture, softened ice cream, peanuts, cooled chocolate mixture, and caramel topping. Freeze for at least 2 hours before serving.

Makes 12 to 15 servings

Ingredients

1 ½   cups powdered sugar

1   cup evaporated milk

½   cup semisweet chocolate pieces

⅓   cup butter

1 ½   teaspoons vanilla

½   gallon vanilla ice cream

25   chocolate sandwich cookies with white filling

½   cup butter, melted

1 ½   cups Spanish peanuts, slightly crushed

2   cups caramel ice cream topping

This elegant dessert features a light lemon-flavored custard on a meringue shell topped with whipped cream and coconut.

Lemon Meringue Dessert

Hildegarde–Sioux Falls, SD

Ingredients

6	egg whites
1½	teaspoons lemon juice
½	teaspoon vanilla
	Dash salt
3½	cups granulated sugar
¾	cup lemon juice
12	egg yolks
2	tablespoons cornstarch
½	teaspoon salt
2	cups whipping cream
3	tablespoons powdered sugar
	Flaked coconut

Prep: 30 minutes **Bake:** 2 hours **Cool:** 30 minutes **Chill:** overnight

Method

1. For meringue crust, preheat oven to 275°F. Grease the bottom of a 13×9×2-inch baking dish; set aside. In a large bowl combine egg whites, the 1½ teaspoons lemon juice, the vanilla, and pinch of salt; beat with an electric mixer on medium speed until soft peaks form. Add 2 cups of the granulated sugar; beat until stiff peaks form. Spoon egg white mixture into prepared baking dish. Bake for 2 hours. Shut off oven but leave baking dish in oven overnight.

2. For custard, in the top of a double boiler combine the remaining 1½ cups granulated sugar, the ¾ cup lemon juice, the egg yolks, cornstarch, and the ½ teaspoon salt. Place over boiling water (upper pan should not touch water); cook until thickened, stirring frequently. Remove from heat; cool for 30 minutes.

3. Spread custard over meringue crust. In a medium bowl combine whipping cream and powdered sugar; beat with an electric mixer on medium speed until soft peaks form. Spread whipped cream mixture over custard. Sprinkle with coconut. Chill overnight before serving.

Makes 15 servings

Tip

Beating Egg Whites Mile-high meringue depends on fluffy egg whites—and the fluffiest egg whites are made when there isn't a speck of fat in them. When beating egg whites, take great care when separating the eggs not to get any yolk in them!

Sliced apples are cooked in juice that is flavored with coffee powder then spooned into crepes, rolled, and topped with a ricotta cheese mixture.

quick French Apple Crepes

Rosemarie—New Port Richey, FL

Start to finish: 30 minutes

Method

1. Slice each apple quarter into ⅛-inch slices. In a heavy medium saucepan combine apples, 1 tablespoon of the coffee powder, and apple juice; bring to a simmer. Cover and cook over low heat about 15 minutes or until apples are tender. Uncover; increase heat to high. Cook about 2 minutes or until some of the juice evaporates. Set aside until lukewarm.

2. Microwave each crepe on 100% power (high) about 10 seconds or just until warm. Place each crepe on a dessert plate. Spoon one-quarter of the cooked apples down one side of each crepe. Roll from the filled side to form a cigar shape.

3. Beat ricotta cheese with a hand mixer or fork about 1 minute to soften. Gently fold in the remaining 2 tablespoons coffee powder, the whipped topping, and cinnamon. Spoon one-quarter of ricotta mixture over each crepe.

Makes 4 servings

Cook's Notes
You may use other fruit if you like.

Ingredients

2 large apples (such as Golden Delicious or Gala, peeled, cored, and quartered)

3 tablespoons instant Austrian-style coffee powder

2 tablespoons apple juice

4 dessert crepes (purchased or homemade)

½ cup ricotta cheese

½ cup frozen whipped topping, thawed

1 teaspoon ground cinnamon

Strawberries are dipped in a prepared no-bake cheesecake mixture. After it sets, the berries are dipped in melted chocolate to create the second layer.

Chocolate Cheesecake Strawberries

Joanna—Davisburg, MI

374

Ingredients

2 16-ounce packages medium to large fresh strawberries, cleaned but with the green tops still attached

1 11.2-ounce package no-bake cheesecake

1 7-ounce container dipping chocolate

Prep: 35 minutes **Chill:** 40 minutes

Method

1. Wash and dry strawberries; they must be completely dry before beginning. Lay berries out on waxed-paper-lined trays or baking sheets, spacing them 1 to 1½ inches apart.

2. Prepare the cheesecake mix according to package directions, except do not prepare the crust. (Save crust for another use or discard it.) Let mixture stand for 3 to 5 minutes or until it thickens slightly.

3. Hold a strawberry by its top and dip it into the cheesecake mixture, covering berry to just under the leafy top. Place on prepared tray. Repeat to dip all the berries. Refrigerate for 10 to 15 minutes. (This will help set the cheesecake.)

4. Remove the tray from the refrigerator and set aside. Melt the dipping chocolate according to package directions. Dip cheesecake-covered berries, one at a time, in chocolate to coat. Place the strawberries back on the tray and refrigerate for 30 minutes.

Makes 20 to 30 strawberries

Cook's Notes
If you don't want to add the layer of melted chocolate, these berries are wonderful just covered in the cheesecake. If you are serving more than 10 people, you may want to double the recipe. Trust me, your friends and family won't be able to put these down!

Surprise guests with bruschetta that's sweet instead of savory. Besides being delicious, this treat is superfast and easy to make.

Sweet Berry Bruschetta

Patricia—Portola Valley, CA

Start to finish: 15 minutes

Method

1. Preheat oven to 350°F. Lightly coat baguette slices with nonstick cooking spray; sprinkle with sugar. Bake until golden.

2. Meanwhile, mix together cream cheese and almond extract; spread on toasted baguette slices. Top with berries, almonds, and powdered sugar.

Makes 4 to 8 servings

Ingredients

8   baguette slices

    Nonstick cooking spray

2   tablespoons sugar

1   8-ounce package nonfat cream cheese

½   to 1 teaspoon almond extract

1   cup fresh blackberries (or a mixture of blackberries, raspberries, and sliced strawberries)

¼   cup slivered almonds

    Powdered sugar

For a fun and healthful after-school snack, halved bananas are brushed with honey and rolled in nuts, coconut, and/or cookie crumbs, then wrapped and frozen.

Frosty Banana Pops

Michelle–Billings, MT

Ingredients

6 firm bananas, peeled

12 wooden craft sticks

Honey

Assorted toppings (such as chopped nuts, shredded coconut, and cookie crumbs)

Prep: 15 minutes Freeze: 1 hour

Method

1. Cut each banana in half crosswise. Insert a stick in the cut end of each half.

2. Using a pastry brush, brush honey over bananas. Roll each banana in desired toppings.

3. Arrange on plate; cover with plastic wrap. Freeze for a least 1 hour.

Makes 12 servings

Cook's Notes
These are fun for parties. You can try other toppings.

Chapter 13
Holiday

For a creepy Halloween treat, cut a block of cream cheese to look like a severed hand. A raspberry preserves mixture is poured over the top for an eerie but tasty dip.

Severed Hand Raspberry Dip (quick)

Nancy—Houston, TX

Ingredients

1	8-ounce package cream cheese
5	smoked almonds
1	cup raspberry preserves
1 ½	tablespoons adobo sauce from canned chipotle peppers in adobo sauce
1 ½	tablespoons raspberry vinegar
	Wheat or melba toast

Start to finish: 15 minutes

Method

1. Place cream cheese in center of serving platter. Using a sharp knife, cut four equally spaced lengthwise slits in cream cheese approximately halfway down the block of cream cheese, cutting all the way through the block of cream cheese.

2. Using your hands, shape five "fingers" from the cut sections of the cream cheese. Round off opposite end of block of cream cheese to resemble palm of hand. Place a smoked almond at the tip of each finger to resemble fingernail. In a small bowl stir together raspberry preserves, adobo sauce, and raspberry vinegar. Pour preserves mixture over palm end of cream cheese. Serve with wheat or melba toast.

Makes 10 to 12 servings

These popular Christmas cookies are loaded with dried cherries, almonds, and white baking pieces. They're perfect to bring to a holiday cookie exchange.

Cherry-Almond Chewies

Sally—Shelby Township, MI

Prep: 20 minutes Freeze: 15 minutes Bake: 10 minutes per batch

Method

1. Preheat oven to 350°F. In a large mixing bowl combine butter and the sugars; beat with an electric mixer on medium speed until creamy. Beat in eggs, vanilla, and almond extract. In a medium bowl stir together flour, salt, baking powder, and baking soda; stir into the butter mixture. Stir in dried cherries, almonds, and white baking pieces. Place bowl in freezer for 15 minutes.

2. Drop dough by spoonfuls onto cookie sheets (line with parchment paper if you wish). Place on center rack of oven; bake for 10 to 12 minutes or until light golden brown. Cool slightly before removing from cookie sheet.

Makes 36 to 48 cookies

Cook's Notes
If cherries are sticky when chopping, dust them with a little powdered sugar.

Ingredients

1 **cup butter**

¾ **cup granulated sugar**

¾ **cup packed light brown sugar**

2 **eggs**

1 **teaspoon vanilla**

1 **teaspoon almond extract**

2½ **cups all-purpose flour**

¼ **teaspoon salt**

1 **teaspoon baking powder**

½ **teaspoon baking soda**

1½ **cups dried cherries, chopped**

1 **cup chopped almonds**

1 **cup white baking pieces**

379

This Thanksgiving sauce is made by cooking fresh cranberries in a sugary syrup. For extra flavor, it is then spiked with candied orange peel and crystallized ginger.

Simply Divine Cranberry Sauce

Barbara—Chapel Hill, NC

Ingredients

1   12-ounce package
    fresh cranberries

¾   cup sugar

¾   cup water

⅓   cup chopped candied
    orange peel

¼   cup diced
    crystallized ginger

Prep: 15 minutes   Cool: 1 hour

Method

1. In a large saucepan combine cranberries, sugar, and water; bring to boiling, stirring frequently. Cook at medium boil for 4 to 5 minutes or until sauce thickens, stirring constantly.

2. Remove from heat; stir in orange peel and ginger. Let stand at room temperature about 1 hour or until cooled, stirring occasionally. Serve at room temperature, or refrigerate until ready to serve.

Makes 6 to 8 servings

Croissants are toasted and crumbled to make this decadent Thanksgiving stuffing. Celery, red onion, and water chestnuts are added for crunch and sensational flavor.

Croissant and Water Chestnut Stuffing

Melissa—Shawano, WI

Prep: 25 minutes Bake: 30 minutes

Method

1. Preheat oven to 350°F. Place split croissants on baking sheet; bake 5 to 10 minutes or until crisp. Remove and let cool; coarsely crumble into a large bowl.

2. In a medium skillet cook celery, red onion, and water chestnuts in hot olive oil and butter until celery is tender. Add salt and pepper to taste. Add 1 cup chicken broth and the sage; simmer for 2 minutes.

3. Toss broth mixture with croissant pieces; add enough additional broth to moisten as desired. Place in a 2-quart casserole. If desired, sprinkle top with Parmesan cheese. Bake for 30 to 45 minutes or until firm and slightly crisp on top.

Makes 6 to 8 servings

Cook's Notes
Keep the croissants crumbled in larger pieces. Use lots of black pepper and not too much salt. Add fresh grated Parmesan cheese on the top of the casserole, if you wish.

Ingredients

12	large croissants, split
1	stalk celery, chopped
1	small red onion, chopped
1	8-ounce can water chestnuts, chopped
1	tablespoon olive oil
1	tablespoon butter
	Salt
	Black pepper
1	to 2 cups chicken broth
1	teaspoon ground sage
	Grated Parmesan cheese (optional)

Tip

Peeling Celery Most stuffing and dressing recipes include celery as an ingredient. If you're not a fan of the fibrous strings on celery—whether you're eating it cooked or raw—it's easy to remove them. Just run a vegetable peeler down the rounded side of each celery stalk, from top to bottom, and the strings will peel right off.

Soaking your Thanksgiving turkey in a brine of water, maple syrup, salt, and brown sugar will make it moist and slightly sweet.

Maple-Brined Turkey

Traci—Port Jervis, NY

Ingredients

24	cups water
1½	cups maple-flavor syrup
1	cup coarse salt
¾	cup packed brown sugar
1	10-pound turkey
	Cooking oil

Prep: 20 minutes Marinate: 12 hours Roast: 2¾ hours

Method

1. In a stockpot large enough to hold turkey combine water, syrup, salt, and brown sugar; stir to dissolve salt and sugar. Rinse turkey. Carefully add turkey to brine. Cover and marinate in the refrigerator for 12 to 24 hours.

2. Preheat oven to 325°F. Remove turkey from brine; discard brine. Rinse turkey; pat dry with paper towels. Place turkey, breast up, on a rack in a shallow roasting pan. Brush with oil. Cover turkey loosely with foil.

3. Roast for 2¾ to 3 hours or until instant-read thermometer inserted in center of an inside thigh muscle registers 180°F, removing foil after first 2¼ hours. Cover turkey and let stand at room temperature for 20 minutes before carving.

Makes 12 servings

Tip

Benefits of Brining Brining, which is soaking meat or poultry in a bath of water, salt, and sometimes sugar and other flavorings, has multiple benefits. The salt solution begins to break down the proteins in the meat, making it more tender. The salt also helps the meat absorb the water, plumping it up and making it superjuicy, even after cooking. The other elements—sugar and seasonings—help flavor the meat. If you've never tried brining, you'll be amazed at the results.

By roasting the turkey breast side down, the juices from the dark meat constantly baste the white meat—with moist and succulent results.

Jim's Upside-Down Thanksgiving Turkey

Marla—Moriarty, NM

Prep: 30 minutes **Roast:** 3 hours **Cool:** 15 minutes

Method

1. Preheat oven to 350°F. For stuffing, in a very large bowl combine bread, broth, bacon, sausage, apple, celery, raisins, cranberries, sage, garlic powder, ½ teaspoon sea salt, and ¼ teaspoon pepper. After removing giblets from cavities, pack as much stuffing as will fit nicely inside the turkey. Put any remaining stuffing in a casserole dish. Cover with foil.

2. Close cavities with skewers. Carefully place turkey in oven bag (helping hands are good for this). Sprinkle flour, additional salt, and additional pepper in and around turkey. Close oven bag. Place turkey in bag breast side down in large roasting pan. Cut a few slits in top of bag. Roast for 3 to 3½ hours or until instant-read thermometer inserted in center of an inside thigh muscle registers 180°F. Place extra stuffing in oven when about 1 hour roasting remains.

3. Remove turkey and extra stuffing from oven. Cool about 15 minutes. Carefully remove turkey from oven bag; if desired, save juices for gravy. Remove stuffing; carve turkey.

Makes 10 to 12 servings

Cook's Notes
What started out as a mistake has become a family tradition. One year my husband volunteered to make the turkey for Thanksgiving. When he got up early to put the turkey in the oven, he accidentally put it in upside down. It turned out to be the moistest turkey ever! Every year since then, we purposely put our Thanksgiving turkey in the oven upside down (breast side down) and enjoy this delicious treat!

Ingredients

5	cups cubed dry bread
2	cups reduced-sodium chicken broth (or broth from boiling the giblets, except the liver, with celery tops)
1	cup crumbled cooked bacon
1	cup cooked maple-sage sausage
1	cup diced unpeeled red apple
1	cup diced celery
½	cup raisins
½	cup dried cranberries
1	teaspoon dried sage
½	teaspoon garlic powder
	Sea salt
	Black pepper
1	16- to 20-pound turkey
1	cooking bag for a large turkey
3	tablespoons all-purpose flour

This sweet potato casserole is a must-have recipe for any Thanksgiving or Christmas dinner. If you want leftovers, be sure to make extra!

Sweet Potato Casserole

Sue—Oviedo, FL

Ingredients

3 large cooked sweet potatoes, cut into small pieces

1 cup granulated sugar

2 eggs

½ cup melted butter

⅓ cup milk

1 teaspoon vanilla

1 cup packed light brown sugar

1 cup chopped pecans

⅓ cup all-purpose flour

⅓ cup butter, softened

Prep: 30 minutes   Bake: 25 minutes

Method

1. Preheat oven to 350°F. In a food processor combine sweet potato, granulated sugar, eggs, ½ cup melted butter, milk, and vanilla; cover and process until smooth. Spoon into a greased 1½-quart casserole.

2. For topping, in a medium bowl combine brown sugar, pecans, flour, and ⅓ cup softened butter, stirring with a fork until crumbly. Sprinkle over sweet potato mixture in casserole.

3. Bake about 25 minutes or until hot in center.

Makes 8 servings

Cook's Notes
The topping mixture could be halved and probably would be enough.

Looking for something new to do with yummy sweet potatoes? Here a mashed sweet potato mixture is piped into mounds, sprinkled with pecans, and baked.

Stuffed Sweet Potato Bundles

Pamela—Parkersburg, WV

Prep: 20 minutes Cook: 25 minutes Bake: 10 minutes

Method

1. Preheat oven to 350°F. Peel and rinse sweet potatoes; cut into cubes. In a large covered saucepan cook sweet potatoes in boiling water about 25 minutes or until tender. Drain; add brown sugar, butter, and cinnamon. Stir in ¾ cup of the pecans. Mix with potato masher or mixer; stir in egg.

2. Line baking sheet with parchment paper. Place potato mixture in a large pastry bag; pipe into cone-shaped mounds on the parchment paper. Sprinkle remaining pecans over. Bake about 10 minutes or until set in center.

Makes 6 servings

Cook's Notes
These are rich tasting and turn out so pretty.

Ingredients

4   medium sweet potatoes

1   cup packed brown sugar

¼   cup butter

½   teaspoon ground cinnamon

1   to 1 ¼ cups chopped pecans

1   egg, beaten

Bite-size tassies are a Christmas classic, and this tasty version is sure to become a new favorite. Rich pastry shells are filled with pumpkin, cranberries, and spices.

Pumpkin-Cranberry Tassies

Carole—Cleveland, OH

Ingredients

½   **cup unsalted butter, softened**

1   **3-ounce package cream cheese, softened**

1   **cup all-purpose flour**

¾   **cup packed light brown sugar**

¼   **cup canned pumpkin (not pumpkin pie filling)**

2   **tablespoons unsalted butter, melted and cooled**

1   **egg yolk**

1   **tablespoon whipping cream**

1   **teaspoon vanilla**

⅛   **teaspoon ground cinnamon**

⅛   **teaspoon ground nutmeg**

3   **tablespoons dried cranberries, finely chopped**

½   **cup pecans, finely chopped**

Prep: 40 minutes   Bake: 23 minutes   Cool: 10 minutes

Method

1. Preheat oven to 325°F. Grease 24 miniature muffin cups; set aside.

2. In a small mixing bowl combine ½ cup softened butter and cream cheese; beat with an electric mixer on medium speed until fluffy. Beat in flour. Shape into 24 balls. Place one ball in each prepared muffin cup. Using your fingers, press dough onto the bottom and up sides of each muffin cup. Bake for 8 to 10 minutes or until edges of dough are light brown. Remove muffin cups from oven.

3. Meanwhile, for filling, in a medium bowl combine brown sugar, pumpkin, 5 teaspoons of the melted butter, the egg yolk, whipping cream, vanilla, cinnamon, and nutmeg. Stir until smooth. Mix in cranberries. Spoon into warm shells. In a small bowl stir together the nuts and the remaining 1 teaspoon melted butter. Sprinkle over the filled cups.

4. Bake for 23 to 26 minutes or until the filling is set. Remove from oven and cool in pan for 10 minutes. Run a knife around edges of muffin cups to loosen. Transfer to wire racks and cool completely.

Makes 24 cookies

Cook's Notes
These are perfect for your holiday cookie trays.

This Christmas recipe is special enough for any company! Roasted duck breast is served with a sauce of ground hazelnuts, pumpkin, and pomegranate juice.

Seared Duck with Pomegranate Sauce

Josie–Chicago, IL

Prep: 30 minutes **Cook:** 40 minutes **Roast:** 5 minutes **Stand:** 10 minutes

Method

1. Preheat oven to 450°F for sauce, spread hazelnuts in a single layer on a baking sheet; bake about 10 minutes or until toasted. Rub skins off with a kitchen towel. In a food processor finely chop toasted hazelnuts. Add pomegranate juice, pumpkin, sugar, the 1 teaspoon salt, the cinnamon, and saffron water. Process until smooth. Transfer sauce to a medium saucepan; simmer, uncovered, over low heat for 40 minutes, stirring occasionally. Mix the butter into the sauce. Keep warm.

2. Meanwhile, score skin of duck breasts in crisscross pattern (do not cut through to meat). Sprinkle duck with additional salt and pepper. Heat a heavy large ovenproof skillet over high heat. Add duck breasts, skin sides down, to dry skillet. Reduce heat to medium; cook about 7 minutes or until skin is golden brown. Turn duck over; transfer skillet to oven and roast for 5 to 10 minutes or until duck is done (155°F.). Transfer duck to cutting board; cover loosely with foil. Let stand for 10 minutes.

3. To serve, cut duck breasts crosswise into ½-inch slices; serve over rice and top with the sauce. If desired, garnish with pomegranate seeds and chives.

Makes 4 servings

Cook's Notes
The savory sauce can be made a day ahead of time and gently reheated while the duck is cooking.

Ingredients

8 **ounces hazelnuts**

3 **cups pomegranate juice**

½ **cup canned pumpkin**

1 **tablespoon sugar**

1 **teaspoon salt**

½ **teaspoon ground cinnamon**

¼ **teaspoon ground saffron threads dissolved in 1 tablespoon hot water**

1 **tablespoon butter**

4 **boneless duck breast halves with skin (about 1½ pounds total)**

   Salt

   Ground black pepper

   Hot cooked rice

   Pomegranate seeds (optional)

   Fresh chives (optional)

This sweet bread ring, filled with cinnamon and walnuts, will become a new favorite holiday tradition.

Holiday Ring

Hildegarde—Sioux Falls, SD

Ingredients

¼ cup warm water

1 tablespoon granulated sugar

1 package fast-rising active dry yeast

1 cup milk

½ cup shortening

½ cup granulated sugar

1 teaspoon salt

4 cups all-purpose flour

4 eggs, beaten

½ cup melted butter

¾ cup chopped walnuts

½ cup granulated sugar

2 tablespoons ground cinnamon

1 recipe Powdered Sugar Icing

Chopped walnuts

Butter

Prep: 45 minutes   Bake: 15 minutes

Method

1. In a small bowl stir together warm water, the 1 tablespoon granulated sugar, and the yeast; let stand for 5 minutes to soften.

2. Meanwhile, in a small saucepan combine milk, shortening, the ½ cup granulated sugar, and the salt; heat and stir just until warm (120°F to 130°F) and shortening almost melts. Cool milk mixture. In a large bowl combine flour, eggs, milk mixture, and yeast mixture; mix well.

3. Cover and let rise in a warm place until doubled in size. Punch down dough; let rest for 15 minutes. Divide dough into three balls. Pat or roll each ball into a ½-inch-thick rectangle.

4. Spread butter over dough rectangles. In a small bowl combine the ¾ cup chopped walnuts, ½ cup granulated sugar, and the cinnamon. Divide walnut mixture among dough rectangles, sprinkling evenly on top of butter. Roll up each dough rectangle, starting at a long side; shape each into a ring, pressing ends to seal. Place dough rings on two large baking sheets. Using kitchen scissors, cut each dough ring at ¾-inch intervals, cutting nearly to the center. Let rise in a warm place until doubled in size.

5. Meanwhile, preheat oven to 350°F. Bake about 15 minutes or until golden. Transfer to wire racks; let cool. Drizzle with Powdered Sugar Icing. Sprinkle with additional chopped walnuts. Serve with butter.

Powdered Sugar Icing: In a small bowl stir together 2 cups powdered sugar, ¼ cup milk or water, and 1 teaspoon vanilla. If necessary, stir in enough additional milk or water to make icing of drizzling consistency.

Makes 3 rings (6 servings each)

Eggnog and nutmeg give these homemade caramels a sensationally sinful flavor. They're great for holiday gift giving ... or keeping for yourself!

Eggnog Caramels

Mary—Ann Arbor, MI

+ · · · + · · · + · · · + · · + + · · · + + · · · + · · · + · · · + · · · + + · · · + · · · + · · · + · · · + · · · + · · · +

Prep: 1 hour **Chill:** 3 hours

Method

1. Line an 8×8-inch baking pan with a double thickness of foil; coat well with nonstick cooking spray. Set aside.

2. In a heavy deep-sided saucepan combine eggnog, granulated sugar, brown sugar, corn syrup, shortening, and nutmeg; attach a candy thermometer to the side of the saucepan. Bring mixture to boiling over high heat, stirring constantly. Reduce heat to medium and continue boiling at a moderate, steady rate, stirring constantly, until mixture reaches 245°F. Immediately pour caramel mixture into prepared pan; cool. Refrigerate for 3 hours or until completely firm.

3. Using foil, lift caramel slab from prepared pan. Pull the foil down from the sides of the caramel. Using a long knife, trim the edges off the caramel slab (these are ideal for nibbling!) and then cut the block of caramel into eight rows. Cut each row into 8 squares (64 caramels total).

Makes 64 caramels

Cook's Notes

You can wrap the caramels in foil wrappers (available at cooking or craft stores). They make beautiful—and delicious— gifts! While the stirring is simple, it takes awhile for the caramel to reach the correct temperature. But when you taste how delicious these are, you'll know it was well worth the wait!

Ingredients

Nonstick cooking spray

2 **cups eggnog**

1 **cup granulated sugar**

1 **cup packed brown sugar**

¾ **cup light-color corn syrup**

½ **cup butter-flavor shortening**

Dash ground nutmeg

Here's a rich and chocolaty way to warm up after holiday activities such as sledding, ice skating ... or just shoveling the sidewalks.

Hot Chocolate quick

Melvina—Laurens, SC

Ingredients

6 ounces semisweet chocolate pieces

2 cups whipping cream

   Dash ground cinnamon

   Whipped cream (flavored with vanilla)

Start to finish: 15 minutes

Method

1. Place chocolate pieces in top of double boiler; place over boiling water (upper pan should not touch water). Heat and stir until chocolate is melted.

2. Stir the 2 cups whipping cream into melted chocolate. Heat and stir just until boiling. Stir in cinnamon. Top servings with whipped cream.

Makes 2 to 4 servings

The green and red from the kiwifruit and raspberries make this cream cheese and gelatin dessert festive—perfect for Christmas!

Fruity Holiday Pretzel Torte

Denise—Milwaukee, WI

Prep: 45 minutes Bake: 10 minutes Chill: 4 hours

Method

1. Preheat oven to 350°F. In a medium bowl stir together crushed pretzels, melted butter, and the 3 tablespoons sugar. Lightly coat a 13×9×2-inch baking pan with nonstick cooking spray. Pat pretzel mixture onto the bottom of the prepared pan. Bake for 10 minutes. Cool completely.

2. In a large mixing bowl combine cream cheese and the 1 cup sugar; beat with an electric mixer on medium speed until smooth. Fold in whipped topping, kiwifruit, and green food coloring. Spread over cooled crust. Cover and chill.

3. In a large bowl dissolve gelatin in the boiling water. Stir in raspberries. Chill until mixture starts to thicken slightly. Spoon thickened mixture over cream cheese layer. Chill about 4 hours or until set.

Makes 16 servings

Ingredients

2 cups crushed chocolate-covered pretzels (4 cups uncrushed)

6 tablespoons unsalted butter, melted

3 tablespoons sugar

   Nonstick cooking spray

1 8-ounce package cream cheese, softened

1 cup sugar

1 8-ounce container frozen whipped dessert topping, thawed

2 kiwifruit, peeled and diced

   Few drops green food coloring

2 3-ounce packages raspberry-flavor gelatin

2 cups boiling water

1 16-ounce package frozen raspberries, slightly thawed

Ricotta cheese and low-fat sour cream and cream cheese make this cheesecake lower in fat but still deliciously rich. A topping of cherry pie filling adds stunning color.

Cherry Cheesecake

Eve—Olympia, WA

Ingredients

Nonstick cooking spray

¾ cup finely crushed graham crackers

2 teaspoons butter, melted

2 teaspoons light-color corn syrup

1 15-ounce container part skim ricotta cheese

1 cup sugar

2 eggs

2 egg whites

½ teaspoon grated lemon zest

1 tablespoon lemon juice

½ teaspoon almond extract

12 ounces reduced-fat cream cheese (Neufchâtel), softened and cut up

1 cup low-fat sour cream

¼ cup all-purpose flour

1 20-ounce can cherry pie filling

Prep: 30 minutes Chill: 3 hours Bake: 50 minutes Stand: 30 minutes

Method

1. Preheat oven to 350°F. Coat a 9-inch springform pan with nonstick cooking spray. Wrap outside of pan with heavy-duty foil. In prepared pan combine crushed graham crackers, butter, and corn syrup; press into bottom. Bake for 8 minutes. Cool on wire rack. Reduce oven temperature to 325°F.

2. In a food processor combine ricotta cheese, sugar, eggs, egg whites, lemon zest, lemon juice, and almond extract; process for 30 seconds. With machine running, add cream cheese, processing until smooth. Add sour cream and flour; pulse until smooth. Pour into crust.

3. Place springform pan in shallow baking pan. Add boiling water to baking pan to come 1 inch up sides of springform pan. Bake for 50 to 60 minutes or just until set in center. Turn off oven; let stand in oven 30 minutes. Refrigerate cheesecake for at least 3 hours.

4. To serve, spread pie filling over top.

Makes 12 to 16 servings

This baked ham is glazed with a Dijon-style mustard and ketchup mixture that is flavored with orange peel and juice. See photo on page 224.

Orange-Glazed Ham

June—Princeton, WV

* * *

Prep: 20 minutes **Bake:** per package directions

Method

1. For glaze, in a small bowl whisk together mustard, orange zest, orange juice, ketchup, brown sugar, oil, and garlic salt; set aside. Preheat oven according to ham directions. Place ham in roasting pan; add the water to pan. Cover loosely with foil. Bake ham according to package directions.

2. About 30 minutes before ham is done, remove from oven and baste with some of the glaze. Reserve remaining glaze.

3. Place orange slices over ham in decorative fashion, using two cloves to attach each orange slice to ham. Bake, uncovered, for 30 minutes more.

4. To serve, remove orange slices and cloves. Slice ham. Serve with reserved glaze.

Makes 16 to 20 servings

Cook's Notes
This recipe makes a great Easter ham or holiday main dish.

Ingredients

- ¼ cup Dijon-style mustard
- Finely shredded zest of 1 large orange
- ¼ cup orange juice
- ¼ cup ketchup
- ¼ cup packed dark brown sugar
- 2 tablespoons cooking oil
- 1 teaspoon garlic salt
- 1 6- to 6½-pound cooked boneless ham
- ½ cup water
- 5 thin slices orange
- 10 whole cloves

When hosting Easter guests for the weekend, avoid last-minute stress with this make-ahead breakfast casserole packed with eggs, potatoes, bacon, and lots of cheese.

Egg Casserole

Michelle—Costa Mesa, CA

394

Ingredients

2 large baking potatoes, unpeeled and cubed

¼ cup margarine

¼ cup all-purpose flour

1 cup milk

1 cup half-and-half or light cream

4 cups shredded cheddar cheese

1 teaspoon dried Italian seasoning, crushed

½ teaspoon ground black pepper

12 hard-cooked eggs, sliced

1 pound bacon, cooked, drained, and crumbled

2 cups soft bread crumbs

3 tablespoons margarine, melted

Prep: 40 minutes Chill: overnight Stand: 30 minutes Bake: 45 minutes

Method

1. In a covered large saucepan cook potato cubes in large amount of boiling water until tender; drain and cool.

2. Meanwhile, for cheese sauce, in a small saucepan melt the ¼ cup margarine; add the flour, stirring until smooth. Gradually add milk and half-and-half; cook and stir until thick and bubbly. Add cheese, Italian seasoning, and pepper, stirring until cheese melts.

3. In a greased 13×9×2-inch baking pan layer half of the egg slices, bacon, and cheese sauce. Top with potato. Layer with the remaining egg, bacon, and cheese sauce. In a small bowl combine bread crumbs and the 3 tablespoons melted margarine; sprinkle over. Cover and chill overnight.

4. Let stand at room temperature for 30 minutes. Meanwhile, preheat oven to 350°F. Bake, uncovered, for 45 minutes to 1 hour or until heated through.

Makes 12 servings

This soufflé is loaded with spices, and it's perfect for your Easter breakfast or even dinner. Serve it piping hot from the oven.

Easter Soufflé

Marjorie—Skaneateles, NY

Prep: 25 minutes Bake: 45 minutes

Method

1. Preheat oven to 350°F. In a large skillet cook onion in hot oil until tender. Set aside.

2. Layer half of the bread in a buttered 13×9×2-inch baking pan. Add half of the grated cheese, half of the onion, half of the ham, and half of the mushrooms. Sprinkle with oregano, garlic salt, and *ground black pepper*. Repeat layers.

3. In a medium bowl beat together milk and eggs. Pour egg mixture over top, making sure all is covered and bread has absorbed the liquid.

4. Sprinkle top with bread crumbs, parsley flakes, additional oregano, and paprika. Bake about 45 minutes or until brown and puffed up. Cut into pieces and serve hot.

*Tip: Make garlic bread by spreading melted butter over slices of bread. Sprinkle with minced garlic and brown under broiler.

Makes 6 to 8 servings

Cook's Notes
I make bread crumbs using the crusts of stale bread. Grind them and add black pepper, salt, garlic powder, parsley, oregano, and a touch of basil.

Ingredients

6	small onions, thickly sliced
2	tablespoons cooking oil
18	slices garlic bread,* crusts removed
12	ounces sharp cheddar cheese, grated
2	cups chopped cooked ham or 1 pound bulk Italian sausage, cooked and well drained
8	ounces fresh mushrooms
	Dried oregano, crushed
	Garlic salt
3	cups milk
4	eggs, beaten
1	cup seasoned fine dry bread crumbs
¼	cup dried parsley flakes, crushed
	Paprika

Holiday

395

Supereasy Soufflé Egg-based soufflés are notorious for being difficult to make, bake, and serve. But since this puffed up masterpiece is more of a cross between a romantic soufflé and a tasty strata, you don't even need to use a special baking dish! A regular 13×9×2-inch pan works perfectly for the layering of the bread, sausage, cheese, and egg.

These little candy "eggs" are made with a mixture of peanut butter and powdered sugar formed into ovals and dipped into melted chocolate to coat.

Peanut Butter Easter Eggs ◆quick◆

Lara—Cincinnati, OH

Ingredients

½ cup peanut butter

¾ cup powdered sugar

1 cup semisweet chocolate pieces

1 tablespoon butter

Start to finish: 25 minutes

Method

1. In a small bowl stir together peanut butter and powdered sugar until well mixed. Shape into 10 to 12 small ovals for "eggs"; place on waxed paper.

2. In a small saucepan combine chocolate pieces and butter; heat and stir over low heat until melted. Dip peanut butter "eggs" into chocolate mixture to coat, turning to coat evenly. Place on waxed paper; let stand until chocolate is hardened.

Makes 10 to 12 servings

Perfect for Halloween parties, these caramel apples can be drizzled with white and/or dark candy coating and a crunchy cashew topping. See photo on page 224.

Decadent Caramel Apples

Patricia—Jefferson, WI

Start to finish: 1 hour

Method

1. Wash and dry apples well. Line a baking sheet with waxed paper. Insert a caramel apple stick about 2 inches into stem end of each apple.

2. Place caramels and milk in the top of a double boiler. Place over boiling water (upper pan should not touch water); heat until mixture is melted and smooth, stirring occasionally. Dip apples in melted caramel mixture, turning to coat two-thirds up sides. Place on waxed paper and let stand until firm.

3. For chocolate drizzle, place chocolate-flavor candy coating in a microwave-safe bowl with the shortening. Microwave on 50% power (medium) about 2 minutes or until melted and smooth, stirring every 30 seconds.

4. Using a spoon, drizzle the candy-coating mixture over apples and/or dip bottoms of apples in nuts (you can also sprinkle the apples with nuts). Let apples stand until hardened.

Makes 10 servings

Ingredients

10 **firm ripe apples (such as Cortland, Gala, or Red Delicious)**

1 **16-ounce package caramels, unwrapped**

3 **tablespoons milk**

4 **ounces chocolate-flavor candy coating (preferably dark chocolate), cut into pieces**

1½ **teaspoons shortening**

1 **cup chopped cashews or pecans**

Cook's Notes

If you can't find caramel apple sticks, cut two 36-inch-long ¼-inch wooden dowels into six pieces each. If you like, you can also make a white drizzle with vanilla-flavor candy coating. To do this, place 4 ounces vanilla-flavor candy coating in a bowl with 1½ teaspoons of the shortening and repeat melting directions for chocolate drizzle. You can either drizzle the apple with one candy-coating mixture or both. If you choose to do both, let the first one harden before drizzling with the second.

This cheddar cheese fondue has an option of white wine or broth, depending on the tastes of your party crowd. The fun dippers bring to mind certain ghoulish ideas.

Halloween Party Fun-due ◆quick◆

Pamela—Parkersburg, WV

Ingredients

½ **cup butter or margarine**

⅓ **cup all-purpose flour**

½ **teaspoon salt**

½ **teaspoon ground black pepper**

¼ **teaspoon dry mustard**

¼ **teaspoon Worcestershire sauce**

1½ **cups milk**

1 **cup whipping cream**

½ **cup dry white wine or chicken broth**

4 **cups shredded cheddar cheese**

Assorted dippers (such as cooked meatballs, cooked breaded chicken breast strips, miniature corn dogs, small cooked sausage links, breadsticks, bread cubes, and/or black- and orange-color tortilla chips)

Start to finish: 20 minutes

Method

1. For cheese fondue, in a large saucepan melt butter over medium heat. Stir in flour, salt, pepper, mustard, and Worcestershire sauce until smooth. Add milk, whipping cream, and wine. Cook, stirring constantly, until smooth. Reduce heat; add cheddar cheese, about 1 cup at a time, stirring constantly. Cook until the cheese melts.

2. Transfer to a fondue pot or small slow cooker. Place the dippers around the pot in Halloween serving dishes. Set out fondue forks or party toothpicks for dipping.

*Note: If the cheese fondue becomes too thick, you can add more milk.

Makes 16 servings

Cook's Notes
For more Halloween fun, label the dippers with names of body parts or creepy ideas. Meatballs can be eyeballs; chicken can be fingers; sausages are monster toes; corn dogs are mummies or cocoons; breadsticks can be bones; and black tortilla chips are bats. There are many other great ideas to use as dipping foods. These were the ones my grandchildren and I came up with when they spent the night with me. To make bone-shape breadsticks, separate dough into sticks and tie each end into a knot; bake as directed.

Kids will love these great Halloween party favors—plastic gloves stuffed with popcorn and candy corn. They're gruesome fun!

Skeleton Hands

Ann —Rochester, NY

+ · · + · · + · · + + · + · + · · · · + · + · + + · + · · + · · + · + + · + · · + · +

Start to finish: 45 minutes

Method

1. Pop popcorn according to package directions. Place in large bowl; let cool.

2. Open up one clear plastic glove and place one candy corn inside the glove all the way down to the tip of a finger. (This is a fingernail.) Repeat with remaining fingers.

3. Place handfuls of the cooled popcorn into glove until the glove is stiff. Make sure to get popcorn into each finger.

4. Tie the end of the glove with ribbon.

Makes 12 servings

Ingredients

3 **packages microwave popcorn**

12 **clear disposable plastic gloves**

60 **pieces candy corn**

Black and/or orange ribbon

Holiday

399

Cook's Notes
When you buy the plastic gloves, read the box to make sure there is no baby powder in them (look for this product in a pharmacy). I used to make these for my kids' Halloween parties. The teachers liked them because there wasn't too much candy.

Both kids and adults will love this colorful and tasty snack mix. Serve it at your next Halloween party.

Spooktacular Snack Sacks quick

Mary—Ann Arbor, MI

Ingredients

8 cups caramel corn with nuts

1 17.25-ounce package candy-coated peanut butter pieces

1 14-ounce package autumn-color candy-coated milk chocolate pieces

1 11-ounce package corn candy

1 6-ounce bag peanut butter-filled pretzel nuggets

16 treat bags

Black and/or orange curling ribbon

Start to finish: 20 minutes

Method

1. In a large bowl combine all ingredients.

2. Divide mixture among 16 treat bags (approximately 1 cup mixture per bag). Tie each bag with both black and orange curling ribbon.

Makes 16 servings

Cook's Notes
This is a ridiculously easy snack to make, but it's festive with the autumn colors and seasonal candy corn. It's great to serve at parties, to give as gifts, or just to snack on.

Index

Note: Boldface page numbers indicate photographs.

402

Best of Hometown Cooking

For more delicious recipes, visit betterrecipes.com

Metric Information

The charts on this page provide a guide for converting measurements from the U.S. customary system, which is used throughout this book, to the metric system.

Product Differences

Most of the ingredients called for in the recipes in this book are available in most countries. However, some are known by different names. Here are some common American ingredients and their possible counterparts:

- Sugar (white) is granulated, fine granulated, or castor sugar.
- Powdered sugar is icing sugar.
- All-purpose flour is enriched, bleached or unbleached white household flour. When self-rising flour is used in place of all-purpose flour in a recipe that calls for leavening, omit the leavening agent (baking soda or baking powder) and salt.
- Light-colored corn syrup is golden syrup.
- Cornstarch is cornflour.
- Baking soda is bicarbonate of soda.
- Vanilla or vanilla extract is vanilla essence.
- Green, red, or yellow sweet peppers are capsicums or bell peppers.
- Golden raisins are sultanas.

Volume and Weight

The United States traditionally uses cup measures for liquid and solid ingredients. The chart below shows the approximate imperial and metric equivalents. If you are accustomed to weighing solid ingredients, the following approximate equivalents will be helpful.

- 1 cup butter, castor sugar, or rice = 8 ounces = $\frac{1}{2}$ pound = 250 grams
- 1 cup flour = 4 ounces = $\frac{1}{4}$ pound = 125 grams
- 1 cup icing sugar = 5 ounces = 150 grams

Canadian and U.S. volume for a cup measure is 8 fluid ounces (237 ml), but the standard metric equivalent is 250 ml.

1 British imperial cup is 10 fluid ounces.

In Australia, 1 tablespoon equals 20 ml, and there are 4 teaspoons in the Australian tablespoon.

Spoon measures are used for smaller amounts of ingredients. Although the size of the tablespoon varies slightly in different countries, for practical purposes and for recipes in this book, a straight substitution is all that's necessary. Measurements made using cups or spoons always should be level unless stated otherwise.

Common Weight Range Replacements

Imperial / U.S.	Metric
$\frac{1}{2}$ ounce	15 g
1 ounce	25 g or 30 g
4 ounces ($\frac{1}{4}$ pound)	115 g or 125 g
8 ounces ($\frac{1}{2}$ pound)	225 g or 250 g
16 ounces (1 pound)	450 g or 500 g
$1\frac{1}{4}$ pounds	625 g
$1\frac{1}{2}$ pounds	750 g
2 pounds or $2\frac{1}{4}$ pounds	1,000 g or 1 Kg

Oven Temperature Equivalents

Fahrenheit Setting	Celsius Setting*	Gas Setting
300°F	150°C	Gas Mark 2 (very low)
325°F	160°C	Gas Mark 3 (low)
350°F	180°C	Gas Mark 4 (moderate)
375°F	190°C	Gas Mark 5 (moderate)
400°F	200°C	Gas Mark 6 (hot)
425°F	220°C	Gas Mark 7 (hot)
450°F	230°C	Gas Mark 8 (very hot)
475°F	240°C	Gas Mark 9 (very hot)
500°F	260°C	Gas Mark 10 (extremely hot)
Broil	Broil	Grill

*Electric and gas ovens may be calibrated using celsius. However, for an electric oven, increase celsius setting 10 to 20 degrees when cooking above 160°C. For convection or forced air ovens (gas or electric) lower the temperature setting 25°F/10°C when cooking at all heat levels.

Baking Pan Sizes

Imperial / U.S.	Metric
9×1$\frac{1}{2}$-inch round cake pan	22- or 23×4-cm (1.5 L)
9×1$\frac{1}{2}$-inch pie plate	22- or 23×4-cm (1 L)
8×8×2-inch square cake pan	20×5-cm (2 L)
9×9×2-inch square cake pan	22- or 23×4.5-cm (2.5 L)
11×7×1$\frac{1}{2}$-inch baking pan	28×17×4-cm (2 L)
2-quart rectangular baking pan	30×19×4.5-cm (3 L)
13×9×2-inch baking pan	34×22×4.5-cm (3.5 L)
15×10×1-inch jelly roll pan	40×25×2-cm
9×5×3-inch loaf pan	23×13×8-cm (2 L)
2-quart casserole	2 L

U.S. / Standard Metric Equivalents

$\frac{1}{8}$ teaspoon = 0.5 ml	
$\frac{1}{4}$ teaspoon = 1 ml	
$\frac{1}{2}$ teaspoon = 2 ml	
1 teaspoon = 5 ml	
1 tablespoon = 15 ml	
2 tablespoons = 25 ml	
$\frac{1}{4}$ cup = 2 fluid ounces = 50 ml	
$\frac{1}{3}$ cup = 3 fluid ounces = 75 ml	
$\frac{1}{2}$ cup = 4 fluid ounces = 125 ml	
$\frac{2}{3}$ cup = 5 fluid ounces = 150 ml	
$\frac{3}{4}$ cup = 6 fluid ounces = 175 ml	
1 cup = 8 fluid ounces = 250 ml	
2 cups = 1 pint = 500 ml	
1 quart = 1 litre	

BetterRecipes.com | Better Recipes, Better Meals.

In the mood to find or share the dishes that inspire the request, "Can I have that recipe?" BetterRecipes.com is an online recipe-sharing community that showcases the recipes that friends share over coffee, neighbors swap over the fence, and mothers pass down to daughters.

What you'll find on betterrecipes.com

1. The most complete collection of great home cooking plucked from the recipe boxes, files, and kitchens from cooks across America.

2. Two monthly recipe contests edited and judged by recipe editors.

Submit your favorite recipe today at betterrecipes.com